The Rise of Asian Firms

The AIB Southeast Asia Series

Series Editor: **T S Chan**, Lingnan University, Hong Kong

The Academy of International Business Southeast Asia Region (AIB-SEAR) series publishes books that aim to inform and inspire academics, researchers and practitioners with an interest in further advancing knowledge and understanding of international business and multinational company behaviour from and within the South East Asia region.

Political changes and financial issues have been at the forefront of international business for several years, yet one trend is clear: the focus of global business is now on Asia. The growth of Asian economies in recent years, in particular China and several other Association of Southeast Asian Nations (ASEAN) countries, has been based on the manufacture and export of goods around the world, especially large quantities of consumer goods exported to Western Europe and North America. The AIB-SEAR series examines these international links, which are essential to the expanding South East Asian economies. Moreover, these Asian countries have emerged as viable and important consumer markets, creating tremendous potential for multinational firms as growth destinations. The focus of the AIB-SEAR book series is on the continuous evolution of international business.

Titles include:

T. S. Chan and Geng Cui (*editors*)
MULTINATIONALS AND GLOBAL CONSUMERS
Tension, Potential and Competition

T. S. Chan and Geng Cui (*editors*)
THE RISE OF ASIAN FIRMS
Strengths and Strategies

The AIB Southeast Asia Series
Series Standing Order ISBN 978–1–137–30726–2

You can receive future titles in this series as they are published by placing a standing order. Please contact your bookseller or, in case of difficulty, write to us at the address below with your name and address, the title of the series and the ISBN quoted above.

Customer Services Department, Macmillan Distribution Ltd, Houndmills, Basingstoke, Hampshire RG21 6XS, England.

The Rise of Asian Firms

Strengths and Strategies

Edited by

T. S. Chan
Shun Hing Chair Professor of Marketing, Department of Marketing and International Business, Lingnan University, Hong Kong

and

Geng Cui
Professor, Department of Marketing and International Business, Lingnan University, Hong Kong

palgrave
macmillan

First published 2014 by
PALGRAVE MACMILLAN

Palgrave Macmillan in the UK is an imprint of Macmillan Publishers Limited, registered in England, company number 785998, of Houndmills, Basingstoke, Hampshire RG21 6XS.

Palgrave Macmillan in the US is a division of St Martin's Press LLC, 175 Fifth Avenue, New York, NY 10010.

Palgrave Macmillan is the global academic imprint of the above companies and has companies and representatives throughout the world.

Palgrave® and Macmillan® are registered trademarks in the United States, the United Kingdom, Europe and other countries

ISBN: 978–1–137–40769–6

This book is printed on paper suitable for recycling and made from fully managed and sustained forest sources. Logging, pulping and manufacturing processes are expected to conform to the environmental regulations of the country of origin.

A catalogue record for this book is available from the British Library.

A catalog record for this book is available from the Library of Congress.

Contents

List of Illustrations

Boxes

Figures

Tables

Preface

The Academy of International Business Southeast Asia Region (AIB-SEAR) forged a collaborative link with Palgrave Macmillan to publish a book series in 2012. The first volume of the series, *Multinationals and Global Consumers: Tension, Potential, and Competition* (2013), emphasized two distinct components: (1) The strategies of multinational firms in advancing global markets among both developed and emerging countries; and (2) The ultimate target for multinational firms – the voracious global consumer. Our second volume, entitled *The Rise of Asian Firms: Strengths and Strategies,* is organized around the schematic theme of international business research in Asia and has two parts: (1) Asian Firms: Environment, Institutions and Management; and (2) Internationalization of Asian Firms: Perspectives and Strategies. It includes selected papers presented at the AIB-SEAR 2013 Conference, as well as several other papers focusing on the growth and expansion of Asian firms in the global arena.

The theme of our 2013 Conference was "International Business Cooperation, Competition, and Coopetition" and featured lively dialogue and discussion on the growth of Asian firms. How and where have Asian firms been expanding their business? What are their growth strategies? What factors motivate the outward flows of foreign direct investment (FDI) from these firms? How are these firms responding to the challenges and competition of the rapidly changing international business environment? The conference papers selected for this book strive to address some of these questions.

Coincidentally, the 2013 AIB-SEAR Conference was held during the same week (in December 2013) and in the same location (in Bali, Indonesia) as the 9th World Trade Organization (WTO) Ministerial Conference. The Bali Round continued with the efforts initiated at the Doha Round in 2001, attempting to reduce trade barriers and create a fairer trade environment that enhances trade opportunities and global economic expansion and development. As global trade continues to grow, more and more countries are utilizing WTO dispute settlement processes to resolve trade issues. Recent rulings by the Dispute Settlement Panel concluded that China breached its WTO obligations by restricting the export of rare earth elements for industrial and high-tech uses, and the United States acted inconsistently with WTO rules in its countervailing and anti-dumping measures towards certain products from China. These rulings, which involve the world's two leading trading nations, are just examples of the increasing complexity of international trade. Moving forward, both multinational and Asian firms must be vigilant in monitoring the evolving international trade and business landscape so they can continue to adapt and stay ahead of the competition.

In light of the increasingly diverse views among the 159 members of the WTO, negotiations do not always deliver the best result. The WTO framework adopts a "single undertaking" approach, meaning that "nothing is agreed until everything is agreed". Therefore, the WTO has been moving very slowly with efforts focusing more on "understanding" and "discussing" issues instead of negotiating to close gaps. While the multilateral approach yields little in terms of results, we are seeing more and more bilateral and regional agreements of regional trade in goods and services. The North American Free Trade Agreement and the European Union are the key examples in the Western world. In Asia, there are two major examples, the South Asian Free Trade Area (consisting of India, Pakistan, Nepal, Sri Lanka, Bangladesh, Bhutan and the Maldives) and the Association of Southeast Asian Nations (ASEAN – with ten member states: Brunei, Cambodia, Indonesia, Laos, Malaysia, Myanmar, the Philippines, Singapore, Thailand and Vietnam). In fact, plans and discussions have been underway for ASEAN to establish closer trade relationships with Australia, China, India, Japan, New Zealand and South Korea (the so-called ASEAN plus Six). In particular, China has signed the China-ASEAN Free Trade Area framework agreement in order to eliminate or scale down tariffs on a large range of products by 2015, and the Korea–Australia Free Trade Agreement announced in April 2014 will eventually remove tariffs on primary products ranging from about 15% to more than 500%.

The emergence of these largely borderless trade blocs has created both challenges and potential for multinational firms. International business is driven by companies with strong capabilities to stand up to global competition in their search for new markets. The growth of some Asian economies, in particular China and India, has been driven by the production of low-cost goods for export around the world. However, we are now seeing more Chinese and Indian firms aggressively engaging in outbound overseas investment. As these leading Asian companies seek to lead an economic transition and move away from export-led growth, there is strong evidence that they are actively seeking out expansion through outbound FDI and strategic alliances.

The various book chapters adopt different focuses and perspectives, as well as different research methodologies – both qualitative and quantitative approaches – in their attempt to explain new trends and phenomena in the internationalization of Asian firms. The key topics involve discussions of internationalization patterns, network relationships and localization, understanding of organizational adaptive capabilities and leadership styles, location choice (developed vs developing countries) and the impact of alternate approaches for outbound FDI (mergers and acquisitions vs greenfield investments). This second volume offers extensive case studies and theory-based research with empirical data. Based on in-depth analyses, the chapters provide insightful suggestions and conclusions that showcase the unique challenges confronting Asian firms and the strengths and strategies of these firms in achieving market success and business performance.

The selected papers in this book highlight some of the current discussions around the issues, trends and challenges among Asian firms and capture the different "Asian" ways of managing international businesses. The findings and conclusions presented within each chapter present the unique styles of management, insights and reflections based on each country's distinct background, and cultural and historical perspectives. Asia has shed its third world status in the global economic arena and transformed into an important player in international trade and investment. In covering countries from China to India, and Singapore to Taiwan, this book reveals the increasing adoption and integration of Western and Asian business concepts by Asian firms in developing a unique style of Asian strategies for international growth and expansion in the 21st century.

T. S. Chan, Chapter Chair
AIB-SEAR

Notes on Editors

T. S. Chan is Shun Hing Chair Professor of Marketing at Lingnan University, Hong Kong. He received his DBA from Indiana University-Bloomington, and BBA and MBA degrees from the University of Wisconsin at Madison. As an active researcher, he has published/edited ten books and over 100 articles and papers in the areas of international marketing strategies, cross-cultural consumer behaviour, joint venture decisions and marketing education. He serves on the editorial board of five international journals. He consults widely for corporations and government agencies in Hong Kong and abroad. His areas of consulting include strategic marketing planning, effective selling, leadership and intercultural communication.

Geng Cui is Professor, Department of Marketing and International Business, Lingnan University, Hong Kong. His research interests include consumer behaviour and marketing in China, foreign direct investment strategies and performance, and quantitative models in marketing. His works have appeared in leading academic journals. He is a leading scholar on Chinese consumer research, which has been widely cited and adopted for marketing practice and teaching. He has been a consultant to local and overseas organizations on China business and marketing strategies.

Notes on Contributors

Ya-Yuan Chang is a PhD candidate in the Department of Business Administration in National Chung Hsing University, Taiwan. Her research interests focus on strategic management and consumer behaviour. She has been an instructor for three years in the department of food technology and marketing management and the department of food and beverage management in Taipei College of Maritime Technology.

Xudong Chen is Professor and Director of the Institute of Global Business at the School of Management, Zhejiang University, Hangzhou, China. She received a Bachelor's and a Master's in Economics from Hangzhou University in China and Indiana University at Bloomington, Indiana, respectively. Her research interests include transnational business activities of small and medium enterprises (SMEs), growth of SMEs and government policy, corporate social responsibility and firm performance, and firm growth in China's private sector.

Ritam Garg is a senior teaching and research associate in the Department of International Management at the Friedrich-Alexander University of Erlangen-Nürnberg, Germany. He is responsible for courses such as intercultural competence and managing intercultural relations. He has been actively pursuing his research in the field of internationalization of firms, and has presented papers at several international conferences. His research interests include firms from emerging markets, indigenous management practices and cross-cultural communication.

Wilfred How is a writer and researcher associated with Singapore Management University. His research interests include Singapore's development strategies and transborder internationalization experiences, and the sociopolitical dimensions thereof. He has published a number of articles on these subjects in various print and online journals.

Robert Graham Jack is Senior Lecturer in International Business at Macquarie University, Australia and is also the Convenor of Macquarie's China Business Research Network (CBRN). He has Master's in both marketing and international business and was awarded his PhD from Monash University in 2007. He specializes in case study research and has undertaken a number of extensive studies on the internationalization patterns of both Australian and Chinese firms. He has published widely in the subject areas of firm internationalization, emerging market multinationals and the internationalization of services.

Wiboon Kittilaksanawong is Associate Professor of Strategy and International Business at Faculty of Management, Nagoya University of Commerce and Business, Japan. He received his PhD in Management from National Taiwan University. He has three and a half years of teaching experience at Zhejiang University and Zhejiang Gongshang University in China. He has 12 years of management and consulting experience in multinational and Thai enterprises. His research interests include global business and strategy, business strategies in emerging markets and international entrepreneurship. His research publications have appeared in *Management and Organization Review, Asian Journal of Technology Innovation* and *Academy of Management Proceedings*.

Sai Lan is Assistant Professor of Management at Peking University HSBC Business School. He earned his PhD in Strategy and Entrepreneurship from the University of Illinois at Urbana-Champaign, USA. His research interests include technology and innovation management, international business and corporate strategy. Before joining academia, he was a seasoned software architect working for high-technology firms in the US. He is currently the associate director of the Center for Innovation and Entrepreneurship at Peking University HSBC Business School.

Ku-Ho Lin is Assistant Professor in the Department of Business Administration in National Chung Hsing University, Taiwan. He currently serves as Deputy Director of Marketing and Consumer Behaviour Research Division, Commerce Development Research Institute, Taiwan. He received a PhD from Royal Holloway, University of London. His research interests focus on internationalization strategy, international marketing and small and medium sized enterprise management.

Denny Meyer is Associate Professor of Statistics in the Faculty of Life and Social Sciences at Swinburne University in Melbourne. She has also held academic appointments in the Institute of Information and Mathematical Sciences at Massey University in New Zealand and the Department of Statistics at the University of the Witwatersrand in South Africa. Denny has published two books, eight book chapters and more than 100 refereed articles in conference proceeding and academic journals. Her main interests are in the area of statistical modelling, using methods such as structural equation modelling, multilevel modelling and time-series models.

Chueh-Chu Ou is a research fellow in the Corporate Synergy Development Center, Taiwan. She received her PhD from National Chung Hsing University. Her research interests focus on marketing management, service marketing and relationship marketing.

Ling Peng is Associate Professor in the Department of Marketing and International Business, Lingnan University, Hong Kong. She received her PhD from the University of Alberta in 2007. Her research, addressing the psychometric theories to measurement issues in new product development and Internet marketing, has appeared in the *Journal of Product Innovation Management, International Journal of Market Research, Journal of Marketing Management* and *Journal of Global Marketing,* among others. Her current research focuses on new product and innovation management, e-commerce and social media.

Lijun (Karl) Qin is a China-born New Zealand citizen who has lived and worked in New Zealand and Australia. Karl has Master's in Engineering and Business Administration. He was appointed CEO of Haier Australia Pty Limited in 2004, at which time he moved to live in Sydney and began to build the Oceania headquarters for China's largest electronic appliance manufacture. Leaving the Haier Group in 2007, Karl founded TDES (Technology Development and Equipment Supply Limited). Karl has been a faculty industry advisory board member in the Faculty of Business and Economics at Macquarie University since 2009.

Christopher Selvarajah is Professor of International Business in the Department of Leadership and Management, Faculty of Business and Enterprise at Swinburne University in Melbourne. He has worked at RMIT University, Massey University in New Zealand, the University of Brunei Darussalam and Deakin University in Melbourne. Professor Selvarajah has published five books, over 20 book chapters, over 100 refereed articles in journals and conference proceedings, and 30 case studies. His interests focus on international business management, in particular on leadership and cultural diversity studies. He has acted as a consultant to companies in the Asia Pacific region.

Suku Sukunesan is Senior Lecturer of Business Designs and Systems in the Department of Information Systems of the Faculty of Business and Enterprise at Swinburne University of Technology. His research interests are mainly in areas related to social media applications and e-business. He has authored more than 50 research articles including refereed journals, international conferences and book chapters.

Wei-Kuo Tseng is doctoral researcher at National Chung Hsing University, Taiwan. He received his MBA from the same school and now is a marketing specialist in POU CHEN Group, the world's largest athletic shoe manufacturer.

R. Venkatapathy is Dean and Director of the Bharathiar School of Management and Entrepreneur Development. Previously, he was the associate dean in the Faculty of Management, Multimedia University, Malaysia. He is the author of seven monographs and over 100 research articles; he has edited 12 volumes of essays. He is a member of the ABEST 21, a Japanese international accreditation organization and UGC, as well AICTE, the policy-formulating bodies of higher education in India. His areas of specialization include entrepreneurial leadership, organizational dynamics and behaviour, microfinance and spiritual intelligence.

Shanshan Xie is research associate at the Institute of Global Business, School of Management, Zhejiang University, Hangzhou, China. She received her Bachelor's in Management from Zhejiang University. Her research interests include globalization of firms from China and other emerging economies. She has many years' working experience in privately owned enterprises in China's Zhejiang province and other multinational enterprises.

Fan Yang is Senior Associate at Citic Securities, a leading investment bank in China. She works in the equity research department, providing consultancy services to the Citic Group and major regulators in the Chinese capital market. She is interested in the development of the domestic and global capital market, and cross-border mergers and acquisitions. She received her dual Master's in Management from Peking University and in Finance from the University of Hong Kong.

Caroline Yeoh received her PhD from the University of Oxford, and currently teaches at the Singapore Management University. She has written extensively in books and journals on internationalization and transborder industrialization in the context of Singapore state-enterprise strategies, particularly with regards to the city-state's industrial parks and more recent internationalization efforts. Her current research focuses on Singapore firms in the Asia Pacific and Middle East regions.

Hua Zhang is Assistant Professor of Marketing at the Guangdong University of Finance and Economies. She received her PhD from the City University of Hong Kong. Her research interests focus on online consumer behaviour and strategic management.

Yuanyuan Zhang is a PhD candidate in Marketing at the City University of Hong Kong. Her research interests are international business, Chinese outward FDI and institutional theory. Her recent works have appeared in *Industrial Marketing Management*. She is currently working on her dissertation, which is a study on institutional theory and the performance of outward mergers and acquisitions by Chinese firms.

Hong (Susan) Zhu is Assistant Professor in Peking University HSBC Business School. Her primary research interests include mergers and acquisitions (M&A), cross-border mergers and acquisitions, Chinese firms' acquisitions, divestitures, and corporate governance and strategic leadership in organizational restructurings (M&As and divestitures). She has contributed articles to *International Business Review, Journal of International Management and Journal of World Business*. She is also one of the co-authors of an *M&A Handbook* (2012).

1

Research on Asian Firms: A Review and Look Forward

Geng Cui, T. S. Chan and Hua Zhang

Asia has a population of approximately 3.5 billion people in over 30 nations spreading east from Europe and Africa, excluding the nations of the Middle East and the Caucasus, and substantive parts of Turkey and Russia (Bruton & Lau, 2008). The economic influence of this region is expanding and growing stronger. With China and Japan as two of the world's largest economies, the Four Tigers (i.e., Singapore, South Korea, Hong Kong and Taiwan) as the newly industrialized economies, and India, another large emerging economy, the GDP of this region is predicted to exceed that of the United States by 2050 (Wilson & Purushothaman, 2003).

Asia's multinational corporations (MNCs) play a significant role in the global market. The 2012 Fortune Global 500 list includes 172 companies from Asian countries, including 73 from China, 68 from Japan, 13 from South Korea, 8 from India, 6 from Taiwan, 2 from Singapore and 1 each from Malaysia and Thailand. Together, these firms account for an increasing proportion of the world's trade and foreign direct investment, and thus have become a major driving force in the world economy. As a result, research on Asian firms has been on the rise, especially in recent years, as the centre of economic growth has shifted to this region of the world.

The objectives of this chapter are: (1) we provide a concise review of the research conducted on firms from the major Asian economies, including the relevant countries' economic development and government policies for outward foreign direct investment, as well as the firms' characteristics; (2) we delineate how research on Asian firms has contributed to the management and international business literature in terms of theoretical development and managerial implications; (3), we explore the opportunities and directions for future research and introduce the chapters contributed by the various authors to this book.

Internationalization of Asian economies and firms

Clearly, it is impractical to mount a comprehensive review of the studies on Asian firms. Instead, we focus on studies from leading academic journals and major publishers. These studies have focused on Japan, the Four Tigers, China and India, among others, largely due to their stage of economic development and internationalization of firms. For a more systematic treatment of these issues and other countries, readers may refer to other works (e.g., Ghymn, 1980; Young et al., 1996).

Japan

Japanese firms began the process of internationalization and started to expand overseas by the early 1960s (Lorriman & Kenjo, 1996). Thus, research on Asian firms began with studies of Japanese companies and focused on several areas, including the role of government, firms' motives for overseas expansion and firm's organizational strategies. The influence of government policy on the growth of Japanese firms has been widely noted (Callon, 1995). From1950 to 1978, the internationalization of Japanese firms was characterized by natural resource-seeking investment (Yang et al., 2009). The outward foreign direct investment (OFDI) of these firms effectively supplemented the country's resource-poor economy (Park, 2003). During this period, the Japanese government and firms resisted the inflow of foreign capital through administrative mechanisms such as the Foreign Exchange and Foreign Trade Control Law and the Foreign Capital Law. Without permits to export to or directly invest in Japan, foreign firms had to invest through licensing their technology (Odagiri & Goto, 1993). These laws facilitated the transfer of technology and provided protection to the uncompetitive domestic firms, in addition to incentives such as subsidies, preferential tax measures and the supply of low-interest loans (Yang et al., 2009). In 1979, the Foreign Exchange and Foreign Trade Control Law was revised to "free" outward FDI (OFDI) for Japanese firms (Yoshida, 1987). Japanese OFDI began to surge in the late 1970s, and has increased tremendously since 1985 due to the rapid appreciation of the yen that followed the G-5 Plaza Accord.

The domestic market in Japan is much smaller than those of other countries with limited resources and market size. Japanese firms invested in other Asian countries mainly to reduce their costs, while looking to the developed economies in search of new markets and technologies (Fukuda, 1993; Yoshida, 1987). According to Yang et al. (2009), Japanese MNCs have two motives to internationalize. First, the competitive and sophisticated industry environment has driven firms to expand abroad. Although some MNCs expanded overseas to acquire critical capability and overcome the domestic market limitations, others reacted to the internationalization strategies of their competitors (Hanssens & Johansson, 1991). When large firms in a *keiretsu* (i.e., conglomeration) expanded abroad, their suppliers in Japan were compelled to follow them overseas (Banerji & Sambharya, 1996) in a move referred to as the "keiretsuization" of Japanese FDI (Peng et al., 2002). Second, resource-seeking motives are evident in Japanese firms' internationalization. Li (1993) found that 94% of subsidiaries of Japanese firms were joint ventures and only 6% were wholly owned subsidiaries. Japanese firms started mergers and acquisitions (M&As) at a much later stage than their Western counterparts, many years after their initial international expansion. FDI is also viewed as providing networks that allow access to technology from different subsidiaries and sharing such technology within the organization (Bartlett & Ghoshal, 1989). It should be noted that the cluster or network model worked outstandingly for Japan. Global learning has been effective in close-knit Japanese *keiretsus* through their overseas subsidiaries. This *keiretsu* advantage comes from cooperative specialization among member firms (Peng et al., 2002).

The Four Tigers

South Korea

South Korea underwent rapid industrialization from the 1960s onward. In comparison with Japanese multinationals, Korean firms' expansion into international markets was relatively late. The evolution of Korea's OFDI policy began in 1968, with the passing of the Act of Foreign Exchange Management, although the laws governing OFDI remained restrictive until much later (Gill, 2013). In 1978, the Korean government established the Guiding Principles of FDI and Post-Investment Management under the authority of the Bank of Korea, and passed the rules for the Approval of Foreign Investments, which required prior approval for invest abroad (Pattnaik, 2006). However, until the late 1980s, Korean firms' international investments were minuscule, relying mainly on exporting locally manufactured products.

In the late 1980s, as domestic labour disputes intensified and competition from low-wage countries such as China and Indonesia increased, Korean firms began investing abroad (Chang & Rhee, 2011). The Korean government simplified foreign investment regulations, eliminated the prior approval of investment plans and relaxed the approval processes and prerequisites for foreign investment between 1986 and 1990 (Gill, 2013). From early 1991, the Korean government passed a series of laws to support OFDI by Korean firms. For example, the Law of Foreign Exchange Management was revised in 1991, and the Korea Development Bank and the Industrial Bank of Korea were also authorized to approve foreign investment. In 1997, Korea became a member of the Organisation for Economic Co-operation and Development. While changes have been made to promote Korean OFDI, smaller firms from the private sector has also joined the move for foreign investment (Kim & Rhe, 2009; Pattnaik, 2006).

Recent empirical studies on South Korea point mainly towards the search for new markets and cheap labour as the prime motives for internationalization, especially in cases of FDI in other developing and emerging economies. According to Moon (2007), Korean OFDI has experienced a saturated home market, cost disadvantages and intense competition. Rising wages, interest and exchange rates, a limited domestic market and regulations were the domestic push factors, while the need for natural resources, export markets, technology and improved efficiency were identified as the global pull factors (Kwak, 2007). Low labour and transport costs were the main reasons behind the concentration of Korea's OFDI in Asia (Yoon, 2007). However, Korean FDI appears to be both capital-intensive and labour-intensive in China, the most popular destination for Korean FDI, accounting for one-tenth of its total FDI (Park & Lee, 2003).

Singapore

Singapore has successfully developed into a newly industrialized country, mainly because of its inbound and outbound FDI. Inbound FDI brings foreign capital and technology, whereas outbound FDI allows Singapore to gain access to cheap labour and natural resources (Moon et al., 1998). In the 1960s and 1970s, Singapore followed export-orientated economic policies and integrated itself with the international order (Zutshi & Gibbons, 1998). The government made tremendous efforts to build scale-efficient capacities and modernize its infrastructure to attract foreign capital. Both private firms and state enterprises flourished in the process, through industrialization and import substitution. From the late 1970s to the mid-1980s, the economy diversified from traditional entrepôt trade to manufacturing, construction, tourism and financial services (Boey & Tyabji, 1980). A decade of high growth resulted in the almost doubling of per capita income, with constant prices and falling unemployment rates (Zutshi & Gibbons, 1998). Singaporean firms began to engage in significant FDI activities in the early 1980s, focusing on replacing labour-intensive operations with knowledge-based industries and services connected with manufacturing, tourism and finance, because of the tight labour market and increasing wages (Tsang & Yip, 2007; Zutshi & Gibbons, 1998).

During the late 1980s and 1990s, in response to the recession of 1985, the government found that MNC-led growth was insufficient and encouraged domestic entrepreneurship, technological development and internationalization (Zutshi & Gibbons, 1998). Therefore, the emphasis shifted to building an external wing for the Singaporean economy in the region. In the 1990s, Singaporean investment abroad increased substantially, mostly in neighbouring low-wage countries such as China. Developing countries currently host more than 80% of Singapore's OFDI stock (Ellingsen et al., 2006). In Singapore, government-linked corporations (GLCs) are the key players in internationalization. After the Public Sector Divestment Committee recommended privatization of some of the GLCs in 1987, many of them became market listed. GLCs are now major economic players in marine and technology-intensive sectors.

Taiwan

As late movers in internationalization, Taiwanese MNCs have grown rapidly to capitalize on overseas manufacturing and enhance their competitiveness since the late 1980s. Sim and Pandian (2003) found that Taiwanese firms expanded overseas for cost-based competencies and other location-based advantages, which were brought together by an extensive web of ethnic networks and assisted by government encouragement and the institutional framework. While cheap labour is the main motivator for moving into Asian countries, market-seeking and strategic asset-seeking are the prevailing motives for moving into developed countries. Makino et al. (2002) found that Taiwanese MNCs with resource exploration motives often locate FDIs in countries that are better developed than those in Taiwan, while those with resource exploitation motives tend to invest in countries that are less developed than Taiwan.

In Taiwan, small and medium sized firms play a key role in internationalization. The size of Taiwanese MNCs generally has a constraining effect on the geographical spread of their internationalization. With limited resources, such firms tend to extend their current products and technologies to nearby countries with similar economic and cultural environments. Government policy has targeted strategic industries (e.g., computer information industry) for internationalization. For political reasons, however, the government imposed constraints on Taiwanese FDI to China. Restrictions on travel to and direct investments (particularly by stock market listed companies) in China led many Taiwanese firms to invest in China via third countries. The government even initiated a "Go South" policy in 1993 to encourage Taiwanese firms to diversify their investments away from China towards South East Asia.

Hong Kong

As an entrepôt between China, East Asia and the world, Hong Kong has experienced rapid industrialization since the 1960s, led by small and medium enterprises (SMEs) in labour-intensive, export-oriented manufacturing. For a long time, Hong Kong has been the largest foreign investor in mainland China, having transferred its manufacturing operations to neighbouring Guangdong province. Many multinationals from other countries have also entered China via Hong Kong. Thus, the processes underlying the internationalization of Hong Kong firms are very different from those in the advanced economies where market expansion is the major motivation. Multinational firms from Hong Kong emerged as a result of production relocation from advanced countries. Therefore, many of these firms started exporting at their inception, as opposed to the general internationalization process described by the Uppsala and innovation models, which assume that strength in a firm's domestic market leads to a gradual process of internationalization (Andersen, 1993). The internationalization process of these firms shifted as Hong Kong developed and then lost its cost competitiveness. Firms were motivated to relocate their production to other lower-cost countries. Their managerial experiences and marketing skills have provided them with a competitive edge compared with local firms in the less developed countries (LDCs). However, a major weakness of Hong Kong firms is that they undertake FDI mainly in overseas production rather than in marketing or brand building (Lau, 2003).

China

Over the past three decades, Chinese firms have undergone significant internationalization in terms of greater participation in international trade, growing outflows of FDI and a recent surge in cross-border M&A activities. In the 1980s and 1990s, the Chinese government devised foreign investment laws to enable state-owned enterprises (SOEs) to receive foreign capital, technology and management systems through joint ventures, licensing agreements and other forms of strategic alliances (Yang et al., 2009). The first wave of Chinese firms began to internationalize from 1991 to 2000, after the Ministry of Foreign Trade and Economic Cooperation (MOFTEC) formalized administrative measures granting permits to large SOEs for outbound FDI projects. Since 1996, the number of overseas Chinese subsidiaries has reached 5,356, dispersed across more than 140 countries (Warner et al., 2004). During the early period, the internationalization of Chinese firms was driven by the need to access natural resources, overcome the low brand image of Chinese products and obtain advanced distribution networks and research and development (R&D) operations in developed countries as quickly as possible (Hong & Sun, 2006). In 2001, China began to accelerate its overseas expansion activities in the form of M&As, partially due to the perceived onslaught of foreign competition after China's entry to the World Trade Organization (WTO) in 2001 (Yang et al., 2009). Chinese overseas acquisitions are more commonly carried out by SOEs, and Chinese overseas investments are more likely to be in primary sectors, notably minerals and energy. Chinese firms increasingly prefer to engage in their OFDI activities alone, rather than seeking joint ventures with local firms in host countries (Buckley et al., 2008). Since 2003, the Chinese government has allowed private firms to invest overseas, triggering another wave of OFDI from China. Today, China has transformed itself from the largest recipient of FDI to the largest source of OFDI from developing countries.

India

India experienced a very different pattern of internationalization than that of China. In the 1950s, India was open to inward FDI, and a substantial stock of foreign capital was built up during this period. In the 1960s, the policy of import-substituting industrialization allowed considerable scope for domestic firms to grow and flourish (Athreye & Kapur, 2009). Thus, Indian outward FDI involved mostly private sector firms, typically large, diversified business conglomerates. The sectorial composition of Indian OFDI progressed from manufacturing in the 1960s and 1970s to both manufacturing and services in the 1980s, and then became more equally spread across the three broad economic sectors (including natural resources) in the 1990s and 2000s (Gammeltoft et al., 2010; Pradhan, 2008).

Partial liberalization of trade and investment policies was introduced in the 1980s, followed by the New Industrial Policy (NIP) in 1991. Indian economic liberalization allowed a cadre of professionally run Indian firms to emerge in skill-intensive sectors, such as information technology and pharmaceuticals, and these firms have been particularly active in overseas markets. Outward FDI from India has spanned investments in a broad range of sectors, including steel, pharmaceuticals, information technology, services and food and beverages. OFDI from India grew from negligible levels in the 1990s to $13.6 billion in 2007, to a stock of $29 billion (Nayyar, 2008). In more recent years, Indian firms have been involved in a growing number of M&As abroad, leading to cross-border purchases by Indian firms averaging $1.5 billion per annum during the 2005–2007 period.

Empirical findings and theoretical contributions

Many studies of Asian firms have explored the organizational management and strategies of Asian firms in the process of internationalization, their strengths in network-building and capability-upgrading and the effects of institutional factors. These studies have contributed to the management and international business literature and enriched our understanding of Asian firms, especially their strengths and weaknesses. The following areas of research and their findings are particularly noteworthy.

Internationalization of firms

Asian economies, especially emerging economies, provide a new context in which to understand the relative strengths and weaknesses of different perspectives on internationalization. Traditional process theory focuses on the internationalization experiences of MNCs in developed countries and suggests that domestic firms start with occasional exports, often via agents, then establish sales subsidiaries in foreign markets and finally invest in production facilities in overseas markets (Johanson & Vahlne, 1977). Another leading theory on international expansion is Dunning's (2001) eclectic paradigm. This theory posits that firms choose the most appropriate entry mode based on their ownership (O), locational (L) and internalization advantages (I). According to these theories, the internationalization of Western MNCs is driven by exploitation of their existing firm-specific assets in the global market.

However, these theories have limited applicability for analysing the internationalization activities of MNCs from Asian economies. The first prominent examples are the Four Tigers, or the so-called export-oriented economies in Asia – South Korea, Singapore, Taiwan and Hong Kong (Gulati, 1992). Due to the small domestic markets in these countries and firms' limited resources, the import substitution policy cannot sustain economic development in the long run. Chen (1995) found that firms in these countries began exporting, manufacturing original equipment or setting up overseas subsidiaries at an early stage, and achieved internationalization in a relatively short period.

Another good example comes from the two biggest emerging economies in Asia – China and India. Compared with developed country MNCs, emerging market MNCs (EMMNCs) tend to suffer from technological disadvantages and resource inadequacy (Bartlett & Ghoshal, 2000; Dawar and Frost, 1999). They often have distinct motives for overseas investment, such as acquiring strategic assets and upgrading capabilities (Buckley et al., 2008; Child & Rodrigues, 2005). Hence, these firms can invest in countries or regions more developed than their own countries to obtain advanced management knowledge or skills, strong brands, new technologies and foreign distribution networks. This trend in FDI towards developed economies occurred in both India and China. The emerging outward orientation of China and India reflects a distinct break from traditional theories. It is notable in two respects. First, the time profile of FDI flow does not conform to the conventional predictions of the "investment development path" taken by developing countries (Athreye & Kapur, 2009). Traditional theories envisage developing countries graduating through various stages, yet both China and India developed their industrial bases through policies of import-substitution without recourse to massive inflows of FDI in the early stages. Outward FDI flows emerged much sooner in both countries than the trajectory of early industrializing nations (Athreye & Kapur, 2009).

Using a springboard analogy, Luo and Tung (2007) suggested that emerging economy enterprises have benefited tremendously from inward internationalization at home by cooperating via original equipment manufacturing (OEM), and joint ventures in particular, with global players. The partners from developed countries have transferred technological and organizational skills, allowing emerging market enterprises to undertake later outward internationalization in some unconventional ways. For example, China's Lenovo and Haier have made substantial inroads in the US, while Tata from India has made high-profile investments in the UK (Athreye & Kapur, 2009). Gill and Singh (2012) also found that the internationalization of firms from China and India has been driven by push factors that enable firms to acquire resources, markets and technologies. Their experiences have inspired alternative interpretations and theoretical explanations of the internationalization of firms.

Network learning and social capital

Some researchers have used the resource-based view to explain firms' internationalization efforts as a means to acquire and control the critical resources that cannot be accessed in the local market or developed within a short period (Child & Rodrigues, 2005). International markets have undergone dramatic changes since the 1980s, including the global dispersal of modern transportation and logistics systems, the fast innovation of new information technologies such as the Internet, the breaking down of trade barriers and the globalization of the world's economies. These factors have made it much easier for today's businesses to acquire knowledge about foreign markets and conduct business across borders. Meanwhile, some researchers have shifted their attention to SMEs, born-global companies and third world multinationals (Ghymn, 1980; Young et al., 1996).

New theoretical frameworks related to organizational learning have emerged, such as the role of communication technologies, networks theory, and social capital theory (Karlsen et al., 2003; Zhou et al., 2007). Peng and Wang (2000) suggested that Asian firms are interested in using R&D-related FDI as a means for organizational learning to gain access to innovations in host countries. Coombs et al. (2006) found that these new ventures often use alliances to tap into the knowledge bases of world-class regional clusters, such as Silicon Valley, in developed economies. Goerzen and Beamish (2005) examined the diversity of alliance networks and performance, while Chang and Park (2005) investigated networking externalities and their effect on location choice. Mathews' (2006) linkage, leverage and learning model (LLL model) extends Dunning's (OLI model) and suggests that the internationalization of MNCs from emerging markets is based on firms' ability to leverage their organizational learning capabilities.

Recent studies have suggested some limitations on networked learning and social capital. Elango and Pattnaik (2007) found that a partner's network is more beneficial for Indian firms that are smaller players in their respective industries. Larger business groups are unable to benefit from network scope to increase international exposure as effectively as their smaller counterparts. Tsang (1998) identified that the constraints of time, money and effort set a practical limit on developing and maintaining close *Guanxi* or relations in China. Pittaway et al. (2004) reviewed the relationships between networking and innovation, and found that many networks appear to encounter problems during expansion, such as inter-partner conflict, displacement, lack of scale, external disruption and lack of infrastructure. Moreover, while networks can and do promote innovation within an existing technological framework, they are subject to disorganization and disintegration during periods of technological change.

Institutional environment

From the institutional perspective it is argued that the internationalization of firms is shaped at least partially by the institutional framework (Baker et al., 2005; Wan & Hoskisson, 2003; Yamakawa et al., 2008). As MNCs from emerging market economies have become major investors in other countries, scholars have expended much effort in exploring the complex relationships between their institutional environments and investment strategies, such as the location choices of EMMNCs (Buckley et al., 2007; Chan et al., 2008; Demirbag & Glaister, 2010; Dunning, 2009; Yuan & Pangarkar, 2010). Among the factors that influence MNCs' location choice, both the home and the host countries' institutions play a critical role (Du et al., 2012; Kang & Jiang, 2012; Kostova et al., 2008). Developed countries ("the North") are characterized by high-quality institutions, such as the efficient bureaucracy and market-supporting rules and regulations in the US, which attract inward FDI from emerging markets (Du et al., 2012; Wei, 2000). The institutions of developing countries ("the South"), in contrast, are typically of limited quality, such as the institutional constraints in China, which supposedly lead to increased OFDI as firms attempt to escape from the misaligned conditions and their disadvantages at home (Buckley et al., 2007; Witt & Lewin, 2007).

Although EMMNCs are naturally attracted to locations with higher institutional quality due to the benefits of reduced risks, protection of private property, and lower transaction costs (Globerman & Shapiro, 2002; Knack & Keefer, 1997), they also face the liability of foreignness and the challenges of institutional obstacles in foreign markets when attempting to access local markets and strategic resources (Cuervo-Cazurra & Genc, 2008). The great institutional distance between developed and emerging markets means that EMMNCs investing in developed countries have to adapt, or even restructure themselves to fit with their host institutions. However, EMMNCs often choose other emerging markets as locations for their FDI, rather than countries with high-quality institutions, because they are more familiar with and easily embedded in the business environment in locations with similar institutional conditions. For example, firms from Hong Kong and Singapore invest in China partly because they share the Chinese culture. Although emerging markets have low-quality institutions, EMMNCs investing in them may overcome the cultural distance by taking advantage of their past management experience when interacting with the relevant government and dealing with different levels of networks in host countries.

Opportunities and directions

Excluding from Japan and the newly industrialized economies, Asia has a number of large emerging market countries, including China, India and Indonesia. These countries have experienced higher growth rates in recent decades and have become a hotbed for growth and a major driving force of the world economy, and promising an "Asia century". Much attention and promise have been directed towards Asian firms. Between 1980 and 2011, 228 articles on international business in Asia were published in leading academic journals (Makino et al., 2013). More recently, research on Asian firms' strategies has been on the rise. Researchers have not only focused on exploring why Asian firms' internationalization processes have developed so quickly, but have also examined the mechanisms through which Asian firms maintain their growth trend. Among the many problems challenging the rise of Asian multinationals, especially those from emerging market economies, several pressing issues warrant greater attention from researchers: (1) How can Asian firms continue to innovate and stay on or move up the value chain? (2) How can they enact effective strategies to overcome their late-mover disadvantages and become viable players in the world markets? (3) How they can emerge from their home institutional environment and become genuine global industry leaders?

For many Asian economies, market liberation and reform have propelled economic development and the expansion of Asian firms in the international markets based on their advantages in mass production. FDI and spillover from Western multinationals have improved local firms' innovational and technological abilities. However, except for Japan, Asian countries are facing the urgent problem of how to cultivate domestic-driven innovations. Low-cost resources, reduced trade barriers and bureaucratic intervention alone do not create sustainable advantages. Emerging market economies have relied on two channels to cultivate domestic-driven innovation (Saxenian, 2005). The first channel, functioning at the country level, operates to take advantage of global labour mobility. Over the years, many people from less developed countries have travelled to developed countries to receive advanced education and work for Western companies. Returning entrepreneurs or foreign-educated venture capitalists can transfer advanced technology, management know-how and international market information to their home countries, which in turn help to develop independent technological capabilities in these countries. For example, India sent thousands of underemployed English speaking engineers to provide software development services for American corporations (Saxenian, 2005). Returning entrepreneurs then identified appropriate market niches, mobilized domestic skills and knowledge, connected to international markets and worked with domestic policymakers to identify and devise strategies to overcome obstacles to further growth. The second channel operates at the firm level. EMMNCs can obtain up-to-date technologies and learn management know-how from the advanced economies via overseas M&As. For example, the Chinese firm Lenovo paid $1.75 billion to acquire IBM's PC and ThinkPad divisions in 2005, and set up research centres in Japan, China and the US. In 2012, Lenovo acquired US-based Stoneware to expand its cloud computing solutions, and in 2014, cooperated with Google to acquire Motorola Mobility's smartphone business. According to the 2013 reports from International Data Corporation (IDC) and Gartner, Lenovo is now ranked the largest PC maker and the third largest smartphone maker in the world.

As the EMMNCs in Asia arose at different times and in different environments from their counterparts in the developed economies, they also differ in many other respects. Thus, a thorough understanding of the paths, processes and performances of EMMNCs requires new perspectives that can take account of their different experiences. In comparison with their counterparts from the developed economies, EMMNCs in Asia are latecomers to the international marketplace and have significant disadvantages in brand power and management expertise in international operations, especially in host countries favouring advanced technology. While EMMNCs have ample experience with low-cost and labour-intensive manufacturing, their internationalization activities are largely motivated by the need to seek natural resources and strategic assets, especially in the advanced economies. Thus, as EMMNCs expand overseas to build their networks of production and innovation, effective latecomer strategies for such firms present a fruitful area of research, including FDI entry mode, location choice and organizational structure and management.

Despite the rapid growth of their domestic economies, the emerging market countries are often associated with tremendous social and economic disparity, corruption and low institutional quality, which present major impediments for further growth. As governments attempt to devise effective strategies to avoid the "middle-income country trap", firms from emerging markets are also battling with the stigma of poor governance. Thus, many EMMNCs are attracted to the better institutional environment in foreign countries, or attempt to avoid the institutional constraints at home (Buckley et al., 2008; Child & Rodrigues, 2005). As they expand into countries with stronger institutions they often face the liability of foreignness and challenges of institutional "constraints" or obstacles in foreign markets. Their credibility and motivations are often questioned when they attempt to acquire strategic assets in advanced economies. Meanwhile, a number of researchers have posited that home country institutional factors may constitute comparative ownership advantages for firms from developing economies, and affect firms' investment decisions in overseas locations (Sun et al., 2012). Perkins (2008) and Dixit (2009) argued that when facing institutional constraints in foreign markets, the unique institutional experience of EMMNCs may provide distinct advantages for them to compete in similar locations. In particular, due to their institutional experience at thome, EMMNCs have more advantages in meeting the challenges of poor governance in foreign locations than those from advanced economies (Dixit, 2011, 2012). Therefore, it is foreseeable that EMMNCs will continue to deal with their institutional embeddedness or imprint from home and the challenges they face in the host institutional environment as they struggle to be taken seriously as credible world-class multinationals.

About this book

The following nine chapters touch upon several emerging issues regarding the rise of Asian firms. The first part includes four chapters on the organizational management and institutional environments that Asian firms face, highlighting their unique characteristics and strengths. These chapters address some of the challenging issues facing EMMNCs raised in this introduction, including entry mode strategies, institutional factors, organizational structure and leadership. The second part focuses on challenges facing Asian firms in different settings of foreign countries and their business strategies, such as M&A vs acquisitions and the paths towards internationalization. Together, they represent Academy of International Business Southeast Asia Chapter's modest contribution to this growing body of literature and serve as a platform to showcase the best research from and on this region and to stimulate further research.

Chapter 2 is an article by Lin, Chang, Ou and Tseng, which examines how both domestic partner relationships and environmental uncertainty have influenced Taiwanese SMEs' localization strategies and assesses whether these strategies influence the performance of these firms. They posit that developing relationships with local partners – or localizing – might be a more fruitful strategy than transplanting domestic networks to a foreign country. Many Taiwanese SMEs have internationalized by utilizing their existing domestic network relationships. By taking this approach, firms take a less incremental route to internationalization because they can access knowledge about the market and new processes from the other network members, which accelerates their internationalization and growth. However, Taiwanese firms' high dependency on resources and technology from the parent country may result in a lock-in effect, which in turn can affect the degree of localization of the firms in their host markets. The authors' analyses show that environmental stability and domestic network partnerships positively influence the degree of localization, and this in turn positively influences a firm's internationalization performance. The majority of Taiwanese firms internationalize to China, a country that is both psychologically and geographically close to Taiwan. However, with their ability to imitate quickly, and with technical support from foreign companies to assist in raising the quality of their output, local Chinese firms have created a more competitive environment for Taiwanese firms with production facilities in China.

In Chapter 3, Zhang, Cui and Chan examine the effect of both host and home country institutional factors on the internationalization of EMMNCs. Based on data from 301 multinational firms from China, the results support the hypotheses that cultural distance and ownership type have significant effects on their entry modes. Moreover, government support from the home country significantly moderates the effects that institutional quality and cultural differences of the host country have on the equity mode. There is also a significant interaction between institutional quality and ownership type. The findings have meaningful implications for understanding the internationalization of EMMNCs and the effect of dual institutional factors on their entry modes in foreign markets.

In Chapter 4, Lan, Yang and Zhu study the imprinting effect of home institutions on Chinese firms' long-term performance in cross-border M&As. Chinese firms may adopt the M&A strategy to effectively capitalize on their financial, domestic market and institutional advantages, and thus create and sustain their competitive advantages in the global market. The authors integrate the imprinting and neo-institutional theories to explain Chinese M&As based on their experience of institutional transitions in China. They find positive and significant abnormal returns for Chinese acquirer firms. Further, they find that the extent of business relatedness, a developed country as the target, and SOE ownership structure have significant positive effects on the long-term performance of Chinese cross-border acquirers. The findings indicate that institutional influence plays an important role in Chinese firms' M&A activities.

In Chapter 5, Selvarajah, Meyer, Sukunesan and Venkatapathy focus on the rise of Indian firms and attempt to shed light on the leadership styles in Indian organizations. Paternalism and nurturing orientations expounded in the philosophy of Dharma, in which discourses on the concepts of virtue and righteousness are embedded, permeate all Indian-based belief systems. Using the four dimensional Asian perspectives on leadership model proposed by Selvarajah et al. (1995), this study identifies key forms of leadership behaviour that influence leader excellence in Indian organizations. The managerial style expected in Indian organizations is that of a leader who is empathetic to workers, keeps abreast of current management knowledge, trusts workers' capabilities, focuses on work needs and uses initiative. Leaders with swift decision-making capabilities are highly valued and important in Indian organizations. A manager who identifies social trends and builds these into the organizational framework, one who checks problems and takes advantage of opportunities, fosters an international perspective and supports a multicultural work orientation clearly contributes to the Indian notion of an excellent leader. This suggests that the Indian workforce supports egalitarianism and downplays the caste and religious angles, at least within the work environment. The study, in effect, supports an environment in which the nurturing of and caring for employees benefits the long-term sustainability of organizations. This conclusion is in contrast to the prevailing idea, especially in the West, that supports stockholder interest as the priority for firms' existence. The Indian leadership excellence model is thus a reflection of a social system that values a paternalistic and nurturing approach to management, which reinforces inter-connectedness and interdependency between employee participation and employer demands. This chapter suggests that paternalism need not be seen as an exploitative approach to management and, if used in the true sense as depicted by Dharma, it can be a powerful management approach that unites the employee and employer for the long-term sustainability of the organization.

Chapter 6 is the first chapter in the second part of the book focusing on the perspectives and strategies regarding the internationalization of Asian firms. How and Yeoh examine the state of Singaporean private enterprises in China. In the largely state-led internationalization strategies over the years, Singaporean firms have enjoyed a strong reputation and possessed systemic efficiency and technical expertise. Private firms often follow on the heels of their government-linked counterparts, which pave the way and sometimes provide partnership and/or support. This partnership or support, however, is possibly a double-edged sword, given the possible weaknesses. Singaporean private firms, while not appearing to suffer endemically from a lack of adaptability, do not seem to fully take the available opportunities, most probably due to a combination of risk aversion and resource constraints. The authors contend that these issues are common among Asian firms from rising economies, and cast doubt on the merit of such an emulation strategy. Additional analysis reinforces the need for a local connection to keep in step with a fast changing business environment, thereby underlining the need for continuous adaptation as the key to internationalization into China.

In Chapter 7, Jack and Qin share their views on Chinese foreign direct investment in Australia. Among the key findings from their research is Chinese firms' use of the Australian market for new product testing, and the ongoing challenges these firms face in building brand preferences for their products. Using an exploratory, multiple case study methodology across a diverse range of Chinese manufacturers in the Australian market, they contribute to the literature on firm internationalization from emerging markets and enhance our understanding of organizational strategies from one of Australia's most important trading partners.

In Chapter 8, Kittilaksanawong, Chen and Xie tackle the issue of acquisition versus greenfield strategies by Chinese privately owned investors in other developing countries. The public sector reforms and the launch of the "Go Global" policy have reduced many of the constraints on overseas investments by Chinese privately owned enterprises

(POEs). Such reforms and policy incentives at home have resulted in the significant rise of Chinese POEs in the global marketplace. Access to capital is a major constraint on the internationalization of POEs. Many Chinese POEs are pushed to invest overseas because of the difficulties of raising capital at home. OFDIs have therefore become an important strategic alternative for Chinese POEs to overcome this particular institutional disadvantage at home, and to increase their resources and experience to that necessary to compete more effectively at home and on the global stage. Since the global financial crisis in 2008, Chinese enterprises have engaged in more acquisitions in many countries due to weakened overseas competition and the more attractive prices of assets in these countries. These acquisitions have enabled many Chinese firms to strengthen their resources and capabilities to compete more effectively at home and on the global stage. This chapter identifies five contingencies that potentially moderate the modes of entry between acquisitions and greenfield investments. Government policies in both China and host developing countries affect the motivations for Chinese POEs to invest in those countries. Particularly, strategic asset and natural resource seeking favour the use of acquisitions and greenfield investments as the mode of entry, respectively.

Chapter 9, by Cui, Chan, Zhang and Peng, examines the patterns of internationalization among Chinese firms by studying four Chinese multinationals, Haier, TCL, Lenovo and Founder. The study shows that by engaging in inward activities, firms may acquire the critical resources that can lead to outward activities and internationalization. The extent of their success in internationalization is conditional upon their entry strategies, the degree of industry internationalization and government support. They are less likely to follow a linear pattern of organic growth in the internationalization process. For these firms, the process of internationalization began with these inward activities some time before they commenced overseas expansion. While inward activities can help firms to acquire the necessary resources for engaging in outward activities, they also speed up the process of resource acquisition and knowledge development and accelerate the pace of outward activities and internationalization. These findings help to advance the development of theories of the internationalization of firms.

In Chapter 10, Garg discusses the trends, motivations and challenges of Indian firms in Germany. Indian firms have been increasingly active in their overseas expansion, including investments through M&As and greenfield investments, especially in Europe. India's OFDI is expected to continue its rapid upward trend, despite the policy paralysis, which strengthens the notion that India is an emerging global power. M&A strategies include buying out distressed firms to establish the acquiring firm in the developed market by creating goodwill and providing employment to negate the country of origin effect. To grow in Germany, Indian firms may have to endure higher costs because it is imperative to have a local presence. Unlike in the US, where IT companies have access to a number of skilled worker visa programmes to bring in inexpensive employees, there are very limited options in Germany and other European countries. Furthermore, it takes a long time for companies to hire someone in Europe, leading to a severe shortage of technology professionals in some European companies . Thus, it is important for Indian firms to stand out against their competitors and to be regarded as attractive employers.

Concluding remarks

While the early research on Asian firms has mostly investigated Japanese companies, recent research effort in this area has shifted to companies from newly industrialized economies (NIEs) and emerging markets, especially China and India. Thus, chapters in the book focus on the rising Asian firms and examine the strengths and strategies of these firms and the challenges they face in the process of internationalization. As their home markets become increasingly open and intertwined with the global economy, these firms have developed rapidly based on myriad inward internationalization activities and risen quickly as viable players in the international market via various channels and modes of operation. But the trajectory of their future is uncertain. Among the many problems challenging the rising Asian multinationals, several pressing issues warrant greater attention. To fulfil their promise, it is imperative that the rising Asian firms continue to innovate, move up the value chain and develop their production and management capabilities. The aspiring Asian multinationals should devise effective strategies to overcome late-mover disadvantages and strengthen their brands and services in the markets around the world. More importantly, while the rising Asian firms may leverage the comparative advantages gained from their home institutional environments, they need to adapt to the host institutional environments, minimize the liability of foreignness and gain legitimacy there in order for them to truly become global players in their respective industries.

References

Andersen, O. (1993). On the internationalization process of the firm: A critical analysis. *Journal of International Business Studies*, 24(2): 209–231.

Athreye, S. and Kapur, S. (2009). Introduction: The internationalization of Chinese and Indian firms' trends, motivations and strategy. *Industrial and Corporate Change*, 18(2): 209–221.

Baker T., Gedajlovic, E., and Lubatkin, M. (2005). A framework for comparing entrepreneurship processes across nations. *Journal of International Business Studies*, 36(5): 492–504.

Banerji, K. and Sambharya, R. B. (1996). Vertical keiretsu and international market entry: The case of the Japanese automobile ancillary industry. *Journal of International Business Studies*, 27(1): 89–113.

Bartlett, C. A. and Ghoshal, S. (1989). *Managing across Borders: The Transnational Solution*. Boston: Harvard Business School Press.

Bartlett, C. A. and Ghoshal, S. (2000). Going global: Lessons from late movers. *Harvard Business Review*, 78(2): 132–142.

Boey, C. K. and Tyabji, A. (1980). External Linkages and Economic Development: The Singapore Experience. *ERC Research Monograph*, 8.

Bruton, G. D. and Lau, C. M. (2008). Asian management research: Status today and future outlook. *Journal of Management Studies*, 45(3): 636–659.

Buckley, P. J., Clegg, L. J., Cross, A. R., Liu, X., Voss, H., and Zheng, P. (2007). The determinants of Chinese outward foreign direct investment. *Journal of International Business Studies*, 38(4): 499–518.

Buckley, P. J., Tan, R. H., and Xin, L. (2008). Historic and emergent trends in Chinese outward direct investment. *Management International Review*, 48(6): 715–748.

Callon, S. (1995). *Divided Sun: MITI and the breakdown of Japanese high-tech industrial policy, 1975–1993*. Stanford University Press.

Chan, C. M., Isobe, T., and Makino, S. (2008). Which country matters? Institutional development and foreign affiliate performance. *Strategic Management Journal*, 29(11): 1179–1205.

Chang, S. J. and Park, S. (2005). Types of firms generating network externalities and MNCs' co-location decisions. *Strategic Management Journal*, 26(7): 595–615.

Chang, S. J. and Rhee, J. H. (2011). Rapid FDI expansion and firm performance. *Journal of International Business Studies*, 42(8): 979–994.

Chen, E. K. Y. (1995). The economic setting. In Lethbrige, D. and Hong, N. S. (eds), *The Business Environment in Hong Kong*, 3rd edition, Hong Kong, : Oxford University Press: 1–51.

Child, J. and Rodrigues, S. B. (2005). The internationalization of Chinese firms: A case for theoretical extension. *Management and Organization Review*, 1(3): 381–410.

Coombs, J. E., Mudambi, R., and Deeds, D. L. (2006). An examination of the investments in US biotechnology firms by foreign and domestic corporate partners. *Journal of Business Venturing*, 21(4): 405–428.

Cuervo-Cazurra, A. and Genc, M. (2008). Transforming disadvantages into advantages: Developing-country MNEs in the least developed countries. *Journal of International Business Studies*, 39(6): 957–979.

Dawar, N. and Frost, T. (1999). Competing with giants: Survival strategies for local companies in emerging markets. *Harvard Business Review*, 77(2): 119–129.

Demirbag, M. and Glaister, K. W. (2010). Factors determining offshore location choice for R&D projects: A comparative study of developed and emerging regions. *Journal of Management Studies*, 47(8): 1534–1560.

Dixit, A. (2009). Governance institutions and economic activity. *American Economic Review*, 99 (1): 5–24.

Dixit, A. (2011). International trade, foreign direct investment, and security. *Annual Review of Economics*, 3:191–213.

Dixit, A. (2012). Governance, development, and foreign direct investment. In Max Weber Lecture No. (2012)/01. Available at https://www.princeton.edu/~dixitak/home/WeberLectFinal. Accessed July 19, 2014.

Du, J., Lu, Y., and Tao, Z. (2012). Institutions and FDI location choice: The role of cultural distances. *Journal of Asian Economics*, 23(3): 210–223.

Dunning, J. H. (2001). The eclectic (OLI) paradigm of international production: Past, present and future. *International Journal of the Economics of Business*, 8(2): 173–190.

Dunning, J.H. (2009). Location and the multinational enterprise: John Dunning's thoughts on receiving the *Journal of International Business Studies 2008* Decade Award. *Journal of International Business Studies*, 40(1): 20–34.

Elango, B. and Pattnaik, C. (2007). Building capabilities for international operations through networks: A study of Indian firms. *Journal of International Business Studies*, 38(4): 541–555.

Ellingsen, G., Likumahuwa, W., and Nunnenkamp, P. (2006). Outward FDI by Singapore: A different animal? *Transnational Corporations*, 15(2): 1–40.

Fukuda, K. J. (1993). *Japanese Management in East Asia and Beyond*. Hong Kong: Chinese University Press.

Gammeltoft, P., Pradhan, J. P., and Goldstein, A. (2010). Emerging multinationals: Home and host country determinants and outcomes. *International Journal of Emerging Markets*, 5(3/4): 254–265.

Ghymn, K. I. (1980). Multinational enterprises from the third world. *Journal of International Business Studies*, 11(2):118–122.

Gill, A. (2013). Internationalization of firms: An analysis of South Korean FDI in India. Working paper. Centre for Development Economics and Innovation Studies (CDEIS), PUNJABI UNIVERSITY. Available at http://www.punjabiuniversity.ac.in/cdeiswebsite/downloads/discussion_papers/1%20INTERNATIONALIZATION%20OF%20FIRMS.pdf.

Gill, A. and Singh, L. (2012). Internationalization of firms from China and India: Theory, evidence and policy. *Millennial Asia*, 3(1): 23–44.

Globerman, S. and Shapiro, D. (2002). Global foreign direct investment flows: The role of governance infrastructure. *World Development*, 30(11): 1899–1919.

Goerzen, A. and Beamish, P. W. (2005). The effect of alliance network diversity on multinational enterprise performance. *Strategic Management Journal*, 26(4): 333–354.

Gulati, U. C. (1992). The foundations of rapid economic growth: The case of the four tigers. *American Journal of Economics and Sociology*, 51(2): 161–172.

Hanssens, D. and Johansson, J. (1991). Rivalry as synergy? The Japanese automobile companies' export expansion. *Journal of International Business Studies*, 22(3): 503–526.

Hong, E. and Sun, L. 2006. Dynamics of internationalization and outward investment: Chinese corporations' strategies. *The China Quarterly*, 187: 610–634.
Johanson, J. and Vahlne, J. E. (1977). The internationalization process of the firm – a model of knowledge development and increasing foreign market commitments. *Journal of International Business Studies*, 8(1): 23–32.
Kang, Y. and Jiang, F. (2012). FDI location choice of Chinese multinationals in East and Southeast Asia: Traditional economic factors and institutional perspective. *Journal of World Business*, 47(1): 45–53.
Karlsen, T., Silseth, P. R., Benito, G. R., and Welch, L. S. (2003). Knowledge, internationalization of the firm, and inward-outward connections. *Industrial Marketing Management*, 32(5): 385–396.
Kim, J. M. and Rhe, D. K. (2009). Trends and determinants of South Korean outward foreign direct investment. *Copenhagen Journal of Asian Studies*, 27(1): 126–154.
Knack, S. and Keefer, P. (1997). Does social capital have an economic payoff? A cross-country investigation. *The Quarterly Journal of Economics*, 112(4): 1251–1288.
Kostova, T., Roth, K., and Dacin, M. T. (2008). Institutional theory in the study of multinational corporations: A critique and new directions. *Academy of Management Review*, 33(4): 994–1006.
Lau, H.-F. (2003). Industry evolution and internationalization processes of firms from a newly industrialized economy. *Journal of Business Research*, 56(10): 847–852.
Li, W. G. (1993). *The Japanese multinational corporations*. Beijing: China Economics Press.
Lorriman, J. and Kenjo, T. (1996). *Japan's Winning Margins: Management, Training and Education*, New York: Oxford University Press.
Luo, Y. and Tung, R. L. (2007). International expansion of emerging market enterprises: A springboard perspective. *Journal of International Business Studies*, 38(4): 481–498.
Makino, S., Chan, T. S., and Cui, G. (2013). International business research in Asia. In TS Chan and Geng Cui. *Multinationals and Global Consumers: Tension, Potential and Competition*, Palgrave Macmillan, Basingstoke, UK: 1–12.
Makino, S., Lau, C.-M., and Yeh, R.-S. (2002). Asset-exploitation versus asset-seeking: Implications for location choice of foreign direct investment from newly industrialized economies. *Journal of International Business Studies*, 33(3): 403–421.
Mathews, J. A. (2006). Dragon multinationals: New players in 21st century globalization. *Asia Pacific Journal of Management*, 23(1): 5–27.
Moon, H.-C. (2007). Outward foreign direct investment by enterprises from the Republic of Korea. In *Global Players from Emerging Markets: Strengthen Enterprise Competitiveness through Outward Investment*, New York: UNCTAD, United Nations.
Moon, H.-C., Rugman, A. M., and Verbeke, A. (1998). A generalized double diamond approach to the global competitiveness of Korea and Singapore. *International Business Review*, 7(2): 135–150.
Nayyar, D. (2008). China, India, Brazil and South Africa in the world economy: Engines of growth?. No. (2008)/05. WIDER Discussion Papers, World Institute for Development Economics (UNU-WIDER).
Odagiri, H. and Goto, A. (1993). The Japanese system of innovation: Past, present and future. In Nelson, R.R. (ed.), *National Innovation Systems: A Comparative Analysis*, Oxford: Oxford University Press: 76–114.

Park, K. H. (2003). Patterns and strategies of foreign direct investment: the case of Japanese firms. *Applied Economics*, 35(16): 1739–1746.
Park, B. and Lee, K. (2003). Comparative analysis of foreign direct investment in China firms from South Korea, Hong Kong, and the United States in Shandong province. *Journal of the Asia Pacific Economy*, 8(1): 57–84.
Pattnaik, C. (2006). Outward foreign investment policy in Korea: A review on policy issues and performance. *Journal of Korea Trade*, 10(3): 171–193.
Peng, M. W., Lee, S. H., and Tan, J. J. (2002). The keiretsu in Asia: Implications for multilevel theories of competitive advantage. *Journal of International Management*, 7(4): 253–276.
Peng, M. W. and Wang, D. Y. (2000). Innovation capability and foreign direct investment: Toward a learning option perspective. *Management International Review*, 40(1): 79–93.
Perkins, S. (2008). When does prior experience pay? Institutional experience and the case of the multinational corporation. In SSRN working paper: No. 1088251.
Pittaway, L., Robertson, M., Munir, K., Denyer, D., and Neely, A. (2004). Networking and innovation: A systematic review of the evidence. *International Journal of Management Reviews*, 5(3/4): 137–168.
Pradhan, J. P. (2008). *Indian Multinationals in the World Economy: Implications for Development*. New Delhi: Bookwell Publisher.
Saxenian, A. (2005). From brain drain to brain circulation: transnational communities and regional upgrading in India and China. *Studies in Comparative International Development*, 40(2): 35–61.
Selvarajah, C. T., Duignan, P., Suppiah, C., Lane, T., and Nuttman, C. (1995). In search of the ASEAN leader: An exploratory study of the dimensions that relate to excellence in leadership. *Management International Review*, 35(1): 29–44.
Sim, A. B. and Pandian, J. R. (2003). Emerging Asian MNEs and their internationalization strategies – case study evidence on Taiwanese and Singaporean firms. *Asia Pacific Journal of Management*, 20(1): 27–50.
Sun, S. L., Peng, M. W., Ran, B., and Yan, D. (2012). A comparative ownership advantage framework for cross-border M and As: The rise of Chinese and Indian MNEs. *Journal of World Business*, 47(1): 4–16.
Tsang, E. W. (1998). Can Guanxi be a source of sustained competitive advantage for doing business in China? *The Academy of Management Executive*, 12(2): 64–73.
Tsang, E. W. and Yip, P. S. (2007). Economic distance and the survival of foreign direct investments. *Academy of Management Journal*, 50(5): 1156–1168.
Wan, W. P. and Hoskisson, R. E. (2003). Home country environments, corporate diversification strategies, and firm performance. *Academy of Management Journal*, 46(1): 27–45.
Warner, M., Sek Hong, N., and Xiaojun, X. (2004). 'Late development' experience and the evolution of transnational firms in the People's Republic of China. *Asia Pacific Business Review*, 10(3/4): 324–345.
Wei, S. J. (2000). Natural openness and good government (No. w7765). *National Bureau of Economic Research*.
Wilson, D. and Purushothaman, R. (2003). *Dreaming with BRICs: The Path to 2050* (Vol. 99). New York: Goldman, Sachs and Company.

Witt, M. A. and Lewin, A. Y. (2007). Outward foreign direct investment as escape response to home country institutional constraints. *Journal of International Business Studies*, 38(4): 579–594.

Yang, X., Jiang, Y., Kang, R., and Ke, Y. (2009). A comparative analysis of the internationalization of Chinese and Japanese firms. *Asia Pacific Journal of Management*, 26(1): 141–162.

Yamakawa, Y., Peng, M. W., and Deeds, D. L. (2008). What drives new ventures to internationalize from emerging to developed economies? *Entrepreneurship Theory and Practice*, 32(1): 59–82.

Yoon, D. R. (2007). Korea's outward FDI in Asia: Characteristics and prospects. Unpublished manuscript, Korea Institute for International Economic Policy, Seoul.

Yoshida, M. (1987). Macro-micro analyses of Japanese manufacturing investments in the United States. *Management International Review*, 27(4): 19–31.

Young, S., Huang, C. H., and McDermott, M. (1996). Internationalization and competitive catch-up processes: Case study evidence on Chinese multinational enterprises. *Management International Review*, 36(4): 295–314.

Yuan, L. and Pangarkar, N. (2010). Inertia versus mimicry in location choices by Chinese multinationals. *International Marketing Review*, 27(3): 295–315.

Zhou, L., Wu, W. P., and Luo, X. (2007). Internationalization and the performance of born-global SMEs: The mediating role of social networks. *Journal of International Business Studies*, 38(4): 673–690.

Zutshi, R. K. and Gibbons, P. T. (1998). The internationalization process of Singapore government-linked companies: A contextual view. *Asia Pacific Journal of Management*, 15(2): 219–246.

Part I

Asian Firms: Environment, Institutions and Management

2

The Impact of Network Relationships, Environment and Localization on the Performance of Taiwanese Small and Medium Sized Enterprises

Ku-Ho Lin, Ya-Yuan Chang, Chueh-Chu Ou and Wei-Kuo Tseng

Introduction

The integration of global production networks has become an important phenomenon in recent times. This trend has also influenced Taiwanese firms to move their production offshore and seek new production bases with lower costs to meet demands from their international original equipment manufacturer (OEM) customers. Since the 1980s, the position of Taiwan's government toward the international flow of direct foreign investment (DFI) has dramatically changed, to the point where Taiwan has become a significant source of foreign direct investment (FDI), especially in the Asian region. Based on Taiwan's FDI in 2007, which accounted for US$11.107 billion, the United Nations Conference on Trade and Development (UNCTAD, 2008) ranked Taiwan as the sixth major FDI outflow country in Asia.

Small and medium sized enterprises (SMEs) have been the most important players in the internationalization of Taiwanese firms, with many Taiwanese SMEs tending to internationalize by utilizing their existing domestic network relationships (Chaney et al., 2004; Johansson & Mattson, 1991). Internationalizing through existing network relationships allows firms to take less incremental internationalization routes because they can access knowledge of the market and new processes from other network members. Hence, internationalization and growth is accelerated (Bell, 1995; Forsgren, 2001).

There has been criticism of employing these networks to develop internationally. Chen (2003) suggests that such relationships are in fact double-edged swords, as they might inhibit the international market development of these firms. Due to the high interdependence of the network partners and the integration of production processes, the firms usually have more difficulty in forming partnerships with local firms (Karagozoglu & Lindell, 1998). Such a lock-in effect can be one of the greatest stumbling blocks confronting firms' internationalization through their domestic inter-firm networks.

The influence of network relationships on a firm's localization process is not fully understood. In particular, little is known about how firms expand or depart from their existing relationships and form new connections after entering a host market. It is argued that a firm's international operations face environmental uncertainties (Forsgren, 2001), and this may impact on the decision to remain within an existing network or seek a local one. Inter-firm networks could be an important way for SMEs to reduce the perceived uncertainties and risks of internationalization (Kirby & Kaiser, 2003; Wu & Huang, 2002). Lambe and Spekman (1997) argue that an uncertain market environment usually encourages firms to form new network partnerships in the market as these relationships offer higher levels of coordination, greater stability and also the flexibility to cope with uncertainties in the new environment.

The objective of this chapter is to investigate how network relationships and industrial environment shape a firm's localization strategy and, in turn, how this strategy influences internationalization performance.

Literature review and hypothesis development

Network relationship

A broad definition of an inter-firm network is various types of vertical and horizontal inter-organizational relationships, including those with suppliers, customers, competitors and other entrants (Gulati et al., 2000). Gilbert et al. (2007) indicate that a network relationship involves sharing resources and the transfer of knowledge between businesses. This is particularly important when trading in a dynamic environment.

Firms in network relationships exchange information and learn from each other. For SME manufacturing firms, a network can provide more efficient coordination and improved communication with suppliers and buyers within and between production, marketing and other business functions. As many Taiwanese SMEs still lack international experience and integration, a network relationship can assist them in penetrating international markets with the intention of establishing successful FDI activities. It is suggested that firms participate in various network relationships for their own specific needs and purposes (Liu et al., 1994) with the intention of gaining reciprocal access to resources controlled by other network participants (Gerlach, 1992). Through networks, Taiwanese manufacturers can efficiently coordinate production, marketing and research and development (R&D) activities with their suppliers and buyers. Based on this resource sharing and pooling and the coordination of production processes, firms can achieve economies of scale and scope and simultaneously avoid the disadvantages of full organizational integration, such as high integration costs and strategic inflexibility (Powell, 1990). In fact, networks have proven so advantageous to Taiwanese SMEs that many are frequently involved simultaneously in more than one business network (Liu et al., 1994).

The development of Taiwan's SMEs in overseas markets has been constrained by limited resources and changing market demands and other uncertainties. Thus, these SMEs rely on strong network relationships with other local firms to increase access to reliable resources or technology channels and achieve stable and long-term growth. However, the development of closer, longer-term relationships with partners is not without problems (Hakansson & Snehota, 1998). These include lock-in effects caused by the development of relationship-specific assets and activity adaptations that reduce a firm's ability to develop more fruitful alternative relationships. The two main forms of lock-in are discussed below.

Resources and technology dependence

Firms that have a high level of interdependence are characterized by a close network relationship developed through resource exchange and technology sharing (Pfeffer & Nowak, 1995). However, relationships within networks are often not entirely balanced. In many situations, one partner will be highly dependent on another partner for resources or technology. The smaller firms and those with limited resources of their own rely more heavily on their partners than vice versa. Fujita (1995) points out that SMEs partnering with large enterprises have a competitive advantage, and this creates a dependency on the relationship. Furthermore, low-level technology manufacturers in high-tech industries have a higher dependency within the network relationship. When the decision to localize is undertaken, the dominant partner is likely to make that decision. The likely scenario is that existing minor partners will be disadvantaged.

Transaction relationship lock-in

When establishing an overseas manufacturing base, a firm usually faces the difficult choice of using local materials in the host country or continuing relationships with its original suppliers. By localizing a supply chain, a firm may obtain several advantages, including fewer shipping risks, savings in delivery time and costs and the establishment of relationships with local firms (Zhang & Goffin, 1999). However, when there is high interdependence on network partners and close integration of production processes, firms usually have difficulties forming partnerships with local firms (Karagozoglu & Lindell, 1998).

This lock-in effect is regarded as one of the major negative impacts of existing network relationships on a firm's internationalization. Gulati et al. (2000) identify that resource constraints and expectations of long-term cooperation are the main causes of this effect. Network firms will try to maintain their position within a network and maintain stable relationships with the other members in order to secure resources, and such an approach is likely to prevent the substitution of new entrants into the network. Loyalty to the network, regardless of resource dependency, is paramount to the existence of the network. Network partners that seek similar activities outside the network are perceived as being disloyal, and trust in that partner is likely to be affected. This is of importance particularly in sectors involved in innovative processes or products.

Industrial environment

It is argued that a firm will not undertake internationalization activities if the perceived risk is higher than a tolerable level (Forsgren, 2001). Studies have pointed out that inter-firm networks could be an important way to help a firm reduce the perceived uncertainties and risks of internationalization (Kirby & Kaiser, 2003; Wu & Huang, 2002). Lambe and Spekman (1997) further argue that an uncertain market environment usually encourages foreign firms to form network partnerships in the market.

According to the Investment Commission of Taiwan's Ministry of Economic Affairs (MOEA) (2007), the majority of Taiwanese firms agreed that "intense competition in the industry" is the main factor causing earnings to decline. It suggested that the development of networks may be a method of counteracting a competitive environment. The networks are likely to be even more important in the international environment as local knowledge of the environment can be shared and adaptations to strategy can be made to the advantage of all partners.

Localization

Understanding the needs of the international environment is of paramount importance to firms embarking on internationalization. There are many uncertainties and risks facing a company's global production and distribution, because of the customs, laws and politics of different regional markets. Therefore, firms must often adopt different strategies for different markets.

When operating in host markets, many Taiwanese manufacturing SMEs undertake a "production first, marketing later" strategy (Liang, 2002), that is, focusing on production in the host country in the initial phase and exploring new marketing channels in later stages. Their operations in the host market are very similar to their Taiwan operations (SMEA, 2001). This strategy also allows the firms to start their internationalization at a low cost as they usually start their production in host countries by bringing their existing production equipment and technology from Taiwan (Gereffi & Pan, 1994).

Heavy sourcing of supplies from Taiwan is another common characteristic of the internationalization process of Taiwanese firms. Having already established long-term relationships and mutual trust with their suppliers in Taiwan, many Taiwanese firms tend to continue these business relationships when they internationalize to other markets. This phenomenon might be caused by the limited ability of firms to internationally source materials and machinery (Chung, 1997). However, it is not a disadvantageous strategy as firms may obtain lower prices when they continue sourcing from Taiwan; original suppliers try to keep their customers by offering competitive prices or additional logistic services (Chou & Lin, 1999).

When firms establish overseas manufacturing centres they must decide whether to import raw materials and components from the parent country or use local materials. Localization of the supply chain can bring many advantages, including lower prices for raw materials and transportation, shorter delivery times and the establishment of partnerships with local firms (Zhang & Goffin, 1999). If the supply of raw materials is from overseas, both the transport and warehousing costs may be increased, and distance might put timely supply at risk (Levy, 1995).

The main objective of Taiwanese companies when setting up their own factories overseas is to quickly establish a competitive manufacturing base both in terms of price and quality. From a global point of view, moving Taiwan's industrial production base to overseas markets that provide lower production costs does incur some degree of localization.

Determinant factors of localization include available resources, economic and social conditions and industrial conditions. These factors lead to either a comprehensive transplantation of a network, transplantation of parts of a network or the establishment of a completely new local network. Taiwanese companies that localize in China build factories and use local resources in their operations have contributed to the Chinese economy. Those companies that merely transplant their home operations and networks may be considered in a poor light, and this could affect their sales performance.

Internationalization performance

Internationalization is one of the most important paths for SME growth. Through broadening customer bases by entering other countries, firms can achieve a larger volume of production and growth, leading to economies of scale (Lu & Beamish, 2001). In the internationalization performance literature, previous studies have tended to focus on SME exporting activities and exporting performances (Shoham, 1998). The performance of SMEs in other internationalization activities (e.g., FDI), however, has received less attention. Obtaining detailed information on SME foreign investments and financial data may be a stumbling block to most researchers (Lu & Beamish, 2001). Furthermore, most of the previous studies of internationalization performance have tended to focus on firm profitability and other financial performance (Lu & Manitoba, 2002). However, the business success of SMEs is not merely related to their financial performance (Kotey & Meredith, 1997). Indeed, accounting measures are usually less reliable in SMEs than in larger firms (Majocchi & Zucchella, 2003). Therefore, in any study of SMEs, other non-financial performance indicators are also worth considering. Delios and Beamish (2001) argue that a firm's performance is a multidimensional construct and should be measured using a number of variables. Employing both financial and non-financial measures is most appropriate in the SME context where financial data is often unavailable or incomplete (Bergeron et al., 2004). This study, therefore, examines firm performance in both financial and non-financial terms.

Hypothesis development

In the internationalization process, Taiwanese firms have a high dependency, in terms of resources and technology, on the parent country. This in turn may result in a lock-in effect, which could affect the degree of localization of firms in host markets. In addition, the industrial environment, in terms of competitors and level of internationalization in the industry, can also impact on the development of Taiwanese firms. Based on the literature review, this study developed the research model shown in Figure 2.1.

According to the network model, the internationalization of a firm begins with the firm engaging in a network that is primarily domestic and then developing business relationships with networks in other countries (Johansson & Mattsson, 1988). The network relationships of a firm can function as bridges to other local networks, with the international firm using these relationships to enter networks in foreign countries (Johansson & Elg, 2002). However, several studies have questioned the benefits of this strategy (Chaney et al., 2004; Chen, 2003). Although existing network relationships can be used by firms to accelerate the internationalization process and facilitate international growth, these same networks may also inhibit the international market development of the firms (Bell, 1995; Coviello & Munro, 1997). Due to the high interdependence of the network partners and the high integration of production processes, firms usually have more difficulty in forming partnerships with local firms (Karagozoglu & Lindell, 1998). Such a lock-in effect can be one of the greatest problems faced by firms internationalizing with their domestic inter-firm networks. When considering the lock-in effect of network relationships, this study developed Hypothesis 1.

> H1: The interdependence of a network with domestic partners would negatively influence a firm's localization in the host market.

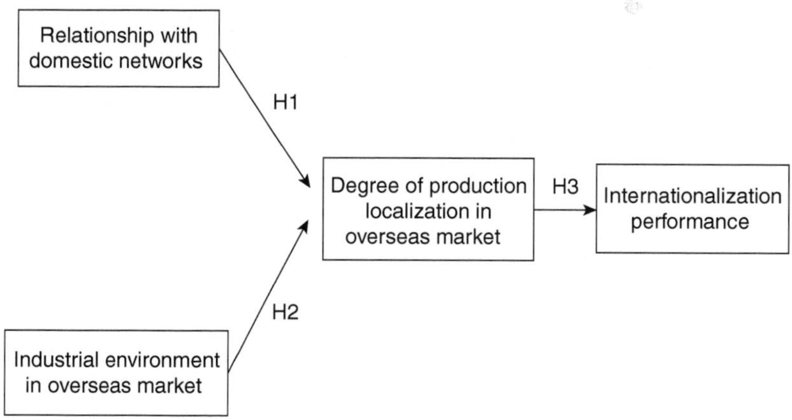

Figure 2.1 Research model of the study

It is argued that a firm's internationalization activities will not be initiated if the perceived risk is intolerable (Forsgren, 2001). Prior studies have pointed out that using inter-firm networks could be an important means to help SMEs reduce the perceived uncertainties and risks of internationalization (Kirby & Kaiser, 2003; Wu & Huang, 2002). Lambe and Spekman (1997) argue that an uncertain market environment usually encourages foreign firms to form network partnerships in the new international market. Such relationships offer higher levels of coordination, greater stability and also the flexibility to cope with the uncertainties of the environment. Accordingly, host market conditions may play an important role in firm localization decisions. Therefore, Hypothesis 2 was developed.

> H2: A lower degree of uncertainty in the industrial environment will positively influence a firm's localization in the host market.

Hu and Jefferson (2002) point out that FDI in both China's large enterprises and SMEs in the electronics and textile industries is tending to follow a localization strategy. Both hiring local personnel and purchasing local raw materials have been shown to lead to significant performance gains (Chen, 1999; Gaba et al., 2002; Luo, 1998). Anderson et al. (2002) point out that a subsidiary of a multinational corporation (MNC) accumulated its business embeddedness and technical embeddedness outside of the network. Suppliers, third-party vendors and customers, etc., will affect the subsidiary's market performance and possibly even affect cooperation between the subsidiary and parent company. Based on the above findings, it is suggested that those Taiwanese firms in China that have a higher degree of localization will in turn have a higher performance level. Based on the above discussion, this study established H3.

> H3: Localization positively influences internationalization performance.

Research method and data collection

Data collection

This study investigated the research propositions by surveying internationalized Taiwanese firms in the electrical engineering and electronics sectors. In the FDI activities of Taiwanese firms in the Chinese market, the electrical engineering and electronics sectors have accounted for nearly 50% of the total investments made by Taiwan in the past two decades. They are sectors of importance to the economy.

The sample frame employed was obtained from annual membership books published by the Association of Electronics Industry, and the company information database constructed by the Investment Commission of the Ministry of Economic Affairs in Taiwan. To ensure the quality of responses, senior managers or managers of relevant departments were selected as key informants and asked to respond to the questionnaire. In order to assess respondents' appropriateness for participation in the questionnaire, a screening question about familiarity with business operations and interactions with partners was also used in the questionnaire. Responses that indicated little familiarity were regarded as invalid and were eliminated.

A total of 800 companies were randomly selected and sent questionnaires by mail, resulting in 87 valid replies, a response rate of 10.8%. In terms of the backgrounds of the replying firms, 72.1% belong to computer peripherals and the electronic components industry, and 62.1% have been established for over 15 years. Of these companies, 38.8% have 201 to 1,000 employees. In addition, 44% of the respondents are in operational management offices, and 15.7% of the respondents are in marketing department management offices.

Two issues pertinent to survey methodology are non-response bias and common method variance. This study evaluated non-response bias by comparing early and late respondents (Armstrong & Overton, 1977) with demographic variables and model constructs. The results revealed no statistically significant differences, suggesting that non-response bias was not a serious issue in this study. Furthermore, to address the potential concerns of common method variance, which may because by the single key informant approach used in this research this study protected respondent anonymity, reduced item ambiguity and listed items for dependent variables before those for independent variables (Morgan & Berthon, 2008). Also, the Harman one-factor test was used to check for common method variance (CMV) after the survey (Podsakoff & Organ, 1986). A factor analysis of the dependent and independent variables yielded nine factors, accounting for 74.66% of the variance. The first component accounted for 24.55% of the variance. Because no one factor accounted for a majority of the variance, we have determined that common method variance is not a serious concern in this study.

Variable definition and measurement

The data were collected through a structured questionnaire. The design and questionnaire items for each construct were based on the existing literature. All items were measured using a 7-point Likert-scale anchored with 1 = "strongly disagree" and 7 = "strongly agree".

Network relationships were further divided into Network relationships were further divided into resource interdependence and transaction relationship. The measure items were adapted from Gulati et al. (2000) and Gemunden et al. (1996). This study operationalized industrial environments as a multidimensional construct that includes industrial competition and industrial internationalization. The items were adapted from Luo (1998). Firm localization was further divided into productive localization and operative localization. Items used to measure them were modified from Gaba et al. (2002). Finally, internationalization performance was measured in a multidimensional construct that includes non-financial and financial performance. The items were adapted from Lin *et al.* (2007).

Age of relationship was included as a control variable to avoid model misspecification. Age of relationship is a simple count of the number of years since an alliance was formed. Organizational age is a simple count of the number of years since the firm was formed. Organizational size is a simple count of the number of employees.

Factor analysis

Exploratory factor analysis (EFA) was used and four factors were extracted, including network relationships, industrial environment, localization and internationalization performance. Using principal components analysis (PCA) as the factor extraction method, the Varimax as an orthogonal rotation method and the eigenvalue greater than 1 helped identify the latent dimensions of the constructs. The Kaiser–Meyer–Olkin (KMO) measure of sampling adequacy (0.6) and Bartlett's test of sphericity ($P = 0.000$) indicated that the results were suitable for the EFA. In the extraction of the items, this study excluded the various components in the factor-loading of items that were less than 0.6. The EFA extracted network relationships using two measures, transaction relationship and resource dependence . The factor solution accounts for 64.877% of the total variance. Industrial environment comprised "degree of industrial competition" and "degree of industrial internationalization", and explained 66.575% of the total variance. Localization was extracted from "production localization" and "management operation localization", and explained 60.825% of the total variance. Internationalization performance was extracted from "non-financial performance" and "financial performance", and explained 70.622% of the total variance. Most factors showed that the Cronbach's α values were greater than 0.7, with the exception of "production localization" (α = 0.66) and "management operation localization" (α = 0.68), thus indicating adequate internal consistency.

Regression analysis

This study used regression analysis to explore the relationship between variables. Initially, Pearson correlation analysis was employed to understand the linkages between the various dimensions. The correlation analysis results revealed that the various dimensions of this study were positively correlated (as shown in Table 2.1) with several being significant: network relationship and industrial environment, localization and industrial environment, and localization and internationalization performance.

The regression analysis explored the impact of the network relationship and industrial environment on the localization, as well as the impact of localization on internationalization performance. Four regression models were established. Model 2 is a regression model for network relationships affecting localization. Model 3 is a regression model in which industrial environment affects localization. Model 4 is a regression model in which localization affects internationalization performance. Adjusted R^2 for the four regression models ranged from 0.162 to 0.199; the F value was significant ($P < 0.01$). Therefore, all four regression models have explanatory power (see Table 2.2).

From the results of the three regression models, it is evident that the impact of network relationships on localization is not significant ($\beta = 0.130$; $P > 0.05$), the impact of industrial environment on localization is significantly positive ($\beta = 0.278$; $^{**}P < 0.01$), and the impact of localization on internationalization performance is significantly positive

Table 2.1 Pearson correlation matrix

Variables	Mean (SD)	1	2	3	4
1. Network relationship	3.339 (0.462)	1.000			
2. Industrial environment	3.697 (0.505)	0.352**	1.000		
3. Localization	3.540 (0.565)	0.216	0.350**	1.000	
4. Internationalization performance	3.176 (0.610)	0.222	0.184	0.225*	1.000

*$P< 0.05$; **$P < 0.01$

Table 2.2 Regression models of the study

	Localization			Internationalization performance
	Model 1	Model 2	Model 3	Model 4
Control variables				
Age of relationship	0.190*			
Organizational age	0.075			
Organizational size	–0.049			
Independent variables				
Network relationship		0.130		
Industrial environment			0.278**	
Localization				0.308***
F	4.222**	8.571***	8.287***	16.715***
Adjusted R^2	0.162	0.186	0.197	0.199

*$P < 0.05$, **$P < 0.01$, ***$P < 0.001$

(β = 308; ***$P < 0.001$). H1 was not supported, but H2 and H3 were supported.

Discussion and conclusions

The association between network relationship and localization

According to the analysis, H1 was not supported, indicating that the lock-in effect of the network relationship on localization is not significant when a Taiwanese firm engages in internationalization through its existing network. This result suggests that dependency on technology and resources from the parent company in Taiwan would not be a barrier to localizing operations. Chen (2003) indicated that in the development stages of internationalization, MNCs initially build relationships within a host country and then seek to expand the new networks. Sasi and Arenius (2008) agree that firms might consider expanding an overseas venture for increased profit and growth by developing the network configuration from a dyadic relationship to a multilateral network with tentacles both in the home and foreign locations. This is evident in the decreasing raw material procurement ratio for the home country of Taiwanese firms. Accessing local suppliers through the development of local networks can lead to more timely input to the production process and more positive relationships with the local markets. This phenomenon is consistent with the views of the network configuration shift (Sasi & Arenius, 2008).

The relationship between industrial environment and localization

The results show that instability in the industrial environment of the host market positively influences a firm's degree of localization. For example, when there is a high level of competition, Taiwanese firms increase their localization activities to counteract that competition. Employing local resources and production processes may be less costly than using resources from Taiwan, affording firms that localize the ability to compete more competitively on price. According to the results of a series of surveys reported by the Ministry of Economic Affairs, Taiwan (2004, 2005, 2007), a majority of Taiwanese firms in the electrical engineering and electronics industries agreed that the competitive environment within the industries was the main cause of reduced profits. Localizing is perceived as a major method of competing in overseas markets such as China where resources are often available at a lower cost than those from Taiwan.

The relationship between localization and internationalization performance

It has been shown that network relationship and business environment can impact on the level of localization of Taiwanese firms. However, the question remains as to whether localizing operations will improve performance. More specifically, this study hypothesized that a high degree of localization can contribute to increased performance in both financial and non-financial terms. Results of the regression support the hypothesis that a firm's degree of localization would positively influence internationalization performance. Two reasons explain this link between localization and performance. First, increased performance may result from the "informational benefits" offered by the local partners, as they enable firms to acquire essential market knowledge and connect with local markets. Second, a localization-performance link can also be a consequence of superior performance by the local interfirm network in the host market, creating more unsolicited demand for the partners. As the globalization trend has increased, relationships between manufacturers and suppliers have become more complex. Previous studies have shown that firms usually have more difficulty localizing if they seek to form partnerships with local firms. This is due to strong interdependence with their original network partners and high level of integration of the production process (Karagozoglu & Lindell, 1998). Taiwanese inter-firm networks are usually characterized as having a heavy dependence on subcontracting relationships among the firms (Hu & Schive, 1996). This lock-in effect has been considered one of the greatest problems faced by firms internationalizing with domestic inter-firm networks. That negative effect was not evident in this study, although it is suggested that the proposition needs to be fully investigated through further research using a larger sample and including other sectors.

Conclusion

This study investigated how network relationships and environmental factors shape an internationalized firm's localization strategy. Previous research has tended to focus on the motivation to internationalize, the choice of entry modes and the internationalization performance, with less emphasis on internationalization strategies after entering overseas markets. This study attempted to fill in the gap regarding factors that might lead to localization and indeed whether localization is associated with better performance.

The study surveyed Taiwanese manufacturers operating in overseas markets, exploring the impact of their existing network relationships on localization strategy and internationalization performance. Traditionally, the collective relocation of a corporate network by Taiwanese enterprises is an important feature of transnational investment. However, the benefits of networking with the firms in host market, such as shortening delivery times, responding more quickly to market changes and demand and reducing production costs, have changed the strategy of many Taiwanese firms to one of localization. The literature suggests there is a lock-in effect due to firm dependency on original domestic networks. However, Taiwanese firms have branched out and developed new relationships with local suppliers in overseas markets.

Industry clusters in Taiwan have been considered a source of industrial competitiveness. The strategy of using network relationships has often been extended to the international environment, with Taiwanese firms following an approach of herd internationalization, entering overseas markets at the same times as firms in their existing domestic networks. This may help firms in the initial period of internationalization as it can reduce the initial risks and costs of entering overseas markets (Lin & Chaney, 2007). However, for long-term sustainability it may be more beneficial to break out of these networks and build relationships with local suppliers and customers.

The majority of Taiwanese firms internationalize to China, a country that is culturally as well as geographically close. However, with their ability to imitate quickly and with technical support from foreign companies assisting in raising the quality of their output, the local Chinese firms have created a more competitive environment for Taiwanese firms that have production facilities in China. Therefore, it is becoming ever more important that Taiwanese firms consider localization strategies that will enable access to resources and the efficient sharing of knowledge and contribute to increased international performance (Ellis & Pecotich, 2001; Harris & Wheeler, 2005; Inkpen & Tsang, 2005; Kraatz, 1998; Uzzi, 1997; Zhou et al., 2007).

This study focused on Taiwanese firms that internationalized to the Chinese market; therefore, the results cannot be generalized to infer the Taiwanese firms internationalized to other countries. Future studies could consider the effects of domestic network relationships on Taiwanese firms that internationalize to countries other than China. In Taiwan and other Asian countries, interfirm networks have played important roles in their business systems, and firms from these countries could be surveyed to assess how their local networks impact on their decisions and performance in overseas markets. This would provide a comparison to the results in this Taiwanese-based study.

References

Armstrong, J. S. & Overton, T. S. (1977). Estimating nonresponse bias in mail surveys. *Journal of Marketing Research*, XIV, 396–402.

Anderson, U., Forsgren, M., & Holm, U. (2002). The strategic impact of external networks: Subsidiary performance and competence development in the multinational corporation. *Strategic Management Journal*, 23(11): 979–996.

Bell, J. (1995). The internationalization of small computer software firms: A further challenge to stage theories. *European Journal of Marketing*, 29(8): 60–75.

Bergeron, F., Raymond, L., & Rivard, S. (2004). Ideal patterns of strategic alignment and business performance. *Information and Managemen*t, 41(8): 1003–1020.

Chaney, I. M., Lin, K. H., & Chaney, J. (2004). The effect of billboards within the gaming environment. *Journal of Interactive Advertising*, 5(1): 54–69.

Chen, H. (1999). International performance of multinationals: A hybrid model. *Journal of World Business*, 34(2): 157–169.

Chen, T. J. (2003). Network resources for internationalization: The case of Taiwan's electronics firms. *Journal of Management Studies*, 40(5): 1107–1130.

Chou, T. C. & Lin, C. (1999). *The Development Mechanism of Taiwan Small and Medium Enterprises*. Taipei, Lien-Gin Press Ltd.

Chung, C. (1997). Division of labour across the Taiwan strait: Macro overview and analysis of the electronics industry. In Naughton, B. (ed.), *The China Circle: Economics and Electronics in the PRC, Taiwan and Hong Kong*. Washington, D.C., Brookings Institution Press: 164–209.

Coviello, N. E., & Munro, H. (1997). Network relationships and the internationalization process of small software firms. *International Business Review*, 6(4): 361–386.

Delios, A. & Beamish, P. W. (2001). Survival and profitability: The roles of experience and intangible assets in foreign subsidiary performance. *Academy of Management Journal*, 44(5): 1028–1038.

Ellis, P. & Pecotich, A. (2001). Social factors influencing export initiation in small and medium-sized enterprises. *Journal of Marketing Research*, 38(1): 119–130.

Forsgren, M. (2001). The concept of learning in the Uppsala internationalisation process model: A critical review. *International Business Review*, 11(3): 257–277.

Fujita, M. (1995). Small and medium-sized transnational corporations: Salient features. *Small Business Economics*, 7(4): 251–271.

Gaba, V., Yigang, P., & Gerardo, R. U. (2002). Timing of entry international market: An empirical study of US Fortune 500 firms in China. *Journal of International Business Studies*, 33(1): 39–55.

Gemunden H. G., Ritter T., & Heydebreck P. (1996). Network configuration and innovation success: an empirical analysis in German high-tech industries. *International Journal of Research Marketing*, 13(5): 449–462.

Gereffi, G. & Pan, M. L. (1994). The globalisation of Taiwan's garment industry. In Bonachin, E. (ed.), *Global Production: The Apparel Industry in the Pacific Rim*. Philadelphia: Temple University Press: 126–146.

Gerlach, M. (1992). *Alliance Capitalism: The Social Organization of Japanese Business*, San Francisco: University of California Press.

Gilbert, N., Ahrweiler, P., & Pyka, A. (2007). Learning in innovation networks: Some simulation experiments. *Physica A*, 378(1): 100–109.

Gulati, R., Nohria, N., & Zaheer, A. (2000). Strategic networks. *Strategic Management Journal*, 21(3): 203–215.

Harris, S. & Wheeler, C. (2005). Entrepreneur's relationships for internationalization: Functions, origins and strategies. *International Business Review*, 14(2): 187–207.

Hakansson, H. & Snehota, I. (1998). The burden of relationships or who's next. In Naude, P. & Turnbull, W. (eds), *Network Dynamics in International Marketing*. Oxford: Pergamon: 16–25.

Hu, A. G. Z. & Jefferson, G. H. (2002). FDI impact and spillover: Evidence from China's electronic and textile industries. *The World Economy*, 25(8): 1063–1076.

Hu, M. W. & Schive, C. (1996). The market shares of Small and Medium-Scaled Enterprises in Taiwan manufacturing. *Asian Economic Journal*, 10(2): 117–131.

Inkpen, A. C. & Tsang, E. W. K. (2005). Social capital, networks, and knowledge transfer. *Academy of Management Review*, 30(1): 146–165.

Johansson, J. & Mattsson, L. G. (1988). Internationalization in industrial systems – a network approach. In Hood, N. & Vahlne, J. E. (eds), *Strategies in Global Competition*, London: Croom Helm: 287–314.

Johansson, J. & Mattsson, L. (1991). Strategic adaptation of firms to the European single market *A Network Approach*, In Mattsson, L., & Stymme, B. (eds), *Corporate and Industry Strategies for Europe*, Amsterdam: Elsevier Science Publications: 263–281.

Johansson, U. & Elg, U. (2002). Relationships as entry barriers: A network perspective. *Scandinavian Journal of Management*, 183: 393–419.

Karagozoglu, N. & Lindell, M. (1998). Internationalisation of small and medium-sized technology-based firms: An exploratory study. *Journal of Small Business Management*, 36(1): 44–59.

Kirby, D. A. & Kaiser, S. (2003). Joint ventures as an internationalisation strategy for SMEs, *Small Business Economics*, 21(3): 229–242.

Kotey, B. & Meredith, G. G. (1997). Relationships among owner/manager personal values, business strategies, and enterprise performance. *Journal of Small Business Management*, 35(2): 37–65.

Kraatz, M. S. (1998). Learning by association? Interorganizational networks and adaptation to environmental change. *Academy of Management Journal*, 41(6): 621–643.

Lambe, C. J. & Spekman, R. F. (1997). Alliances, external technology acquisition, and discontinuous technological change, *Journal of Product Innovation Management*, 14(2): 102–116.

Levy, D. (1995). International sourcing and supply chain stability. *Journal of International Business Studies*, 26(2): 22–28.

Liang, R. H. (2002). *Business Strategy of Small and Medium Sized Enterprises*, Taipei: National Open University Press.

Lin, K. H. & Chaney, I. M. (2007). The influence of domestic interfirm networks on the internationalization process of SMEs, *Asian Pacific Business Review*, 13(4): 565–583.

Lin, K. H., Wu, M. T., & Lee, T. F. (2007).The influence of interfirm networks on the process of the firm's internationalisation and localisation: a study of Taiwanese SMEs. *Jouranl of International Business Studies*, R.O.C., 1(1):205–228.

Liu, P. C., Liu, Y. C., & Wu, H. L. (1994). *Emergence of New Business Organization and Management in Taiwan*. Taiwan: Industry of Free China.

Lu, W. J. & Beamish, P. W. (2001). The internationalization and performance of SMEs. *Strategic Management Journal*, 22(6/7): 565–586.

Lu, W. J. & Manitoba, W. (2002). The Internationalization and Growth of SMEs. Administrative Science Association Canada (ASAC) Conference. Winnipeg, Manitoba, 25–28 May 2002.

Luo, Y. (1998). Timing of investment and international expansion performance in China. *Journal of International Business Studies*, 29(2): 391–407.

Majocchi, A. & Zucchella, A. (2003). International and performance: Findings from a set of Italian SMEs. *International Small Business Journal*, 21(3): 249–268.

Ministry of Economic Affairs (MOEA), Investment Commission (2004). Annual Survey on the Operation of Taiwanese Firms in Abroad Markets Available at: http://www.moeaic.gov.tw.

Ministry of Economic Affairs (MOEA), Investment Commission (2005). Annual Survey on the Operation of Taiwanese Firms in Abroad Markets Available at: http://www.moeaic.gov.tw.

Ministry of Economic Affairs (MOEA), Investment Commission (2007). Annual Survey on the Operation of Taiwanese Firms in Abroad Markets Available at: http://www.moeaic.gov.tw.

Morgan, R. E. & Berthon, P. (2008). Market orientation, generative learning, innovation strategy and business performance inter-relationships in bioscience firms. *Journal of Management Studies*, 45(8): 1329–1353.

Pfeffer, J. & P. Nowak. (1995). Joint venture and interorganizational interdependence. *Research Policy*, 24(3): 398–418.

Podsakoff, P. M. & Organ, D. W. (1986). Self-reports in organizational research: Problems and prospects. *Journal of Management*, 12(4): 531–544.

Powell, W. (1990). Neither market nor hierarchy: Network forms of organization. *Research in Organizational Behavior*, 12: 295–336.

Sasi, V. & Arenius, P. (2008). International new ventures and social networks: Advantage or liability? *European Management Journal*, 26(6): 400–411.

Shoham, A. (1998). Export performance: A conceptualization and empirical assessment. *Journal of International Marketing*, 6(3): 59–81.

Small and Medium Enterprise Administration (SMEA), MOEA (2001). *White Paper on Small and Medium Enterprises in Taiwan*, Taipei: MOEA.

United Nations Conference on Trade and Development (UNCTAD) (2008). World Investment Report. Available at: http://www.unctad.org/en/docs/wir2008_En.pdf.

Uzzi, B. (1997). Social structure and competition in interfirm networks: The paradox of embeddedness. *Administrative Science Quarterly*, 42(1): 35–67.

Wu, R. I. & Huang, C. C. (2002). Entrepreneurship in Taiwan, Turning Point to Restart, research paper for Entrepreneurship in Asia programme, The Maureen and Mike Mansfield Foundation. Available at: http://www.mcpa.org/programs/program_pdfs/ent_taiwan.pdf.

Zhang, L. & Goffin, K. (1999). Joint venture manufacturing in China: An exploratory investigation. *International Journal of Operations and Productions Management*, 19(5/6): 474–490.

Zhou, L., Wu, W. P., & Luo, X. (2007). Internationalization and the performance of born-global SMEs: The mediating role of social networks. *Journal of International Business Studies*, 38(4); 673–690.

3

The Internationalization of Emerging Market Multinationals: Effects of Host and Home Country Institutional Factors

Yuanyuan Zhang, Geng Cui and T. S. Chan

Introduction

The globalization of the world's economies has sparked an increasing number of studies on firms' internationalization. In recent decades, multinational corporations (MNCs) from emerging market economies, many of which lack firm-specific advantages (FSAs), have expanded rapidly in international markets. The expansion of emerging market multinational corporations (EMMNCs) has attracted much interest from scholars in the international business field. The leading theories of internationalization, including the transaction cost perspective (Anderson & Gatignon, 1986), the ownership, location and internalization (OLI) framework (Dunning, 1988), and the knowledge development process model (Johanson & Vahlne, 1977), are largely based on studies of firms from developed economies and emphasize FSAs and the gradual process of knowledge development. These theories are inadequate for explaining the internationalization strategies of firms from less developed countries. The expansion of EMMNCs offers a unique opportunity for theoretical development and empirical study of the factors that drive the internationalization of firms (Child & Rodrigues, 2005).

Recent development in this area has shifted attention to the role of institutional factors on the overseas investment strategies of EMMNCs (Peng et al., 2008). These studies have considered the effects of the host country's institutional factors and those of the home country separately. In this study, we examine simultaneously the influence of institutional factors from both the host country (i.e., institutional quality and cultural distance) and the home country (i.e., government support and ownership type), especially their interactive effects on the foreign market entry modes of EMMNCs. Based on data from 301 multinationals from China, we test our hypotheses concerning the effects of dual institutional factors on their foreign market entry modes. The findings provide implications for understanding the internationalization of firms and directions for future research in this area.

Research background

Economic theories

One of the most important issues in internationalization concerns how firms choose a suitable entry mode into a foreign market. Several theories have been proposed to explain the entry mode choices of firms. The transaction cost theory posits that in choosing entry modes, firms make trade-offs between control (or the level of integration) and the cost of resource commitment (Anderson & Gatignon, 1986). When their asset specificity is high, firms prefer internal integration or wholly owned subsidiaries because the costs of vertical integration can be offset by the benefits derived from such arrangements. When asset specificity is low, firms refrain from integration because the benefits of control do not justify the cost of attaining it.

The OLI framework suggests that the choice of entry mode into a target market is influenced by three factors: the ownership advantages of a firm, the internalization advantages of integrating transactions within the firm and the location advantages of the market (Dunning, 1988). Ownership advantages suggest that the firm possesses superior assets and skills and has the capabilities necessary to develop differentiated products. Thus, the existence of multinational firms is based on the assumption of market imperfections and the firm's ability to internalize the market transactions. This approach, which attempts to analyse the who, where and why of foreign direct investment (FDI) activities in terms of OLI advantages, has dominated international business research for the last two decades. The theoretical perspective is based on transaction cost considerations and mainly emphasizes the FSAs of Western MNCs in the internationalization process.

Behavioural theories

Another popular theory of the internationalization of firms is the process theory, also known as the knowledge development model (Johanson

& Vahlne, 1977). Saturation of the domestic market is considered one of the primary reasons for firms to expand overseas. Other motivations may include profit maximization and risk reduction. In the internationalization process, firms first begin to export to foreign countries. Then, once they develop more knowledge about foreign markets and international business, they may establish foreign sales subsidiaries and then overseas manufacturing operations by direct investment. The Uppsala model posits that firms expand internationally through various stages: from a low-risk, low-commitment mode of entry – direct exporting – to high-risk, high-commitment modes of entry – foreign sales and manufacturing subsidiaries (Johanson & Wiedersheim-Paul, 1975). Thus, the knowledge development process is primarily a linear model based on outward activities.

Other perspectives on firms' internationalization include the adaptation of organizational learning theory and the resource-based view in the internationalization context. Organizational learning theory explains the incremental process of knowledge development (Szulanski, 1996). Organizations not only hold specialized knowledge, but also have the opportunity to learn from other organizations. However, even though the knowledge is available, organizations may not be able to access such knowledge because they may not have the same learning capability to absorb and apply it for their own use. Differences in their absorptive capabilities then explain the probability of local firms developing knowledge of international business (Tsang, 1999).

Based on the concept of economic rent, the resource-based view (RBV) suggests that the performance of firms is determined by their sustainable competitive advantages, which derive from the firms' resources that are rare, valuable, imperfectly imitable and not substitutable (Barney, 1991). Firms can enhance their performance by acquiring or developing intangible rent-generating assets through pre-empting scarce and valuable resources and monopolistic power. Researchers in the international business field have adapted the RBV to explain firms' internationalization efforts as a means to acquire and control critical resources that cannot be accessed in the local market or developed within a short period (Child & Rodrigues, 2005).

While previous research on the internationalization of firms has focused on outward activities such as exporting or setting up overseas subsidiaries, several researchers have recognized that there is an equivalent process of inward activities as multinational firms engage in foreign sourcing activities (Luostarinen & Welch, 1997). These researchers emphasize that inward activities play a key role in the process of knowledge development and resource acquisition among local firm and greatly affect their outward internationalization (Welch & Luostarinen, 1993). They suggest that domestic firms can begin the knowledge development process by engaging in inward activities, such as becoming a distributor of foreign products or forming a joint venture (JV) with a foreign company (Bjorkman & Kock, 1997). Firms may also become integrated into the global economy through inward or up-stream internationalization. The inward internationalization process is very relevant for multinationals from less developed economies, where firms often begin their initial contact with the international markets by becoming a customer, supplier or distributor for multinationals from advanced economies.

Institutional factors

While studies of conventional firm-specific factors have been criticized for offering a narrow view of organizational activities and focusing only on the technical environments of individual transactions, there is a greater need to take country-specific factors into consideration based on the institutional environment. Institutions are characterized by shared, collective understandings or rules of conduct reflected in laws, rules, governance mechanisms and capital markets (DiMaggio & Powell, 1983; North, 1990). Institutional factors include elements of the technical environment and also cognitive and sociological elements such as the norms, standards and expectations shared by relevant members. Each organization is embedded in both its own internal institutional environment, which include the structures, systems and practices established in the past, and its external institutional environment such as cultural and legal systems.

Extant studies from the institutional perspective focus on three main areas: institutional quality, institutional profile and cultural distance. Institutional quality refers to the institutional factors that support an effective market mechanism (North, 1990). These factors include market-supporting factors such as government stability, socio-economic conditions, conflict resolution mechanisms, protection of property rights, and information systems. The institutional profile includes various aspects of a country such as its cultural norms, social knowledge, rules and regulations and so on. Kostova (1997) introduced a three-dimensional country institutional profile that includes a country's government policies (a regulatory dimension), widely shared social knowledge (a cognitive dimension) and value systems (a normative dimension). The cultural context can help to define the profit potential and/or risks associated with a specific country market. The cultural distance refers to the cultural differences between the host country and home country. Previous studies examining location-specific factors have used it to represent the institutional profile of the host country in contrast to that of the home country. Many of these studies were based on Hofstede's cultural dimensions and found that cultural distance affects the entry mode choice and the performance of multinational firms (Morosini et al., 1998).

While the institutional quality and investment incentives of the host country can help to attract foreign investors, the home country's institutional factors, such as government support and the ownership type of firms, may also affect firms' internationalization strategies, especially those of firms from emerging market economies such as China (Peng et al., 2008). Most studies of institutional factors have focused on the attributes of the host country in the internationalization process and have largely neglected the role of the home country's institutional factors. This study takes into account the host country's and the home country's institutional factors and their interactive effects on the foreign market entry modes of EMMNCs.

Hypotheses development

Firms face two types of risks when entering a foreign market. First, firms with ownership advantages face contractual risks and with high transaction costs when they engage in international transactions. Second, firms face environmental risks when they enter an unfamiliar market. When faced with these dual risks, firms must make a trade-off between high-control modes that can help to protect their particular know-how and minimize their transaction costs, and low control modes that allow them the flexibility to adapt their strategies in an uncertain environment. According to conventional theoretical thinking, firms without ownership advantages, such as those from less developed countries, are expected either to avoid entering foreign markets or to use a low control mode such as exporting.

In recent years, however, multinationals from emerging market economies such as China, India and Brazil have undergone rapid expansion in the international markets in search of market opportunities, natural resources and strategic assets such as brands, technologies, and distribution channels (Child & Rodrigues, 2005). Although these firms may lack firm-specific advantages, they have been observed to enter foreign countries with high-control modes such as JVs and wholly owned subsidiaries (WOS). While the usual location-specific factors remain an important variable in explaining firms' entry mode choices, they are mostly related to factors in the host country. In recent years, location-specific factors have been extended to include home country factors and particularly the home country institutional environment. The home country institutional environment is especially important for firms from less developed countries, which often leverage their relationship networks and incentives and support from their home governments in their overseas expansions. In the absence of FSAs, these home country institutional factors may entail certain comparative ownership or country-specific advantages (CSAs), which can shed light on the entry mode strategies of firms from emerging market economies (Cantwell et al., 2010; Sun et al., 2012).

In this study we examine how the institutional factors in both the host country and the home country influence the foreign entry modes of EMMNCs. Regarding the host country's institutional factors, we focus on the institutional quality and cultural distance because these reflect the environmental risks in the host countries. Government support and ownership type represent the home country's institutional factors. We examine the main effects of these institutional factors and their interactive effects. We argue that home government support and ownership type not only affect firms' entry modes choice by changing the risk tolerance of the decision-makers in the firms, but also moderate the effects of the host country's institutional factors. Meanwhile, although firms from emerging market economies may enjoy the advantages of cheap labour and resources, they often lack world-class technology and innovation ability. Thus, the licensing mode for outward investment is almost non-existent. In this study we do not consider licensing, but focus on the choice between the equity-based mode (FDI: JV and WOS) and non-equity-based mode (export).

Institutional quality

In any given country environment, the institutional arrangements are "strong" if they support the voluntary exchanges underpinning an effective market (Meyer, 2001). Conversely, the institutions are "weak" if they fail to ensure an effective market or even undermine the market (e.g., corrupt business practices). From the transaction cost perspective, the institutional quality of a target country influences foreign entrants' entry mode decisions by moderating the costs of alternative organizational forms. High institutional quality helps to decrease various costs in international transactions, such as the costs of monitoring, managing and inspecting performance, which are often associated with the equity-based modes of overseas investment. Everything else being equal, a strong institutional framework lowers the costs of doing business, albeit making the equity mode more attractive for EMMNCs.

From the environmental risk perspective, high institutional quality may decrease the risk perceived by the firms' decision-makers. Based on data from 31 developing countries, Jun and Singh (1996) find that political risks significantly affect the entry modes of firms, and those countries with higher political risks attract less FDI. Lower corruption and nationalization risk levels and better contract enforcement can lead to higher FDI inflows. Furthermore, a stable environment decreases investors' perceptions of risk (Gastanaga et al., 1998). Frequent changes in institutional arrangements create chaos and may reduce the opportunity to make the necessary organizational changes to compete effectively in foreign markets, thus making equity-based modes more risky and costly. When a host country has low institutional quality, firms react to such volatility by avoiding ownership, and attempt to retain flexibility and shift the risk to outsiders. Therefore, the non-equity-based export entry modes should be preferred over their equity-based counterparts in countries with low institutional quality.

> **Hypothesis 1.** The higher the institutional quality of the host country, the more firms favour the equity mode (FDI) over the non-equity mode (export) when entering foreign markets.

Cultural distance

Cultural distance indicates the differences between the home country and the target country's cultural institutions (Kogut & Singh, 1988). Cultural differences play a major role in the managerial effectiveness of using firm-specific advantages in a specific location (Hofstede, 2001). However, there are two opposing views on the effect of cultural distance on a firm's entry mode choice. One stream of literature posits that greater cultural distance between the home market and the foreign market leads to a higher level of equity ownership in a firm's entry mode choice (Tihanyi et al., 2005). This positive relationship between cultural distance and equity investment is based on the control and transaction cost perspective. Because cultural distance leads to greater information asymmetry and thus increases the costs of information and monitoring, firms prefer equity entry modes that allow them to exert greater control and thus minimize transaction costs. The alternative perspective argues that there is a negative relationship between cultural distance and equity investment (Gatignon & Anderson, 1988). Under conditions of great cultural distance, firms restrict their resource commitment and thus reduce their risk of exposure in these markets. In this case, MNCs may require greater flexibility, resulting in preferences for entry modes with lower control, such as export.

Given that firms from emerging markets often lack transaction-specific assets and technology advantages, we argue that the first theoretical perspective, which emphasizes minimizing the costs arising from cultural distance, may not be applicable. First, firms without FSAs may have less control over reducing the contractual risks than their counterparts with such ownership advantages. Moreover, the level of control is often based on the choice between JV and WOS, or between licensing and FDI. In this study we focus on the choice between export and equity entry modes. As entering a country with a greater cultural distance increases transaction costs, such as the costs of information and monitoring, the export mode should be preferred as it is less influenced by these factors. Thus, we propose that there is a negative relationship between cultural distance and equity investment.

> **Hypothesis 2**. When entering a foreign market, the lower the cultural distance between the host and home countries, the more firms favour the equity mode (FDI) over the non-equity mode (export).

Home government support

Government support is regarded as an influential institutional factor in studies of entry mode choices. Overall, a positive relationship has been found between government support and equity investment overseas (Hitt et al., 2004). Most studies, however, have focused on government policies and incentives in the host countries and have not paid sufficient attention to the role of the home country government. As EMMNCs become more involved in overseas markets, home government bodies have provided various incentives and administrative mechanisms to encourage firms to move abroad for growth and expansion. Consequently, the home government often plays a key role in outward FDI activities by providing favourable policies, financial support and government connections in host countries. In 2003, for instance, the Chinese government launched a "going out" campaign to encourage firms to move outward in the pursuit of advanced technologies, research and development (R&D) capabilities or strategic assets such as brands and distribution channels. In Guangdong province, the government even subsidizes companies that visit developed countries to study business practices and enhance their R&D capabilities. In addition to providing incentives for firms to move outward, government support helps to lower the perceived environmental risks and boosts firms' confidence about engaging in overseas investment activities, pursuing technological advances and upgrading their R&D capabilities via foreign market entry. Therefore, we expect home government support to have a positive effect on the equity-based entry modes.

> **Hypothesis 3.** Firms with government support in the home country are more likely to adopt the equity mode (FDI) than the non-equity mode (export) when entering foreign markets.

Ownership type

In emerging market economies, firms with different ownership arrangements vary greatly in their (dis)advantages as a result of the variations in institutional constraints across different types of enterprises (Zhou & van Witteloostuijn, 2010). In countries such as China, state-owned enterprises (SOEs) enjoy greater government support than private firms. They are often the beneficiaries of government protection and are less subject to market competition. In contrast, private firms do not have these advantages and operate more under market economy principles; thus, they tend to be more risk aversive and conservative. Moreover, SOEs are often much bigger firms and have a longer operating history. Large SOEs account for an overwhelming majority of the total outward FDI from China. Up to 2006, the proportion of outward FDI made by SOEs was as high as 81%, and the top ten enterprises based on overseas asset holdings were all SOEs. While benefiting the most from government support, SOEs also suffer from a bureaucratic mentality and culture of dependency, soft budget constraints and a lack of management autonomy (Wilkinson et al., 2006). Meanwhile, they are expected to be more responsive to the government's agenda, including the "going out" policy, and are often less concerned with the transaction costs of international business and the efficiency of capital utilization.

> **Hypothesis 4.** SOEs are more likely than private firms to adopt the equity mode (FDI) when entering foreign markets.

Interactive effects of institutional factors

Home country factors moderate the effects of host country factors on firms' entry mode decisions by altering their risk tolerance levels. First, we argue that home government support moderates the effect of host country institutional factors on the entry modes of firms. Despite the high transaction costs and greater risks caused by low institutional quality and high cultural distance, firms with greater home government support are likely to have a higher level of risk tolerance. These firms are often cushioned when they fall. Collectivism acts as a form of implicit mutual insurance against catastrophic losses, hence members from strong social collectives tend, quite accurately, to perceive the hazards of risky options to be smaller (Weber & Hsee, 1999). In China, the government acts as a timely helper for firms, which boosts their confidence about adopting the equity mode in foreign market entry. Therefore, when facing the environmental risks stemming from the host country's institutional factors, firms with greater home government support should have a higher risk tolerance and be more likely to choose the aggressive mode of foreign market entry. These firms are likely to be less prudent than they should be in taking on the environmental risks, because they believe that the government will bail them out if they run into difficulties. Second, in the drive toward internationalization, home country governments often act as a champion for their home-grown multinationals. They often serve as the agent or promoter of these firms, for instance by leading investment tours, building business and government connections, overseeing negotiations, solidifying agreements, offering language training and cultural immersion programmes and providing market research and other types of services. In other words, government support helps to mitigate the environmental risks in the host country and minimize the effect of cultural distance. Firms under the auspices and support of their home governments are often better received and better treated in the host countries. Therefore, when there are greater environmental risks in the host country, whether due to institutional quality or cultural distance, firms with greater home government support will be more likely to adopt the more risky equity mode of entry than those without government support.

Hypothesis 5. The institutional quality of the host country has more positive effects on the adoption of the equity mode of entry for firms with government support than for those without such support.

Hypothesis 6. The negative effect of cultural distance on the adoption of the equity mode of entry is smaller for firms with government support than for those without such support.

The ownership type of firms also moderates the effect of the host country's institutional factors on the entry mode of firms. Firms with different types of ownership may vary in their resources and abilities to deal with environmental uncertainties in foreign markets. As SOEs are often larger firms with more experience and more resources, they are less concerned with environmental uncertainty in overseas markets. Moreover, while SOEs enjoy greater government support and preferential policies, they are also more responsive than private firms to the home government's agenda on the internationalization of firms. Thus, SOEs are more able to cope with the environmental risks and are less subject to the institutional constraints in overseas markets. In contrast, private firms are often smaller and less resourceful in dealing with environmental uncertainty in overseas markets. Meanwhile, as many private firms are stock-ownership companies and are responsible to multiple stakeholders, they are more concerned about the risks associated with overseas investment, the costs of equity investment and the challenges of operating across national boundaries. Thus, private firms should be more subject to the institutional constraints in a host country characterized by low institutional quality and/or great cultural distance. Therefore, we propose that firms' ownership type significantly moderates the influence of the host country's institutional factors on the entry mode of firms expanding overseas.

> **Hypothesis 7.** The positive effect of the host country's institutional quality on the adoption of the equity mode of entry is greater for SOEs than for private firms.
>
> **Hypothesis 8.** The negative effect of cultural distance on the adoption of the equity mode of entry is greater for SOEs than for private firms.

Methodology

The data

The data on firms' foreign market entry modes and their home institutional factors were collected through a survey of mainland Chinese firms. A major multinational research company was commissioned to conduct the survey using its proprietary panel of executives from 1,500 Chinese companies that had international businesses at the end of 2009. The companies were selected from four major manufacturing sectors: food and beverages, textile and apparel, electric machinery and electronics, and transportation and other equipment. Firms from sectors in natural resources, finance, banking and business services were excluded because their outward FDI often reflects the government's agenda rather than firm behaviour.

The questionnaires were delivered to the top executives of these companies, who were familiar with their international operations. Follow-up phone calls and email reminders were sent out two weeks later to those panellists who had not responded. Finally, 301 completed questionnaires were collected, resulting in a response rate of 21%. At the end of the survey, research assistants placed phone calls to 10% of the respondents, randomly selected, to verify their identities and responses to the survey. The data on the host country's national institutions were collected from the PRS Group's *International Country Risk Guide*, which provides measures of a country's institutional quality (Dikova et al., 2010).

Measurement

We use the entry mode – non-equity (export) versus equity (FDI, including WOS and JV) – as the dependent variable. Firms that adopt an equity mode when entering a foreign market are denoted as 1, and those that adopt the non-equity mode are denoted as 0. The host and home country institutional factors are the independent variables. Home government support and ownership type are indicators of the home institutional factors. We used five indicators to measure government support: (1) the Chinese government implemented a series of policies encouraging us to explore overseas markets; (2) the Chinese government helped us to negotiate with the host country government when we encountered problems in our overseas market; (3) the Chinese government helped us to realize our goal in the host country through developing close relationships with local governments; and (4) the Chinese government helped us to find appropriate projects in overseas markets; (5) the Chinese government has implemented relevant policies to help us obtain financing with favourable terms for our overseas expansion. These items were measured on a 7-point Likert scale, with 7 as the highest score. The five items were subjected to a factor analysis, which showed good conceptual validity. We use the resulting factor score to represent home government support. For ownership type, SOEs in which the government is the sole or the largest owner are denoted by 1, while private firms of various types are coded as 0.

The host institutional factors include institutional quality and cultural distance. Institutional quality is measured using the data from the PRS Group's *International Country Risk Guide* (Dikova et al., 2010). This guide measures the composite country risks for foreign businesses, including both economic and politic risks. We use the average score 74 as the boundary for the 25 countries in our study. Countries with a risk score higher than 74 are deemed to have good institutional quality and vice versa. Cultural distance is measured by Hofstede's (2011) five culture dimensions: power distance, individualism, masculinity, uncertainty avoidance and long-term orientation. Using the index scores from these five dimensions can help to avoid the problems of common method variance and retrospective evaluation of a national culture, which are often attributed to the same individuals answering questions about firm performance and about national cultures. We use the multi-dimensional measure to arrive at the cultural distance between China and the other countries along Hofstede's five indices of cultural differences (Morosini et al., 1998):

$$CD_J = \sqrt{\sum_{i=1}^{5}(I_{ij} - I_{ic})^2}$$

where CD_j denotes the cultural distance for the *j*th country, I_{ij} denotes Hofstede's culture score on *i*th cultural dimension in the *j*th country, and *c* denotes the home country of China.

The control variables include industry category, firm age and firm size. Industry category is denoted by three dummy variables: (1) electric equipment and electronics, (2) food and beverages and (3) textile and apparel, versus transport and other equipment. Firm age is measured as the number of years since it began operations, while firm size is measured by the total number of employees.

Results

Among the respondent firms, 49% of them are SOEs, while the rest are various types of private firms. Most of the firms come from manufacturing industries in electric and electronics (31.9%), machinery (14.6%), and textile and apparel (11.5%) fields, with the remainder coming from other sectors. The number of employees among these firms ranges from 100 to more than 100,000, thus representing firms of various sizes. On average, the firms generate 33.2% of total sales from exports, 23.9% of total sales from overseas subsidiaries (excluding exports) and 25.6% of their total assets from overseas divisions. Their international business operations cover 25 host countries in different parts of the world.

Altogether, they include 2,368 export entry modes and 1,068 cases of equity-based investment. Table 3.1 presents the descriptive statistics and correlations between the key variables.

Main effects of institutional factors

Using binary logistic regression, with the equity mode denoted by 1 and the non-equity mode denoted by 0, we first test the main effects of the host and home institutional factors on firms' probability of adopting the equity-based entry modes (JVs and WOS). The main effects of the variables are shown under Model 1 in Table 3.2. For the host country institutional factors, institutional quality has a significant positive effect on the equity mode ($\beta = 0.072$, $P \leq 0.001$). This suggests that the higher the institutional quality in the host country, the more likely firms are to adopt the equity mode (FDI). As expected, cultural distance has a small and significant negative effect on the equity entry mode ($\beta = -0.010$, $P \leq 0.001$). Thus, the smaller the cultural distance between China and the host country, the more likely firms are to adopt the equity mode. For the home institutional factors, government support has a significant positive effect on the choice of equity mode among Chinese multinationals ($\beta = 0.650$, $P \leq 0.001$). Meanwhile, ownership type (i.e., SOEs) also has a significant positive effect on the equity mode of entry ($\beta = 0.126$, $P \leq 0.1$). Thus, SOEs are more likely to adopt the equity mode (FDI) than private firms.

Moderating effects of home institutional factors

To examine the interactive effects among the variables, we first assess multicollinearity. The variance inflation factor (VIF) ranges between 1.013 and 1.445, far below the critical value of 10, thus indicating no problems with multicollinearity among these variables. According to the results of Model 2 in Table 3.2, the main effects of government

Table 3.1 Descriptive statistics and correlations among variables

	Mean	SD	1	2	3	4	5	6
1. Entry mode	0.31	0.46						
2. Govern support	4.27	1.01	0.092**					
3. Ownership type	1.72	0.79	−0.025	−0.101**				
4. Institutional quality	72.30	14.08	−0.017	0.000	0.000			
5. Cultural distance	91.92	30.27	−0.051**	0.039**	−0.024	0.392**		
6. Firm size	3.69	1.19	−0.002	0.102	0.139**	0.000	0.003	
7. Firm age	10.74	14.86	0.023	0.033**	−0.282	0.000	0.200**	0.337

Note: $^{**}P \leq 0.05$

Table 3.2 Results of logistic regressions on the choice of equity entry modes

Variable/Model	**Model 1**	**Model 2**
Control variables		
Firm size	–0.005	–0.014
Firm age	0.002	0.002
Electronics industry	–0.037	–0.015
Food & beverage industry	0.060	0.042
Apparel & textile industry	–0.005	–0.011
Institutional quality (IQ)	0.072*	0.0392**
Cultural distance (CD)	–0.010***	–0.587***
Government support (GS)	0.650***	0.249
Ownership type (OT): SOE	0.126*	–0.022
IQ*GS		0.481**
CD*GS		0.053
IQ*OT		0.305**
CD*OT		–0.167

Note: *$P \leq 0.10$, **$P \leq 0.05$ and ***$P \leq 0.001$

support and ownership type are no longer significant once the interactions among institutional factors are included. Thus, hypotheses 3 and 4 are no longer supported. It is possible that government support and ownership type alone do not have a significant influence on firms' entry modes choice. However, the main effects of institutional quality and cultural distance remain significant, thus providing support for hypotheses 1 and 2 (Table 3.2).

Furthermore, Model 2 and the interaction plots (Figures 3.1 and 3.2) indicate a significant interaction effect between home government support and host country institutional quality on the equity entry mode (β for IQ*GS = 0.481). Hence, the positive effect of institutional quality on the probability of adopting the equity mode is greater for firms with strong home government support than for those lacking such support; thus, hypothesis 5 is supported. However, the interaction effect between cultural distance and government support is not significant, which indicates that home government support does not significantly mitigate the negative effect of cultural distance on the probability of firms adopting the equity mode. In other words, even when there is strong home government support, the cultural distance between China and the host country remains a barrier for firms adopting the equity mode (FDI), thus hypothesis 6 is not supported.

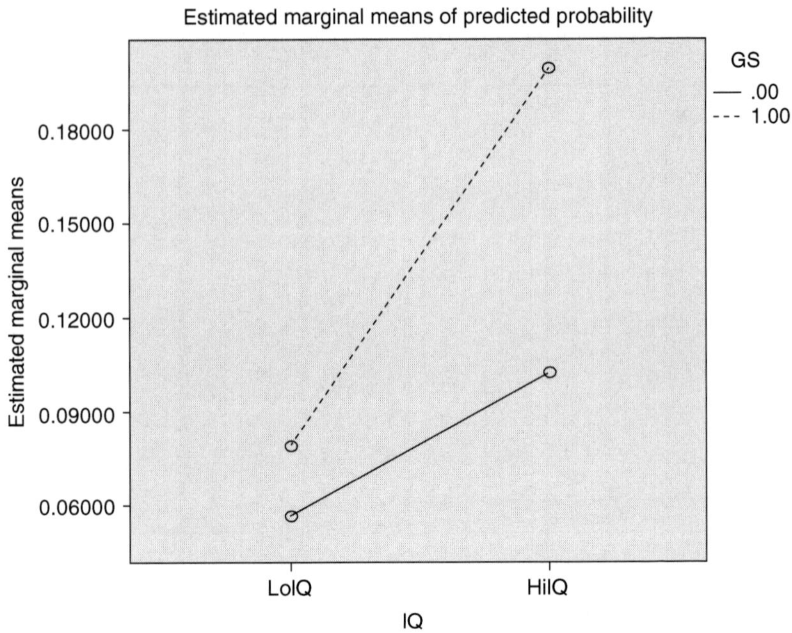

Figure 3.1 The interaction between institutional quality (IS) and government support (GS)

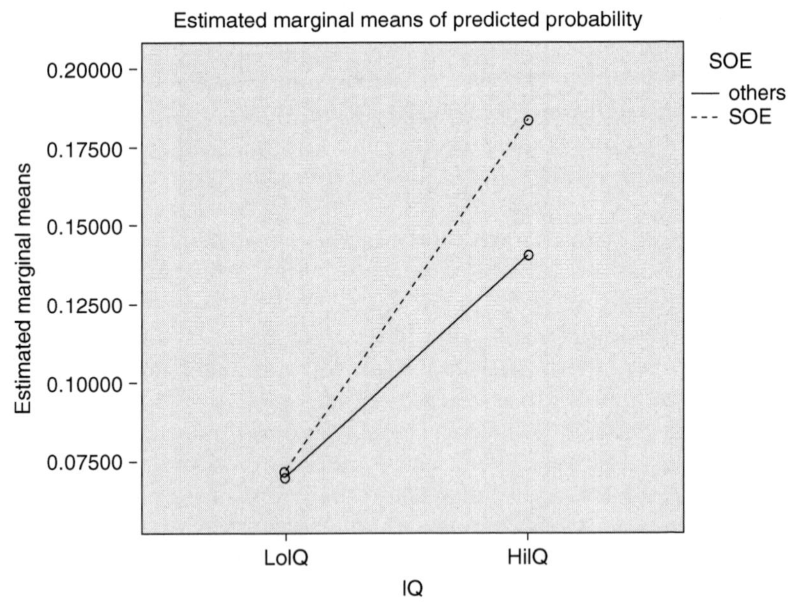

Figure 3.2 The interaction between institutional quality and ownership (SOE)

Perhaps China's deep cultural background means that cultural difference is a very important factor for Chinese firms when choosing an entry mode, and remains a barrier even when the government shares firms' risks.

The interaction between institutional quality and ownership type is also significant (β for IQ*OT = .305), thus supporting hypothesis 7 and suggesting that SOEs tend to adopt the equity mode of entry when expanding into countries with a high level of institutional quality. However, the interaction between cultural distance and ownership type is not significant; thus hypothesis 8 is not supported. This lack of an interaction effect may be due to the fact that the effect of cultural difference on entry mode choices does not differ significantly between SOEs and private firms.

Discussion

The results of this study suggest that the institutional quality of a host country and support from the home government do not, on their own, have significant effects on firms' entry mode choices. Perhaps Chinese firms are not quite ready to invest in host countries of high institutional quality. Neither does government support alone propel firms to engage in foreign direct investment. Cultural distance remains a significant barrier against EMMNCs investing directly in foreign markets. With home government support, however, firms are more likely to adopt the equity or FDI mode in markets with higher institutional quality and greater cultural distance. Furthermore, SOEs are more likely than their private counterparts to adopt the equity mode when expanding into countries with high institutional quality.

Therefore, aside from the host country environment, home country institutional factors, such as the level of government support and type of ownership, are critical factors in the outward movement of Chinese multinationals, given their institutional embeddedness in the home country. Moreover, the effect of government support is even greater when firms enter countries with higher institutional quality and greater cultural distance. Thus, in contrast to multinationals from advanced economies, the home country institutional environment plays an important role in the internationalization of EMMNCs and moderates the effects of host country institutional factors on the entry modes of these firms. SOEs from these emerging market countries are also more inclined than private firms to invest directly in unfamiliar institutional environments. Governments from emerging market economies can strategically support the expansion of firms in certain country markets when firms are pursuing important opportunities or assets there.

These findings on the effect of home country institutional factors shed new light on the entry mode choices of firms from emerging market countries, and indicate the need for more empirical studies of outward internationalization of EMMNCs. However, this study is limited because it includes data from only one home country and thus the findings may not apply to firms from other emerging market economies. Future research could include firms from other emerging market economies and provide more convincing evidence on the effects of institutional factors on the entry mode choices of multinationals from less developed economies. The effects of these host and home institutional factors on the management strategies and performance of EMMNCs in overseas markets with different institutional environments also warrant systematic investigation.

References

Anderson, E. & Gatignon, H. (1986). Modes of foreign entry: A transaction cost analysis and propositions. *Journal of International Business Studies*, 17(3): 1–26.

Barney, J. (1991). Firm resources and sustainable competitive advantage. *Journal of Management*, 17(1): 99–120.

Bjorkman, I. & Kock, S. (1997). Inward international activities in service firms-illustrated by three cases from the tourism industry. *International Journal of Service Industry Management*, 8(5): 362–376.

Cantwell, J., Dunning, J. H., & Lundan, S. M. (2010). An evolutionary approach to understanding international business activity: The co-evolution of MNEs and the institutional environment. *Journal of International Business Studies*, 41(4): 567–586.

Child, J. & Rodrigues, S. B. (2005). The internationalization of Chinese firms: A case for theoretical extension? *Management and Organization Review*, 1(3): 381–410.

Dikova, D., Sahib, P. R., & van Witteloostuijn, A. (2010). Cross-border acquisition abandonment and completion: The effect of institutional differences and organizational learning in the international business service industry, 1981–2001. *Journal of International Business Studies*, 41(2): 223–245.

DiMaggio, P. J. & Powell, W. W. (1983). The iron cage revisited: Institutional isomorphism and collective rationality in organizational fields. *American Sociological Review*, 48(2): 147–160.

Dunning, J. H. (1988). The eclectic paradigm of international production: A restatement and some possible extensions. *Journal of International Business Studies*, 19(1): 1–31.

Gastanaga, V., Nugent, J. B., & Pashamova, B. (1998). Host country reforms and FDI inflows: How much difference do they make? *World Development*, 26(7): 1299–1314.

Gatignon, H. and Anderson, E. (1988). The multinational corporation's degree of control over foreign subsidiaries: An empirical test of a transaction cost explanation. *Journal of Law, Economics, and Organization*, 4(2): 305–336

Hitt, M. A., Ahlstrom, D., Dacin, M. T., Levitas, E., & Svobodina, L. (2004). The institutional effects on strategic alliance partner selection in transition economies: China vs. Russia. *Organization Science*, 15(2): 173–185.

Hofstede, G. (2001). *Culture's Consequence: Comparing Values, Behaviors, Institutions, and Organizations across Nations* (2nd edn). Thousand Oaks, CA: Sage Publications.

Johanson, J., & Wiedersheim-Paul, F. (1975). The internationalization of the firm: Four Swedish cases. *Journal of Management Studies*, 12(3): 305–322.

Johanson, J. & Vahlne, J. E. (1977). The internationalization process of the firms: A model of knowledge development and increasing foreign market commitments. *Journal of International Business Studies*, 8(1): 23–32.

Jun, K. & Singh, H. (1996). The determinants of foreign direct investment in developing countries. *Transnational Corporations*, 5(2): 67–105.

Kogut, B. & Singh, H. (1988). The effect of national culture on the choice of entry mode. *Journal of International Business Studies*, 19(3): 411–432.

Kostova, T. (1997). Country institutional profiles: Concept and measurement. *Academy of Management Best Paper Proceedings*, Briarcliff Manor, NH: Academy of Management: 180–189.

Luostarinen, R. & Welch, L. (1997). *International Business Operations* (3rd edn). Helsinki: Helsinki School of Economics.

Meyer, K. E. (2001). Institutions, transaction costs, and entry mode choice in Eastern Europe. *Journal of International Business Studies*, 32(2): 357–367.

Morosini, P., Shane, S., & Singh, H. (1998). National cultural distance and cross-border acquisition performance. *Journal of International Business Studies*, 29(1): 137–158.

North, D. C. (1990). *Institutions, Institutional Change and Economic Performance*. Cambridge, MA: Harvard University Press.

Peng, M. W., Wang, D. Y. L., & Jiang, Y. (2008). An institution-based view of international business strategy: A focus on emerging economies. *Journal of International Business Studies*, 39(5): 920–936.

Sun, S. L., Peng, M. W., Ran, B., & Yan, D. (2012). A comparative ownership advantage framework for cross-border M&As: The rise of Chinese and Indian MNEs. *Journal of World Business*, 47(1): 4–16.

Szulanski, G. (1996). Exploring internal stickiness: Impediments to the transfer of best practice within the firm. *Strategic Management Journal*, 17(Winter): 27–44.

The PRS Group. International Country Risk Guide, www.prsgroup.com

Tihanyi, L., Griffith, D. A., & Russell, C. J. (2005). The effect of cultural distance on entry mode choice, international diversification, and MNE performance: A meta-analysis. *Journal of International Business Studies*, 36 (May): 270–283.

Tsang, E. W. K. (1999). Internalization as a learning process: Singapore MNCs in China. *Academy of Management Executive*, 13(1): 91–101.

Weber, E. U. & Hsee, C. K. (1999). Models and mosaics: Investigating cross-cultural differences in risk perception and risk preference. *Psychological Bulletin & Review*, 6(4): 611–617.

Welch, L. S. & Luostarinen, R. K. (1993). Inward-outward connections in internationalization. *Journal of International Marketing*, 1(1): 44–56.

Wilkinson, B., Eberhardt, M., & Millington, A. (2006). On the performance of Chinese state-owned and private enterprises: The view from foreign-invested enterprises. *Journal of General Management*, 32 (Sept.): 65–80.

Zhou, C. & van Witteloostuijn, A. (2010). Institutional constraints and ecological processes: Evolution of foreign-invested enterprises in the Chinese construction industry, 1993–2006. *Journal of International Business Studies*, 41(April): 539–556.

4

Imprinting Home Institutional Influence: Chinese Firms' Long-Term Performance in Cross-Border Mergers and Acquisitions

Sai Lan, Fan Yang and Hong (Susan) Zhu

Introduction

The rise of China

Over the past three decades, China has experienced rapid economic growth and social development. China's gross domestic product (GDP) per capita grew dramatically, from US$279 in 1982 to US$6,767 in 2012,[1] lifting billions of people out of poverty.[2] In 2010, China overtook Japan to become world's second largest economy.[3] Institutional reform has played an important role in the dramatic change (Peng, 2003). China has been transitioning its economic system from a Soviet-style planned economy to a market-oriented economy since 1978. During the early stage of economic liberalization, Chinese government reformed state-owned enterprises (SOEs) to improve their efficiencies, while allowing privately owned enterprises (POEs) to re-enter the economy. At the same time, China adopted the open-door policy in 1978, aiming to attract more foreign direct investments (FDIs). In the second stage of reform that started in 1992, many market institutions, such as stock exchanges, were established to provide a more level playing field for both SOEs and POEs. China's entry into the World Trade Organization (WTO) marked the beginning of China's third stage of economic development that, started in 2011 – the globalization stage – in which China's institutions are increasingly shaped by global standards. Since then, China has experienced a great acceleration of global trade and economic growth.

As a result, Chinese firms have developed ambitions to become global players, which necessarily involve more outward foreign direct investments (OFDIs).

Chinese firms' cross-border mergers and acquisition (CBMA)

As one of the major vehicles for OFDI, CBMAs pose both great opportunities and great challenges for acquiring firms who use that method to gain value. There has been steady growth of China's OFDI in recent years. In 2010, China overtook Japan and the United Kingdom to become the fifth-largest global investor. China's OFDI surged in 2011 to US$60 billion, 37% of which was realized through CBMAs (including 16 large transactions, each valued at more than US$1 billion[4]). Figure 4.1 illustrates the value and number of Chinese CBMA deals from 1997 to 2010. This figure shows a general trend of growth of Chinese CBMAs after 2005, with a major boost in both numbers and value of CBMA deals around 2008, when the global financial crisis took place.

The major players in the CBMA market used to be multinational firms from developed countries such as the US. Studies of long-term CBMA value creation in the context of Western stock markets have generated heated debates and inconsistent findings (Dutta & Jog, 2009; King et al., 2004; Mitchell & Stafford, 2000; Shimizu et al., 2004). Some scholars find positive outcomes (Chakrabarti et al., 2009; Morosini et al., 1998),

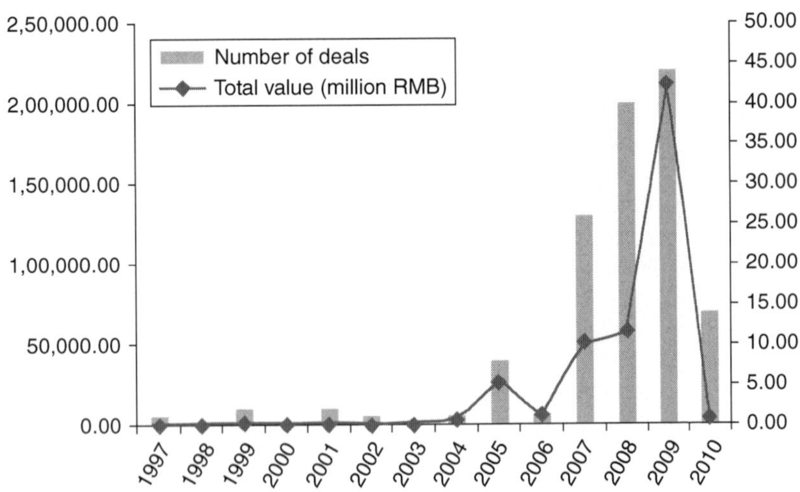

Figure 4.1 Value and number of CBMAs (1997–March 2010) (Unit: million RMB)
Source: Adapted by authors from WIND database

while others find negative results from CBMAs (Uhlenbruck, 2004). However, the research on the long-term value creation of Chinese CBMAs is very limited (Boateng et al., 2008; Shimizu et al., 2004). This study thus investigates whether and how Chinese acquiring firms create value from CBMAs in the long term.

Based on the concept of imprinting and neo-institutional theory, we examine whether and how market investors react to Chinese firms' CBMAs in the long term (DiMaggio & Powell, 1983; Marquis & Tilcsik, 2013; Scott, 1995). We argue that market investors' reactions to CBMAs are based on their prior experience and knowledge of Chinese firms' growth during institutional transition and industrial restructurings in China. Imprinted and influenced by such experience and knowledge, they tend to react to certain salient characteristics in CBMAs, which include the business relatedness between acquiring and acquired firms (Rau & Vermaelen, 1998), target nation in developed or developing countries (Uddin & Boateng, 2009) and ownership structure of acquiring firms – SOEs or POEs.

Our study makes several contributions to the literature. First, our study is one of the first studies to theoretically and empirically examine the long-term value creation of CBMAs by Chinese firms. Our theories and findings suggest that institutional transition, economic reforms, industrial restructurings and organizational changes in China have strong imprinting influences on market investors in China. Such institutional imprinting influences subsequently affect these market investors' reaction to CBMAs by Chinese firms. Second, we provide a nuanced understanding of Chinese firms' CBMA value creation by examining market investors' reaction to three key and salient CBMA characteristics, including the ownership structure of acquiring firms (firm level), business relatedness between acquiring and acquired firms (deal level) and the choice of target nation (country level). Third, using a representative sample of Chinese CBMAs in recent years, our findings provide strong support for our theory. Fourth, by examining the long-term stock market value creation, we provide a more reliable and valid value creation measure of Chinese CBMAs by addressing the market inefficiency issue such as information leakage in the short window of the Chinese stock market. Last but not least, since China is the largest developing country in the world, many of the Chinese CBMAs signify an emerging trend of market entry from developing countries to the developed world. Hence, a deeper understanding of this phenomenon may add to the general knowledge of the international business literature.

Theoretical development

Strengths and strategies of Chinese firms in CBMAs

CBMAs offer Chinese firms not only new business opportunities in foreign markets, but also strategic and value-adding resources to use to restructure their organizations to become competitive in the global market. In particular, Chinese firms may have a number of strengths when pursuing CBMAs.

First of all, the Chinese economy has performed relatively well and smoothly compared to Western economies in recent years. While both US and European firms have been struggling with the aftermath of the 2008 financial crisis and 2009 Eurozone crisis, some Chinese firms find they have plenty of cash in hand and that there are relatively inexpensive potential acquisition targets all around the world. Hence, leveraging such financial advantages may be an effective strategy for Chinese firms when carrying out CBMAs.

Second, during decades of economic growth, China gradually developed a huge domestic market with immense purchasing power. The strong customer base at home may be one of the biggest strategic assets for many Chinese acquirer firms pursuing CBMAs. They may leverage their advantages in the domestic market using various strategies, such as transferring the technology they acquired abroad to strengthen their competitiveness in the domestic market, achieving huge economies of scale through global integration of the domestic and overseas markets, etc. For example, after its acquisition of IBM's PC business in 2004, Lenovo successfully integrated its domestic market and overseas markets to become a global leader in PC manufacturing. With greatly enhanced resources and international competitiveness, Lenovo in 2014 purchased both IBM's low-end server business and Motorola Mobility. Therefore, an important strategy for Chinese firms in CBMAs is to leverage their domestic market advantages, and to achieve global competitiveness.

Third, institutional support also plays a major role in Chinese firms' CBMAs. The Chinese government has always tried to help Chinese firms to reach out to the global market. For instance, the Chinese Ministry of Commerce has a number of public policies encouraging Chinese firms to engage in CBMAs. And the State Administration of Foreign Exchange of China, which controls the largest foreign reserve in the world, is always willing to offer financial help to Chinese CBMA acquirer firms. Thus, seeking government guidance and support would be another effective strategy for Chinese firms to achieve success in CBMA transactions.

In summary, the strong economic growth of China, the institutional support and the increasingly competitive resources and capabilities of firms constitute the main strengths of Chinese firms in the global CBMA market. CBMAs provide hopes for market investors that Chinese firms may find new business opportunities and new strategic assets to renew their growth. The strengths of Chinese firms in CBMAs may further enhance market confidence, thus leading to positive abnormal returns.

Prior studies mainly adopt a short-term event study approach to study the CBMA value creation of Chinese acquirer firms and demonstrated positive value creation. For example, Boateng et al. (2008) analyse a sample of acquirers listed in Chinese stock exchanges and that participated in CBMAs from 2000 to 2005. Based on a short time window of (–20, +20) in their event study, they find a significant average positive cumulative abnormal return (CAR) of 4.43% for the acquiring firms, and positive wealth gains for the shareholders). Chi et al. (2011) examine the financial performance of CBMAs made by public firms in mainland China between 1998 and 2003. They find significant positive abnormal returns before and around the announcement date of the M&A deal, and insignificant returns in the post-M&A period (Chi et al., 2011).

These studies reinforce the short-term positive reactions in the market toward Chinese firms' CBMAs. It is also expected that Chinese firms are able to achieve positive long-term performance. Accessing and leveraging the strategic resources of acquired foreign targets and new market opportunities in host countries can help to strategically restructure Chinese firms to achieve high growth and market power in the global market in the long term. Therefore, we expect a positive long-term CBMAs performance of Chinese acquirers.

> **Hypothesis 1**: The Chinese acquirer firms in CBMAs are likely to achieve positive abnormal returns in the long run.

Determinants of Chinese CBMA long-term performance

While we expect market investors in general to react positively to Chinese firms' CBMAs in the long term, we also propose that investors may react differentially to Chinese firms' CBMAs based on various deal-specific characteristics at different levels. First, we follow extant literature in identifying the potential factors that influence market investors' reaction to Chinese CBMAs. Since empirical research about the long-term performance of Chinese CBMAs is scarce, we mainly refer to relevant studies in Western contexts to gain some insights about these factors. Thus, we examine classic factors including (1) *business relatedness* and (2) *target nation* (Rau & Vermaelen, 1998; King et al., 2004; Uddin & Boateng, 2009; Teerikangas & Very, 2012).

Second, it is also important to note that many Chinese CBMAs represent a new and different kind of FDI than Western CBMAs, that is, from developing countries to developed countries. China's unique context necessitates the examination of some context-specific factors, such as the *ownership structure* of the acquirer firm (Bhabra & Huang, 2013). Furthermore, certain factors may no longer be applicable in the context of China. For example, the method of payment is an important performance determinant in Western CBMA studies, because firms tend to pay for the acquisition by stocks when their stock is overvalued (Andre et al., 2004). However, due to the lack of liquidity of Chinese stocks in the global market, Chinese acquirers overwhelmingly choose to rely on cash payments in CBMAs, which makes the variance of this variable too small for testing. Next, we will take a closer look at each of the three major factors identified above.

Business relatedness

In addition to institutional transition, Chinese government also started industrial restructuring through M&As of firms within similar industries. Merged firms can achieve economies of scale and increase their efficiency and productivity. Thus, observing Chinese institutional transition and industrial restructurings through M&As, market investors who had experiences in Chinese markets tend to expect that when the acquirer firms have significant business overlaps with the target firms, the combined firms increase their efficiency and productivity. This expectation is also consistent with the theory and findings in studies conducted in the Western countries. Many classic empirical studies provided support for the relatedness hypothesis. Some scholars propose that value creation in related acquisitions derives from increases in economic efficiencies, such as economies of scale and scope, and from operating efficiencies as well as market power (Seth, 1990). Others similarly contend that non-conglomerate acquisitions are more inducive to value creation, based on increasing economies of scale, scope effect and market power (Singh & Montgomery, 1987).

Although some scholars argue that unrelated acquisitions may also create value based on risk diversification (Hughes et al., 1984; Reed & Luffman, 1986) and internal capital market (Stulz, 1990), there is much empirical evidence against the value creation argument for unrelated acquisitions. Some researchers find insignificant negative abnormal returns from unrelated M&As and significant positive abnormal returns from related acquisitions (Maquieira et al., 1998). Others find that both related and unrelated acquisitions result in underperformance of the acquirers in the long run, yet the abnormal return is more negative for unrelated acquisitions than related ones (Agrawal et al., 1992). Scholars suggest that managers may engage in unrelated acquisitions for reasons of self-interest and at the expense of shareholder value (Kroll et al., 1990; Morck et al., 1990). Further, unrelated M&As may have negative influences on R&D efficiency and overall stock performance (Hitt et al., 1991). Taken together, the literature considers that the potentially negative effects of unrelated M&As tend to offset their value creation effects, if any.

Although these empirical findings were mostly grounded in Western M&A studies, the relatedness hypothesis is based on the generally applicable principles of economic efficiency, operation efficiency and market power in Chinese institutional transition, industrial restructuring and organizational change. Therefore, we hypothesize that in the context of Chinese CBMAs, market investors react positively to the CBMAs in which targets have business relatedness with acquirer firms.

> **Hypothesis 2**: Chinese acquirer firms that engaged in related CBMAs tend to achieve more positive long-term abnormal returns than those that engaged in unrelated CBMAs.

Target nation

As discussed above, CBMAs break the path for Chinese firms to quickly access new market opportunities, strategic resources and frontier technologies. Facing dynamic and fierce domestic as well as global competition, it is difficult for Chinese firms to develop global distribution channels and the frontier technologies from scratch. Such development requires not only financial capital, but also time. Technology development, in particular, requires a long-term vision, accumulated basic research facilities and experiences, and intangible capabilities of R&D management. For many young Chinese firms first entering into the global arena, it is almost impossible to build up these capabilities in a short time window.

In such circumstances, acquisitions of value-adding resources become the quickest way for Chinese firms to access the frontier technologies and to strengthen their competitiveness (Buckley & Casson, 1976; Shimizu et al., 2004). Often these value-adding resources are located in developed countries. Chinese firms that acquire target companies in developed countries are not limited to the low-profit-margin manufacturing sectors but expanded to access strategic resources and capabilities such as brand, advanced technologies. Accessing strategic resources can help them win the battle in the global competitive markets in the long run.. These Chinese firms are able to access more advanced technologies, R&D capabilities, global distribution channels to best leverage their production capabilities, but also to gradually move to high-profit-margin sectors that compete based on innovation (Errunza & Senbet, 1981). Compared to acquisition of assets in developing countries, investors in China respond more positively to the acquisition of strategic assets in developed countries because such strategic assets can help firms to develop significantly and to sustain their competitiveness in the both global and domestic market.

Prior studies in Western countries also demonstrated the positive reactions of market investors to the acquisitions of targets in developed countries. For example, based on an UK sample of 3,260 CBMAs from 1984 to 2000, researchers find higher abnormal returns for firms acquiring European targets than those acquiring targets in less developed countries (Conn & Michie, 2001). They interpret the results by postulating that developed countries allow the acquirer firms to obtain more advanced technology, protect patents and expand international markets, all of which may benefit the acquirer firms in the long term.

Fosfuri and Motta (1999) build a dynamic game model on international investment decisions, and propose that countries with low technology can improve their technological capabilities through direct investment to countries with advanced technology, which is called the *reverse spillover effect*. According to this perspective, the acquirer firms in the low technology home countries benefit from OFDI to high technology target countries by means of technology diffusion, imitation, industrial linkage and human resource training (Fosfuri & Motta, 1999).

There have not been many empirical studies on the reverse spillover effect for Chinese firms engaging in OFDI. Nevertheless, there is some empirical evidence that supports this effect. Zhao et al. (2006) analyse the interaction between Chinese OFDI and technology development in China. They find that China's OFDI to R&D-intensive countries shows substantial reverse spillover effect. Li and Liu (2012) find that the performance of OFDI varies, based on the acquirer firms' geographic locations – significantly positive reverse spillover effect can be observed in the more developed eastern provinces in China. These evidences of reverse spillover effect in China lead us to expect higher long-term performance for Chinese CBMAs to developed countries than developing countries.

Hypothesis 3: Chinese acquirer firms that engage in CBMAs to developed countries tend to achieve more positive long-term abnormal returns than those that engage in CBMAs to developing countries.

Ownership structure

In the early years of Chinese CBMA, the majority of deals were carried out by SOEs. With more and more POEs being listed on Shanghai and Shenzhen stock exchanges, many of these POEs, including Lenovo, Geely and Sanyi, etc., became actively engaged in CBMAs.

Although China has been opening its market to the world, the Chinese governments have used institutional legacy to control strategic assets in China through SOEs. It is estimated that the Chinese government holds more than 50% of voting rights in approximately 31% of Chinese firms, suggesting the significant position of SOEs in the Chinese economy (Chen & Young, 2010). Further, the Chinese governments also implement their national economic restructuring policies through SOEs. As discussed above, realizing the relatively weak competitiveness of Chinese firms globally, the Chinese government initiated industrial restructuring through M&As. The institutional logic – defined as the organizing principles that guide the action of individuals and organizations (Thornton & Ocasio, 2008) – is "the larger, the stronger". As a result, SOEs in China often are a monopoly or national champion in their respective industries so that they can compete in the global market. With the institutional logic of "the larger, the stronger", these SOEs have also recently started to acquire targets in foreign countries to increase their size and global competitiveness. These acquired foreign targets with strategic assets directly add value to their Chinese acquirer firms in terms of firm size and combined resources. Thus, market investors tend to respond positively to these state-sponsored and resource-rich SOEs, based on their monopoly status in the Chinese market and their market power in the global market.

Further, these have responsibility for national economic development and social stability, they receive preferential policies compared to POEs in China. First, SOEs enjoy favourable government treatment, particularly in the context of OFDI. Prior literature has proposed that government connections should be treated as a policy-related asset because they secure national level support and protection for acquiring scarce resources. For example, Chinese SOEs typically enjoy tax credit benefits and other valuable government subsidies in their international expansions (Child & Rodrigues, 2005; Wang et al., 2012). These benefits and subsidies are needed in post-acquisition integration processes, and can help to build up investors' confidence in the success of post-acquisition integration and value creation.

Second, it is also important to note that SOEs partially operate following market rules. The purpose for Chinese government to regulate SOEs partially in the market is to use the market-based system to monitor SOEs and thus reduce the agency problems in SOEs and increase their competitiveness in the global market. Last but not least, since 2008, the central government has been tightening its control of Chinese SOEs' overseas investments. SOE's are closely scrutinized before their CBMAs are authorized. The government's careful screening processes may help to filter out potentially value-destroying deals for SOEs. Overall, we expect a more positive performance of SOEs than POEs in CBMAs in the China context.

> **Hypothesis 4**: Chinese SOE acquirer firms that engaged in CBMAs tend to achieve more positive long-term abnormal returns than POE acquirer firms that engaged in CBMAs.

Methods

Sampling

We obtained our data from the WIND database. We collected details of all the Chinese CBMAs between 1997 and 2010. Our data collection was based on the following criteria: (1) the transactions were completed by March 2010; (2) the acquirer firms were listed on China's A-share stock market before their CBMAs took place; (3) if the acquirer firm undertook more than one CBMAs during the time window, all the transactions are included in the dataset and (4) the firms have detailed firm-specific and deal-specific data available in WIND database, including ownership structure, Standard Industrial Classification (SIC) Code, target country, etc. Our final sample consists of a total of 140 transactions undertaken by 86 acquiring firms. The descriptive statistics of the sample is shown in Table 4.1 below.

Statistical analysis

Extant empirical studies on Chinese CBMAs are mostly concerned with short-term stock market performance, and mostly produce consistent positive findings (Boateng et al., 2008; Chen & Mao, 2011; Cheng &

Table 4.1 Descriptive statistics for Chinese CBMAs (1997 to March 2010)

Panel A. Transaction distribution by year

	Total value (million RMB)	**Number of deals**	**Average value (million RMB)**
1997	29.62	1	29.62
1998	0.00	0	0.00
1999	1,031.99	2	515.99
2000	0.00	0	0.00
2001	6.57	2	3.29
2002	2.53	1	2.53
2003	0.00	0	0.00
2004	3,138.80	1	3,138.80
2005	26,281.76	8	3,285.22
2006	5,790.00	1	5,790.00
2007	50,691.37	26	1,949.67
2008	57,854.71	40	1,446.37
2009	211,457.14	44	4,805.84
2010	3,746.13	14	267.58

Panel B. Transaction distribution by industry

Industry	**No. of transactions**	**Total value (million RMB)**	**Average value (million RMB)**
Nature resources	17	175,602.00	10,329.53
Coal and steel	18	67,241.00	3,735.61
Financial services and real estate	18	33,063.00	1,836.83
Transportation	16	4,235.00	264.69
Metal and iron ore	14	13,851.00	989.36
Utilities	13	11,837.00	910.54
Industrial	12	32,377.00	2,698.08
IT products and services	11	986.00	89.64
Consumer goods	9	2,207.00	245.22
Automobile	2	1,184.00	592.00
Others	10	21,824.61	2,182.46
Total	140	360,030.61	2,571.65

Panel C. Frequency distribution

		No. of transactions	**%**
Business relatedness	Related	67	47.9
	Non-related	73	52.1

Continued

Table 4.1 Continued

Ownership structure	SOE	93	66.4
	Private	47	33.6
Target nation	USA	22	15.7
	Australia	20	14.3
	Canada	10	7.1
	Russia	8	5.7
	Japan	7	5.0
	Singapore	7	5.0
	UK	5	3.6
	Holland	4	2.9
	France	3	2.1
	Belgium	3	2.1
	South Africa	3	2.1
	Italy	3	2.1
	Indonesia	3	2.1
	Germany	2	1.4
	Brazil	2	1.4
	Bermuda	2	1.4
	Finland	2	1.4
	Kazakhstan	2	1.4
	Luxembourg	2	1.4
	Thailand	2	1.4

Zhang, 2006; Liu, 2011). Since extant literature has generally agreed that the Chinese stock market does not satisfy the efficient market hypothesis (Fama, 1970), a long-term stock market performance would be a more valid and accurate means to reveal the real economic impacts of Chinese CBMAs.

Our empirical test involves two steps. In the first step, we apply long-horizon event study methodology to calculate the monthly CARs of Chinese CBMAs acquirer firms, in order to test our H1. Next, we will test our hypotheses, H2 through H4, through subsample regression analysis.

Long-horizon event study of Chinese CBMAs

In our examination of the long-term stock market performance of Chinese CBMAs, we face a few methodological choices. We will explain next how we arrive at our final choice of the calendar time approach, based on Fama-French model.

Short-term vs long-term abnormal return

The Chinese stock market is relatively young and immature. The underlying assumption for valid short-term event study is that the stock market does not violate the efficient market hypothesis (Fama, 1970). Yet, prior researchers have mostly agreed that the Chinese stock market is generally inefficient (Liu et al., 1997; Mookerjee & Yu, 1999; Wang et al., 2009), which renders the short-term event study approach to CBMA performance unreliable and unconvincing. Therefore, in this study we use a long-term approach to evaluate the Chinese CBMAs performance, rather than the short-term event study approach. The long-term approach may be the only justifiable test of stock market performance in the Chinese context.

Event time vs calendar time approach

There are generally two ways to measure the long-term stock market performance – calendar time approach and event time approach. As indicated by Andre et al. (2004), the results from calendar time and event time results are often not significantly different from each other. Dutta and Jog (2009) also report similar results using either of the two approaches.

The calendar time approach has three advantages over the event time approach. First, calendar time is less likely to suffer from the "bad model problem". Second, monthly portfolios can be used to examine the cross-correlation among companies. Third, monthly portfolios are better for statistical inferences (Fama, 1998; Mitchell & Stafford, 2000). Thus, we use the calendar time approach in our study.

Specifically, we adopt the Fama-French model (F-F model) (Barber & Lyon, 1997; Fama & French, 1993) when calculating the monthly abnormal return in the following model. Note that the constant value α is the monthly abnormal excess returns, driven by the CBMA event.

$$R_{p,t} - R_{f,t} = \alpha + s * HML_t + \beta * (R_{m,t} - R_{f,t})$$

Dependent variable ($R_{p,t} - R_{f,t}$) is calculated for each calendar month t, by the monthly stock price return on this calendar time portfolio minus the risk-free rate. Risk-free rate is the monthly return rate of five-year government bonds issued in the corresponding year. We look back from month t to preceding k years ($k = 1, 2, 3$), and put all the acquirer firms into the portfolio. SMB_t and HML_t are the monthly return of the two control portfolios we constructed in keeping with F-F model, mimicking the size and book-to-market ratio risk factors that are common to all the stocks in the current market. The term ($R_{m,t} - R_{f,t}$) is the overall market return minus the risk free rate.

Weighted least squares vs ordinary least squares

If two calendar months have different numbers of CBMAs in the preceding k (k = 1, 2, 3) years, intuitively they contribute to the value of α to varying extents. To account for potential heteroskedasticity issues, we use weighted least squares (WLS) in the statistical analysis rather than an ordinary least squares (OLS). We assign weights to each calendar month t by the square root of the number of transactions N_t in that month.

Value-weighted vs equal-weighted portfolio

A value-weighted (VW) instead of equal-weighted (EW) portfolio will be adopted. The underlying rational is that when we construct a specific portfolio, we normally try to mimic the proportions of different stocks in the stock market, rather than buying same number shares for different stocks. An EW portfolio is also hard to implement in the real world. We provide equal-weighted results for robustness checks.

Determinants of Chinese CBMAs long-term performance

In the second step, we examine the determinants of Chinese CBMAs performance. To test the impact of various firm-specific and deal-specific characteristics on the long-term performance of CBMAs, we conduct subsample regression using a Fama-French three-factor model similar to the first step. We estimate the α from a F-F model over three years.

We classify all the transactions into subgroups based on relatedness of acquiring and target firms, target firm nation and the ownership structure of the acquirer firm. We will explain below how these subsamples are constructed.

Business relatedness of acquiring and target firms

Most of the prior literature uses Standard Industrial Classification (SIC) code to test whether two firms are running related businesses or not. We categorize related CBMAs and non-related CBMAs based on SIC codes collected from the WIND database. We then calculate abnormal returns for each subsample and the difference of the abnormal returns between the two subsamples.

Target nation

We categorize all the CBMAs into two subsamples based on whether the target nation is a developing country or a developed country. The classification of developing and developed country is in accordance with the latest classification scheme specified by the International Monetary Fund (IMF). Based on that standard, there are 29 developed countries, including

USA, UK, France, Italy, Singapore, Japan, Korea, etc. We divide our sample into two subsamples, based on whether the target firm is in developed or developing countries, and then compare their performance differences.

Ownership structure

We first identify all the CBMAs undertaken by Chinese SOEs, and apply the calendar time event analysis. The rest of the sample consists of CBMAs made by POEs. We calculate the long-term abnormal return similarly, using the calendar time approach. Lastly, we calculate the differences between the returns of the SOEs' CBMAs and POEs' CBMAs for each calendar month, which is similar to testing the return of a new investment portfolio where we long the SOEs' CBMAs deals and short the POEs' CBMA deals.

Results

Long-term performance of Chinese CBMAs acquirer firms

First of all, we present the correlation matrix for the four dependent variables in the F-F model in Table 4.2. Since some of the variables in our model are correlated, we further run a variance inflation factor (VIF) test to see the overall level of multicollinearity.

The result of Table 4.3 shows that the overall level of model multicollinearity is not high with an average VIF value of 1.09.

Table 4.2 Correlation matrix

	$R_{p,t} - R_{f,t}$	SMB_t	HML_t	$R_{m,t} - R_{f,t}$
$R_{p,t} - R_{f,t}$	1.0000			
SMB_t	0.1368	1.000		
HML_t	–0.0305	0.4297*	1.0000	
$R_{m,t} - R_{f,t}$	–0.6879*	–0.0574	0.0046	1.0000

*Significant at 1% level

Table 4.3 VIF test

Variable	VIF	1/VIF
HML	1.13	0.884202
ExRm	1.10	0.912781
SMB	1.05	0.955716
Mean VIF	**1.09**	

One-year post-acquisition performance

Due to data gaps in early years, for a one-year time window, our sample only includes observations from 2005 to 2010 (N = 72). Using the VW method, all three independent variables from the F-F model are significant. The monthly abnormal return is 0.830%, although it is not statistically significant (t = 1.02).

Two- and three-year post-acquisition performance

For two- and three-year time windows, we have a complete sample including all the earlier year data (N = 123), since data gaps are no longer a concern. For the two-year window, the acquirer firms earn a positive average monthly abnormal return of around 1.12% (t = 1.66). For the three-year window, the monthly abnormal return is 1.10% (t = 1.65).

Robustness checks

For robustness checks, we test CBMAs acquirer performance with EW portfolios and non-overlapping deals (if more than one CBMA was undertaken by the same firm within our time windows, we only include the first transaction and exclude the subsequent ones). As pointed out by Lyon et al. (1999) and Loughran and Vijh (1997), the overlapping deals may increasingly influence the regression results when using a long event window. The non-overlapping sample becomes smaller with 95 CBMAs. The results are presented below in Tables 4.4 and 4.5.

Loughran and Ritter (2000) and other scholars have argued that abnormal returns may decrease or even disappear with the VW method, because the VW abnormal returns are likely to be driven by largest transactions. So we further investigate whether the VW abnormal returns are driven by certain of the largest deals in our sample. In terms of market capitalization, the top three largest acquirers in our sample are Petro China (601857.SH), Industrial and Commercial Bank of China (601398.SH) and Bank of China (601988.SH). Together, these largest acquirer firms have a total market capitalization of RMB 4.305 trillion, accounting for 17.8% of the A-share market (based on the market data at 31 March 2010). Using a non-overlapping three-year window, the results show that after taking out the big three firms, the long-term abnormal return for Chinese acquirer firms engaged in CBMAs are significantly positive at 1.93% per month (t = 2.45).

Based on these results, we can see significantly positive long-run abnormal returns for Chinese CBMAs acquirer firms. The results are robust across various scenarios. Our findings are in line with the few

Table 4.4 Abnormal returns using Fama-French calendar time portfolio regression (overlapping case, WLS regressions)

Holding period (years)	**Value-weighted calendar time portfolio**						**Equal-weighted calendar time portfolio**					
	α (%)	*s*	*h*	**β**	**Adjusted** R^2	*N*	**α (%)**	*s*	*h*	**β**	**Adjusted** R^2	*N*
1#	0.830	0.297***	–0.271**	–0.689***	0.818	72	1.254*	–0.348***	–0.158	–0.922***	0.861	72
	(1.02)	(3.83)	(–2.10)	(–14.90)			(1.71)	(–4.83)	(–1.35)	(–21.58)		
2	1.122*	0.299***	–0.295***	–0.698***	0.773	123	2.415***	–0.399***	–0.263***	–0.949***	0.865	123
	(1.66)	(4.13)	(–2.93)	(–17.31)			(3.72)	(–5.73)	(–2.72)	(–24.51)		
3	1.103*	0.276***	–0.343***	–0.693***	0.771	123	2.206***	–0.409***	–0.301***	–0.922***	0.869	123
	(1.65)	(3.92)	(–3.50)	(–17.27)			(3.57)	(–6.31)	(–3.34)	(–25.02)		

Note: *t* statistics in parentheses; *$P < 0.10$, **$P < 0.05$, *** $P < 0.01$; #one-year regression uses the purged sample

Table 4.5 Abnormal returns using Fama-French calendar time portfolio regression (non-overlapping case, wls regressions)

Holding period (years)	Value-weighted calendar time portfolio						Equal-weighted calendar time portfolio					
	α (%)	s	h	β	**Adjusted R^2**	N	**α (%)**	s	h	β	**Adjusted R^2**	N
1#	1.573	0.278***	–0.324**	–0.817***	0.801	72	1.406*	–0.387***	–0.174	–0.950***	0.848	72
	(1.56)	(2.94)	(–2.04)	(–14.44)			(1.78)	(–5.01)	(–1.38)	(–20.66)		
2	0.902	0.234***	–0.296***	–0.763***	0.760	123	2.875***	–0.438***	–0.330***	–0.963***	0.842	123
	(1.24)	(2.98)	(–2.76)	(–17.39)			(4.03)	(–5.68)	(–3.13)	(–22.40)		
3	1.051	0.244***	–0.345***	–0.787***	0.769	123	2.384***	–0.451***	–0.339***	–0.946***	0.852	123
	(1.44)	(3.17)	(–3.27)	(–17.84)			(3.55)	(–6.41)	(–3.51)	(–23.40)		

Note: t statistics in parentheses; *$P < 0.10$, **$P < 0.05$, ***$P < 0.01$; #one-year regression uses the purged sample

Table 4.6 CBMA performance excluding largest three acquirers (non-overlapping case, WLS regression)

Holding period (years)	Value-weighted calendar time portfolio					
	α (%)	s	h	β	Adjusted R^2	N
3	1.930** (2.45)	0.101 (1.21)	−0.461*** (−4.05)	−1.004*** (−20.90)	0.818	123

Note: t statistics in parentheses; *$P < 0.10$, **$P < 0.05$, ***$P < 0.01$

Table 4.7 CBMA performance determinants

Variables	α (over three years) (%)	t statistic	Adjusted R^2	N
Business relatedness				
Related (non-conglomerate) (1)	1.576**	2.29	0.777	112
Non-related (conglomerate) (2)	0.849	1.03	0.729	123
(1) – (2)	1.408*	1.79	0.342	112
Target nations				
Developed countries (1)	1.446*	1.88	0.721	123
Developing countries (2)	−0.851	−1.36	0.537	95
(1) – (2)	2.433**	2.50	0.431	95
Ownership structure				
SOE (1)	1.327*	1.94	0.785	111
None-SOE (2)	−1.042	−1.59	0.046	114
(1) – (2)	2.538***	3.07	0.644	111

Note: t statistics in parentheses; *$P < 0.10$, **$P < 0.05$, ***$P < 0.01$

extant CBMAs studies that examine long-term performance of the Chinese acquirers (e.g., Bhabra & Huang, 2013).

Determinants of Chinese CBMA long-term performance

Following Andre et al. (2004), we test the differences between the returns of two subsample portfolios based on the F-F model. The t statistics of α of each subsample and the differences are presented below in Table 4.7 (three-year window).

First of all, related acquisitions (also known as non-conglomerate acquisitions) result in a significant positive abnormal return of 1.58% ($t = 2.29$). The average monthly abnormal return for non-related acquisitions (also known as conglomerate acquisitions) is 0.85%, though it is not significant ($t = 1.03$). However, the difference between the two subsamples is significantly positive ($t = 1.79$), suggesting that related CBMAs do generate higher long-term abnormal returns than non-related CBMAs. Thus, our Hypothesis 2 is supported. This finding is consistent with extant literature (Agrawal et al., 1992; Choi and Russell, 2004; Uddin and Boateng, 2009). Jensen (1986) believes that shareholders do not want the acquirer firms to diversify their operations. Therefore, acquisitions between unrelated businesses are likely to underperform.

Second, we find significant difference between deals involving target firms in developed vs those in developing countries. Chinese CBMAs involving developed country targets significantly outperform those involving developing country targets. The average monthly abnormal return for deals involving developed country targets is significantly positive, at 1.45% (t = 1.88). Meanwhile the difference between developed and developing country targets is also significantly positive (t = 2.50). Hence, Hypothesis 3 is supported.

Finally, when we analyse the ownership structure of the Chinese CBMAs acquirer firms, the results indicate that SOEs significantly outperform the POEs by 2.54% per month (t = 3.07), and SOE acquirers earn a significant 1.33% abnormal return per month (t = 1.94). Thus our Hypothesis 4 is supported. This result is also consistent with Wu and Xie (2010), who find a positive relationship between proportion of state-owned shares and post-M&A stock market performance.

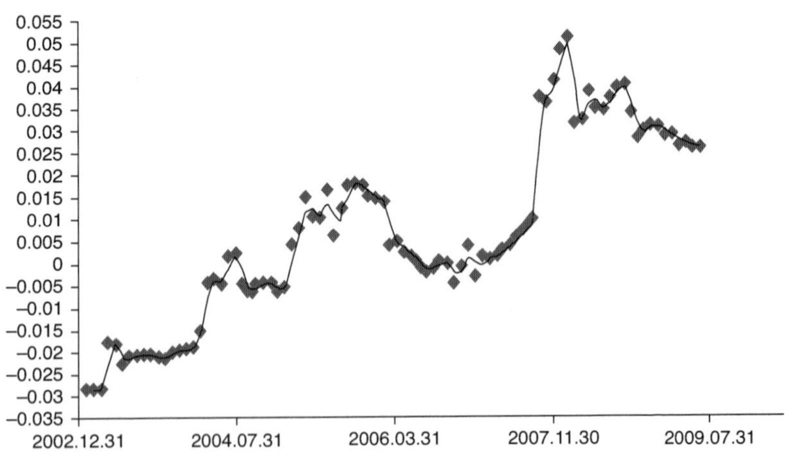

Figure 4.2 Trend of three-year abnormal return

Source: Self-calculation

The trend of the abnormal returns

We are further interested in testing the moving trend of the monthly abnormal return. Base on the "moving average", we run our regression for every three-year periods (36 months for each regression) and plot the distribution and evolutionary trend of abnormal returns, the α value. Results are shown below in Figure 4.2.

From Figure 4.2, we can see that the long-term CBMAs performance of Chinese acquirers has generally been improving. In August 2008, the three-year abnormal return value reaches a peak value of 5.095% per month. The decline afterwards may have to do with the global financial crisis in 2008, which caused substantial damage to firms that were acquired through Chinese CBMAs. Nevertheless, the generally increasing trend of abnormal returns during the past decade reflects a healthy improvement of the Chinese CBMAs.

Discussion and conclusion

The rise of China has reached the globalization stage. Chinese firms are the newcomers in the global market. Although lacking in CBMAs experience, they bring with them unique strengths and strategies that leverage these strengths, while making remarkable progresses in pursuing their global ambitions through CBMAs. This study examined their CBMAs performance so far, using a relatively long time window. Our long-horizon event study of the stock market performance of Chinese CBMAs finds significantly positive abnormal returns for Chinese acquirer firms. Further, we identified several determinants of the long-term stock market performance of the Chinese CBMAs acquirers. The empirical results indicate that: (1) business relatedness is positively related to long-term Chinese CBMAs performance; (2) Chinese CBMAs involving targets in developed countries outperform those with targets in developing countries; and (3) SOE acquirers outperform POE acquirers.

This study has just scratched the surface of research in this burgeoning field. There are some limitations of our research. First, we have only examined publicly listed acquirer firms, which may not account for the entire population of Chinese firms engaging in CBMAs. Some prominent Chinese CBMAs deals were carried out by unlisted companies, such as Huawei Technology and Dalian Wanda Group. Second, as a large-sample empirical study, our research does not touch upon the internal aspects of the Chinese CBMAs acquirer firms, including their motives for CBMAs and how they handle post-merger integration challenges caused by liability of foreignness, etc. These may be interesting future research questions, which were beyond the scope of this study. Last but not least, the methodologies of long-horizon event studies are not without flaws. For example, Kothari and Warner (2005) argued that the Fama-French three-factor model may be subject to model specification problems, which are typically indicated by low adjusted R^2 values. Fortunately, our model has very high explanatory power, with all adjusted R^2 greater than 0.76. This may alleviate the concern about the model misspecification problem.

Nevertheless, the findings of this study do have some important theoretical and practical implications. First of all, this study provides a different perspective from the traditional CBMAs studies that are mainly focused on acquirer firms from developed countries. Considering the key institutional characteristics of China, our theory is built upon the concept of imprinting and neo-institutional theory because institutional transition has strong imprinting influence on social actors such as market investors in China. In contrast to the mostly negative long-term effects of Western CBMAs, the significantly positive long-term performance of Chinese CBMAs suggests that CBMAs indeed add value to Chinese firms in general, perhaps because many of them are facing bottlenecks in their growth domestically.

Second, the findings of our study also reveal some uniquely Chinese characteristics of CBMAs. For example, SOEs still dominate in Chinese CBMAs, and most target nations are developed countries. Thus, one potential interpretation of the overall positive long-term performance of Chinese CBMAs may be related to the role of the government. Although the Chinese market reform has been carried out for over 30 years, the visible hand of the Chinese government may still be playing a more important role than the invisible hand of the market. We cannot rule out the possibility that institutional forces are both driving many of the Chinese CBMAs, as well as providing institutional supports for their success. Such institutional dependence may serve as a double-edged sword for Chinese firms in their globalization process. On the one hand, institutional guidance and support represents a unique strength of Chinese acquirer firms that may be effectively leveraged as a strategy in CBMAs transactions. On the other hand, blindly following government instructions without due diligence on their own part may hamper the rational judgement of Chinese acquirer firms engaged in CBMAs, thus causing future losses. Therefore, a potentially interesting future research question would be to gain in-depth understanding of the trade-offs of these institutional forces influencing the Chinese CBMAs transactions.

Third, we found that Chinese firms gain value from CBMAs especially when the target firms are located in developed countries. This may indeed suggest a positive reverse spillover effect. Potentially interesting future research questions might be how such effects really take place, and how sustainable are such effects. Fourth, we used a novel, long-horizon event study method to test the post-M&A performance of Chinese CBMAs. This long-term approach represents a significant improvement over prior short-term event studies, due to the widely acknowledged fact that the Chinese stock market may not satisfy the efficient market hypothesis necessary for short-term event studies. With China's increasing OFDI, as well as growing presence in international markets, we expect more and more Chinese CBMAs to take place in the future. Our study represents an initial attempt to shed some new light on this important emerging field. A lot more intriguing research questions remain to be explored. We hope to inspire future studies in this promising research area.

Notes

1. National Bureau of statistics of China 2012
2. National Bureau of statistics of China 2012
3. Wall Street Journal, 14 February 2011
4. 2011 Chinese Merger and Acquisition Review and Prospect, issued by PWC

References

Agrawal, A., Jaffe, J. F., & Mandelker, G. N. (1992). The post-merger performance of acquiring firms: A re-examination of an anomaly. *The Journal of Finance*, 47(4): 1605–1621.

Andre, P., Kooli, M., & L'her, J.-F. (2004). The long-run performance of mergers and acquisitions: Evidence from the Canadian stock market. *Financial Management*, 33(4): 27–43.

Barber, B. M. & Lyon, J. D. (1997). Detecting long-run abnormal stock returns: The empirical power and specification of test statistics. *Journal of Financial Economics*, 43(3), 341–372.

Bhabra, H. S. & Huang, J. (2013). An empirical investigation of mergers and acquisitions by Chinese listed companies, 1997–2007. *Journal of Multinational Financial Management*, 23(3): 186–207.

Boateng, A., Qian, W., & Tianle, Y. (2008). Cross-border M&As by Chinese firms: An analysis of strategic motives and performance. *Thunderbird International Business Review*, 50(4): 259–270.

Buckley, P. J., & Casson, M. (1976). *The Future of Multinational Enterprise*. New York: Holmes & Meier Publishers.

Chakrabarti, R., Jayaraman, N., & Mukherjee, S. (2009). Mars-Venus marriages: Culture and cross-border M&A. *Journal of International Business Studies*, 40: 216–237.

Chen, G. R., & Mao, W. (2012). An empirical research on cross-border mergers and acquisitions by Chinese listed companies, *Exploration*, 12: 29–31 (in Chinese).

Chen, Y. Y. & Young, M. N. (2010). Cross-border mergers and acquisitions by Chinese listed companies: A principal–principal perspective. *Asia Pacific Journal of Management*, 27(3): 523–539.

Cheng, H. F. & Zhang, K. Y. (2006). Wealth effect on cross-border mergers and acquisitions by Chinese listed companies. *World Economics*, 29(12):74–80 (in Chinese).

Chi, J., Sun, Q., & Young, M. (2011). Performance and characteristics of acquiring firms in the Chinese stock markets. *Emerging Markets Review*, 12(2): 152–170.

Child, J. & Rodrigues, S. B. (2005). The internationalization of Chinese firms: A case for theoretical extension?[1]. *Management and Organization Review*, 1(3): 381–410.

Choi, J. & Russell, J. S. (2004). Economic gains around mergers and acquisitions in the construction industry of the United States of America. *Canadian Journal of Civil Engineering*, 31(3): 513–525.

Conn, C. & Michie, J. (2001). *Long-run share performance of UK firms engaging in cross-border acquisitions*. ESRC Centre for Business Research, University of Cambridge.

DiMaggio, P. J. & Powell, W. W. (1983). The iron cage revisited: Institutional isomorphism and collective rationality in organizational fields. *American Sociological Review*, 48(2): 147–160.

Dutta, S. & Jog, V. (2009). The long-term performance of acquiring firms: A re-examination of an anomaly. *Journal of Banking & Finance*, 33(8), 1400–1412.

Errunza, V. R. & Senbet, L. W. (1981). The effects of international operations on the market value of the firm: Theory and evidence. *The Journal of Finance*, 36(2): 401–417.

Fama, E. F. (1970). Efficient capital markets: A review of theory and empirical work. *Journal of Finance*, 25(2): 383–417.

Fama, E. F. (1998). Market efficiency, long-term returns, and behavioral finance. *Journal of Financial Economics*, 49(3): 283–306.

Fama, E. F. & French, K. R. (1993). Common risk factors in the returns on stocks and bonds. *Journal of financial economics*, 33(1): 3–56.

Fosfuri, A. & Motta, M. (1999). Multinationals without advantages. *The Scandinavian Journal of Economics*, 101(4): 617–630.

Hitt, M. A., Hoskisson, R. E., Ireland, R. D., & Harrison, J. S. (1991). Effects of acquisitions on R&D inputs and outputs. *Academy of Management Journal*, 34(3): 693–706.

Hughes, A., Mueller, D. C., & Singh, A. 1984. *Hypotheses about Mergers*: Cambridge: University of Cambridge, Department of Applied Economics.

Jensen, M. (1986). Agency cost of free cash flow, corporate finance, and takeovers. *American Economic Review*, 76(2): 323–329.

King, D. R., Dalton, D. R., Daily, C. M., & Covin, J. G. (2004). Meta-analyses of post-acquisition performance: Indications of unidentified moderators. *Strategic Management Journal*, 25: 187–200.

Kothari, S. P., & Warner, J. (2006). Econometrics of event studies. *Handbook of Empirical Corporate Finance*, 1: 3–36.
Kroll, M., Simmons, S. A., & Wright, P. (1990). Determinants of chief executive officer compensation following major acquisitions. *Journal of Business Research*, 20(4): 349–366.
Li, M. & Liu, S. C. (2012). Geographic difference and threshold effect in Chinese ODI reverse spillover effect. *Management World*, 1: 21–32 (in Chinese).
Liu, X., Song, H., & Romilly, P. (1997). Are Chinese stock markets efficient? A cointegration and causality analysis. *Applied Economics Letters*, 4(8): 511–515.
Liu, Y. (2011). An empirical research on cross-border mergers and acquisitions by Chinese listed companies. *Commercial Research*, 6: 106–111 (in Chinese).
Loughran, T. & Ritter, J. R. (2000). Uniformly least powerful tests of market efficiency. *Journal of Financial Economics*, 55(3), 361–389.
Loughran, T. & Vijh, A. M. (1997). Do long-term shareholders benefit from corporate acquisitions? *The Journal of Finance*, 52(5): 1765–1790.
Lyon, J. D., Barber, B. M., & Tsai, C. L. (1999). Improved methods for tests of long-run abnormal stock returns. *The Journal of Finance*, 54(1): 165–201.
Maquieira, C. P., Megginson, W. L., & Nail, L. (1998). Wealth creation versus wealth redistributions in pure stock-for-stock mergers. *Journal of Financial Economics*, 48(1): 3–33.
Marquis, C. & Tilcsik, A. (2013). Imprinting: Toward a multilevel theory. *Academy of Management Annuals*, 7: 195–245.
Mitchell, M. L. & Stafford, E. (2000). Managerial decisions and long-term stock price performance*. *The Journal of Business*, 73(3): 287–329.
Mookerjee, R. & Yu, Q. (1999). An empirical analysis of the equity markets in China. *Review of Financial Economics*, 8(1): 41–60.
Morck, R., Shleifer, A., & Vishny, R. W. (1990). Do managerial objectives drive bad acquisitions? *The Journal of Finance*, 45(1): 31–48.
Morosini, P., Shane, S., & Singh, H. (1998). National cultural distance and cross-border acquisition performance. *Journal of International Business Studies*, 29: 137–158.
National Bureau of statistics of China (2012). *China Statistical Yearbook*. Beijing: China Statistics Press.
Peng, M. W. (2003). Institutional transitions and strategic choices. *Academy of Management Review*, 28(2): 275–296.
PwC (2011) Chinese Merger and Acquisition Review and Prospect. Available at: http://wenku.baidu.com/link?url=VCr1GW0SKcYgjvY8SgXLVsqwMTechFp5fAuU3VKc3GocB0WlYIiWKBFfRp_EgnULo3W0S_AumcR-e1K4oX-PoW2sMejoPgGhb_3RLmBFfdC.
Rau, P. R., & Vermaelen, T. (1998). Glamour, value and the post-acquisition performance of acquiring firms. *Journal of Financial Economics*, 49(2): 223–253.
Reed, R. & Luffman, G. A. (1986). Diversification: The growing confusion. *Strategic Management Journal*, 7(1): 29–35.
Scott R. (1995). *Institutions and Organizations*. Thousand Oaks, CA: Sage.
Seth, A. (1990). Sources of value creation in acquisitions: An empirical investigation. *Strategic Management Journal*, 11(6): 431–446.
Shimizu, K., Hitt, M. A., Vaidyanath, D., & Pisano, V. (2004). Theoretical foundations of cross-border mergers and acquisitions: A review of current research

and recommendations for the future. *Journal of International Management*, 10(3): 307–353.

Singh, H. & Montgomery, C. A. (1987). Corporate acquisition strategies and economic performance. *Strategic Management Journal*, 8(4): 377–386.

Stulz, R. (1990). Managerial discretion and optimal financing policies. *Journal of Financial Economics*, 26(1): 3–27.

Teerikangas, S. & Very, P. (2012). Culture in mergers and acquisitions: A critical synthesis and steps forward. In Faulkner, D., Teerikangas, S., & Joseph, R. J. (eds), *The Handbook of Mergers and Acquisitions*. Oxford: Oxford University Press: 392–430.

Thornton, P. H. & Ocasio, W. (2008). Institutional logics. In Greenwood, R., Oliver, C., Suddaby, R., & Sahlin-Andersson, K. (eds) *The Sage Handbook of Organizational Institutionalism*, SAGE Publications: 99–129.

Uddin, M. & Boateng, A. (2009). An analysis of short-run performance of cross-border mergers and acquisitions: Evidence from the UK acquiring firms. *Review of Accounting and Finance*, 8(4): 431–453.

Uhlenbruck, K. (2004). Developing acquired foreign subsidiaries: The experience of MNEs in transition economies. *Journal of International Business Studies*, 35: 109–123.

Wall Street Journal (14 February 2011). Available at *http://online.wsj.com/news/articles/SB10001424052748703361904576142832741439402*

Wang, C., Hong, J., Kafouros, M., & Wright, M. (2012). Exploring the role of government involvement in outward FDI from emerging economies. *Journal of International Business Studies*, 43(7): 655–676.

Wang, Y., Liu, L., & Gu, R. (2009). Analysis of efficiency for Shenzhen stock market based on multifractal detrended fluctuation analysis. *International Review of Financial Analysis*, 18(5): 271–276.

Wu, C. & Xie, N. (2010). Determinants of cross-border merger & acquisition performance of Chinese enterprises. *Procedia-Social and Behavioral Sciences*, 2(5): 6896–6905.

Zhao, W., Gu, G. D., & He, Y. Q. (2006). Outward FDI and Chinese technology development. *Management World*, 7: 53–60 (in Chinese).

5

Rise of the Indian Firm: Understanding Leadership in Indian Organizations

Christopher Selvarajah, Denny Meyer, Suku Sukunesan and R. Venkatapathy

Introduction

There has been phenomenal growth of India's multinational companies (MNCs) since 2000. Bloomberg data reported that between 2000 and 2012, there were 1,995 acquisitions by Indian firms, at total value of US$116 billion (Goswami, 2013). This was an increase of 251% compared to 2007 with 223 mergers and acquisitions valued at $US33 billon and a 300% increase from 2006 (Raghavan, 2008). This growth has produced a need for an understanding of how the Indian mind works and of Indian organizational behaviour in order to facilitate cultural exchange with and within Indian MNCs.

India's MNCs, as Raghavan (2008) reports, have resorted to mergers and acquisitions as their pathway to a global presence. Tata, Infosys, Reliance, Mahindra and Mahindra, Aventis Pharma, Hindalco, Suzlon, Bharat Forge and Sundram Fasteners are some of the companies that have ventured onto the international stage (Cappelli et al., 2010a; Raghavan, 2008). This scale of development of Indian MNCs, in a very short time frame, is just the beginning and, as the Indian economy develops, as it is poised to do, the management of these companies and the cultural values that Indian managers bring will become topical as we have seen in the past for US, Japanese and, more recently, Chinese management styles. As implied by Raghavan (2008, p. 61), "they have to go global and take charge in a very short time". It is from this perspective that the study reported in this chapter is discussed. It is from these premises we explore how modern Indian management and leadership operates in large companies in India, which we hope will provide the basis for understanding managerial values that these managers, as Indian expatriates, bring to their MNCs.

Despite the increasing attention on India's development as a global economic powerhouse, literature on Indian human resources development is perceived to be lacking (Bhawuk, 2008; Budhwar, 2009; Pio, 2007; Ramaswami & Dreher, 2010). In pursuit of discovering how the largest Indian-based companies, such as the multinationals Tata, Infosys, Reliance, Mahindra and Mahindra, Aventis Pharma, lead their organizations to high performance, Cappelli et al. (2010a) discovered the emergence of a distinct Indian model, where emphasis is on employee interconnectedness rather than on stockholder interest, a model that these researchers believe is exportable. Jain et al. (2012, p. 1006), in a survey of human resources professionals in Indian MNCs and foreign MNCs, concluded that "Indian MNCs are clearly focussed on managing performance from within, and have put in place innovative culture-building practices", while foreign MNC are focused on keeping the balance between parent and subsidiary and standardizing the human resources management innovation (HRMI) practices in various global areas". Again emphasizing the family-oriented value systems that permeate many Asian organizations, Chandra (2012) refers to differentiating values in the work–life balance between Eastern and Western perspectives. Som (2007), when exploring innovative practices to support organizational commitment in Indian firms, found that linking employee participation strategies with corporate strategies, investing in career development, having an open and transparent work atmosphere and decentralizing organizational processes improved employee motivation and morale. This emphasizes the importance of the interconnectedness of employee harmony and support for the organization with an organization's performance.

The Indian MNCs, such as Wipro, MindTree Consulting and Sasken, provide insights into the employee-centred approach that is increasingly seen operating in Indian-based organizations (Jain et al., 2012). The organizational culture in these organizations emphasizes high performance with equally high caring. The interests and welfare of families are included in the caring orientation. Paternalistic nurturing is back in vogue within an innovative HR practice system that is geared toward the recognition of employees as a strategic and most important resource for sustained organizational performance. Herald (2011) supports this assertion in his research of five Indian MNCs, which are business process outsourcing (BPO) firms, where promotion based on the recognition of good work, feeling valued in the company and being encouraged to take new initiatives/risks increased managers' satisfaction with reward and recognition policies.

In this chapter we discuss the employee-centred notion and provide evidence based on research conducted across India about Indian managerial behaviours associated with excellent leadership. The results contradict the accepted Western notion of what constitutes good managerial leadership. In this research, we seek a leadership style that will provide high performance in Indian-based and Indian-led organizations. However, gaining an understanding of the usefulness and application of this leadership style in an international context is not the aim of this research, but gaining an understanding of the value system that Indian managers will bring with them to their international assignments is. It is from this perspective that this chapter addresses Indian managers perceptions about leadership.

The sociocultural environment in India is unique. Its peculiarities mould the personality of the management practitioners and influence management practices. One of the salient features of Indian management is the emphasis on the personality of the leader of the organization. Most studies on Indian management highlight the paternalistic nature of the leader (see, Mathew and Jones, 2013; Northouse, 1997; Pellegrini et al., 2010; Sanyal, 2008; Sinha, 1990). The essential requisite for paternalism appears to be unity in the leadership, and a single, identifiable source of power. What has not been properly researched is how the concept of power is utilized. This implication on how power becomes critical to the understanding of the Indian work environment because, as Das (2002) explains, foreign investment into India has impacted on the traditional view of work and the working environment. It is therefore important to know in what way this new environment, this India in the 21st century, is different.

The Indian social system has exaggerated the power and control of authority over people through both a familial structure and the parallel caste structure. It is this duality that often spawns patronage and friction. As emphasized by Rao (2007, p. 1817), "the Indian managers often confuse their professional role in an objective, rational, organizational system with their social hierarchical role with expectations of conformity and paternalism". The value dilemmas in the Indian managerial roles are further exaggerated as India progresses as a dynamic participant in a global environment.

Realizing the unique features of Indian behaviour and developing workable strategies that suit the environment is, therefore, the challenge for international business. As Rao (2007) adds in support of Sparrow and Budhwar (1997), the performance management process in Indian managerial practices is underemphasized and there is a dire need to study this phenomenon. It is argued that deference to familiarity, seniority, age and open-door communication, be it in a multinational or public sector organization, a traditional family-owned company or a government department, are management features that augur well in Indian organizations.

Based on the study of over 40 organizations of various types in India, it has been found that management in India is characterized by a peculiar dualism (Virmani & Guptan, 1991; Virmani, 2000). There is a distinct difference between the professed policies and the actual practices followed in Indian organizations. This is due to the conflict that arises from having foreign systems thrust on resident Indian practices and expectations. Indian management can absorb principles unfamiliar to it, but these principles should be modified to suit Indian conditions. If such a blending is not done, then conflicts arise in management styles, and the compromises in regard to policies and principles may fail to work.

The theoretical framework for excellent leadership

In an article in the *Leadership Quarterly*, Dorfman et al. (1997, p. 233) explain that although "the phenomenon of leadership is widely considered to be universal across cultures, the way in which it is operationalized is usually viewed as culturally specific". Terms to circumscribe the universality of the phenomenon and discrete differentiation of culturally specific experiences have been covered in the management literature. Etic and emic traits (see Jayakody, 2008), generalizable and idiosyncratic (see Morrison, 2000) and rationalist and culturalist views (see Marcoulides et al., 2004) have been used to describe behaviour within universal and culturally specific experiences. These assumptions are reflected in studies such as the GLOBE (Global Leadership and Organizational Behaviour Effectiveness) study (Den Hartog et al., 1999) and are also the basis for the Selvarajah et al. (1995) framework. The framework is based upon the assumption that there are leadership factors that are universal (etic), but that these factors are manifested in various overt behaviours, which depend on the cultural (emic) context, thereby sidestepping the etic-emic dilemma (Javidan & Carl, 2004; Jong et al., 2009; Smith et al., 1989). The concept of excellence in leadership is seen by Selvarajah et al. (1995) as a combination of factors that are desirable for good leadership within a cultural context framework.

The Asian Perspectives on Excellence in Leadership APEL model

Selvarajah et al. (1995) developed 94 'excellence in leadership' value statements. In their theoretical framework, 'excellence' is defined as "surpassing others in accomplishment or achievement" (Taormina & Selvarajah, 2005, p. 300). Excellence is examined in terms of *behaviours* exhibited by someone in a managerial position, rather than in terms of personal traits or personal characteristics, as the latter are difficult to observe (Taormina & Selvarajah, 2005).

The statements were formulated based on an in-depth study of literature on leadership and management excellence, using both Western and Eastern literature. Subsequently, four broad dimensions were identified: (1) environmental influences, (2) personal qualities, (3) managerial behaviours and (4) organizational demands (see Selvarajah et al., 1995 for more details and the methodologies used to select the 94 value statements).

Environmental influences refer to the way managers react or respond to external factors that influence the operation and the success of the organization. They emphasize the importance of scanning and evaluating the external environment for opportunities and threats. *Personal qualities* are the personal values, skills, beliefs and qualities of an individual with regard to leadership, irrespective of profession or organization. These are the deep-rooted, personal factors that determine a person's approach to leadership in general, not just to management. They emphasize morality, religion, interpersonal relationships and communication. *Managerial behaviours* cover a person's attitudes, actions and styles that are specific to the performance of the managerial task. They emphasize executive-level decision-making rather than participative management. *Organizational demands* include the ways a manager reacts or responds to the organization's goals, objectives, structures, issues, demands, pressures and rewards. They emphasize the importance of organizational prosperity. The dependent variable, the *excellent leader* scale then includes the combination of behaviours and attitudes desirable for good leadership within a certain cultural context as shown in Figure 5.1 (also illustrated, e.g., in Selvarajah et al., 2012, 2013a, 2013b; Selvarajah and Meyer, 2006, 2008a, 2008b).

Following the identification of the leadership dimensions, the 94 excellence in leadership value statements were subjected to a Q-sort technique (Kerlinger, 1973), using the above four dimensions as the framework for categorization. For the Q-sort procedure, all statements were printed three

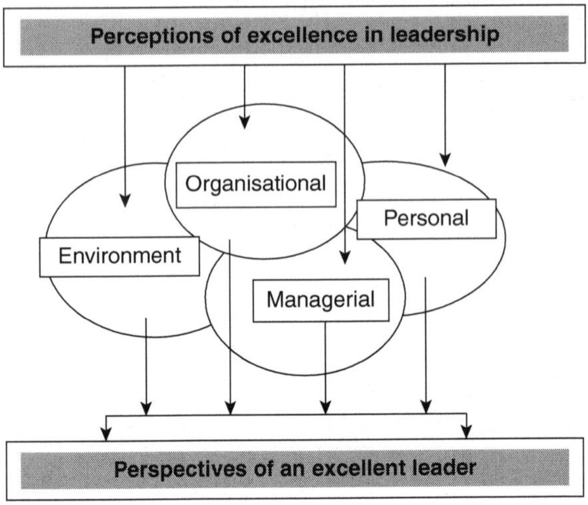

Figure 5.1 Conceptual framework for the study of excellence in leadership
Source: Selvarajah et al. (1995)

times on small cards, and the respondents were asked to sort the three sets of cards in three different ways. The first sorting was used to determine the order of importance of each statement for excellence in leadership. The second sorting was used to determine to which of the four dimensions each statement belonged, and the third sorting was used to determine the importance of each statement in terms of its chosen dimension (i.e., the importance of each statement versus the other statements assigned to the same dimension)., studies by Selvarajah have shown that by using the most important statements for each dimension valid measures have been developed from these items for several Asian countries, such as Cambodia (Selvarajah et al., 2012); Singapore (Selvarajah et al., 2013a); Thailand (Selvarajah et al., 2013b);; Malaysia (Selvarajah and Meyer, 2006, 2008a); China (Selvarajah and Meyer, 2008b); and in a regional context, such as ASEAN (Taormina and Selvarajah, 2005). More specifically, it was found in these studies that the factor loadings of the items onto the distinguished dimensions differed across Asia, thus providing cultural insights into leadership behaviours and values in these countries.

The concept of cultural modelling

The theory underlying our approach is similar to the cultural modelling presented by Hinton (1998), which also studies the influence of culture, predicting how it affects organizational functions and adaptability.

Culture is therefore seen as a determinant of behaviour within organizational units and as a macro-level determinant of leadership behaviour that is environment specific. It is based on this understanding that cultural models for APEL country studies are developed, theorized and discussed. Each country's model is therefore unique, but builds on the same generic four-dimensional APEL model.

From this perspective, the unique dimensions for each country are seen as cultural quotients measured on a continuous scale, rather than as a bipolar attempt to categorize national culture (e.g., masculine versus feminine). In this chapter, we similarly explore leadership behaviour in Indian organizations, employing structural equation modelling to study the dimensions of leadership excellence. Similar to Selvarajah et al. (2012, 2013b), where the four-dimensional APEL model for two Mekong nations provided, respectively, eight and seven distinct cultural constructs that described excellent leadership in organizations, this current study in India has seven constructs.

This study shows that the APEL model is sufficiently robust to allow cultural interpretations for understanding leadership behaviours in India, as it has for many other countries.

Literature review

In a recent article titled "Leadership lessons from India", published in the *Harvard Business Review* (Cappelli et al., 2010a, p. 92), it was shown that Indian business leaders prioritized key responsibilities and ranked the top four as:

1. chief provider of business strategy
2. keeper of organizational culture
3. guide, teacher, or role model for employees
4. representative of owner and investor interests.

The findings in the study were in stark contrast to US executives, who rank shareholder interest as number one (Cappelli et al. 2010a). Appropriate leadership behaviour in the Indian context supports the concept of excellence within a family and a communal framework. The interpretation by Cappelli et al. (2010a) is somewhat similar to the framing of familial thinking based on the *runas* – the manager in the Indian context is seen as god-like – a strategist, a parent-like keeper of organizational culture, a teacher, a selfless role model, and lastly, a representative of the organizational sustainability interest. From the manager's perspective, this involves the creation of a 'social mission' as the basis for mutual dependency. The article stresses a personal style that establishes dependability, trustworthiness, consistency in personal relationships, respect for individuals and acceptance that people make mistakes, and thereby supports transparency and accountability.

The article also recognizes the importance of communication and decision-making as valued attributes of an excellent leader. Empowering employees to communicate and enabling employees down the ranks to participate in decision-making are viewed as essential for a good leader.

Research in leadership and decision-making was popularized by Vroom and Yetton in 1973 with the publication of their book *Leadership and Decision Making*. Vroom (2000, p. 83) argues that "theories of decision-making intersect with theories of leadership", and he quotes the work of Tannenbaum and Schmidt (1973), which defines styles of leadership as being influenced by "area of freedom afforded subordinates" (cited in Vroom, 2000, p. 83). He refers to organizational cultural boundaries within which leadership decision-making operates. Dickson et al. (2003) provide insights into universal values and those that are culture specific – not only when compared between the West and the East, but also within a region.

One of the earlier attempts to search for an appropriate effective leadership style in the Indian context was made by Sinha and Chowdhary (1981). Based on their extensive research, mainly in East India, they reported that in the Indian context the Nurturant-Task Leadership (NTL) style was found to be most effective. The style is characterized by leaders who are both task- and person-centred.

According to Sinha (1990, 1994), the NTL model has been found to be more congruent with Indian cultural values and behaviour dispositions. The style is essentially paternalistic, drawing heavily on the patterns of interaction typifying family dynamics in India. In this respect, a study done by Karla and Gupta (1995) supported the nurturance aspect and showed that effective managers were rated high on nurturing dimensions. However, the study also showed that effective managers were rated low on task obsession and they were seen as moderately prescriptive. Therefore, in this sense, they were nurturing and moderately prescriptive, but not task oriented.

In the Indian context, the paternalistic or the authoritative benevolent leader seems to be repeatedly emphasized as a leadership construct highly valued in society (see Aycan et al., 2000; Chhokar, 2008; Mathur et al., 1996; Sinha, 1990). While Gelfand et al. (2007, p. 493) defined paternalism as a "hierarchical relationship in which a leader guides professional and personal lives of subordinates in a manner resembling a parent, and in exchange expects loyalty and deference", Northouse (1997, p. 39) says that US-based literature portrays paternalism as "benevolent dictatorship".

Paternalistic leadership suggests people in authority assume the role of parents. The leader's benevolence is coupled with a controlling authority, which requires loyalty to the authority figure (James et al., 1996; Pasa et al., 2001). Farh and Cheng (2000, p. 91) define paternalistic leadership as "a style that combines strong discipline and authority with fatherly benevolence". Studies have shown that paternalistic leadership, in collectivistic and high-power-distance cultures, has positive impact on employees' attitudes (see, e.g., Aycan, 2006; Aycan et al., 2000: Farh & Cheng, 2000; Sinha, 1997). The organizational culture based on the concept of mutual dependency establishes the importance of organizational prosperity as a valued long-term objective of the leader and subordinate. Benevolence, mentoring and supporting employees in the interest of the organization is all about organizational demand.

As India develops and takes its place in world economic affairs as a super-power, Indian management values and leadership is bound to influence global thinking (Cappelli et al., 2010a, 2010b), as have Western, Japanese and, more recently, Chinese management philosophies. Greater understanding of dharmic values and the cultural values of the Indian social system is bound to happen. What the *Harvard Business Review* article by Cappelli et al. (2010a) has alluded to, and what we have highlighted above, is the integral nature of a value system that has been passed down through generations of Indians and exists today in modern-day India. What was poorly understood in the past is today making a breakthrough as a management and leadership value that may provide the answers on how to build a sustainable and enduring leadership behavioural paradigm. The notion of preserving traditions while emphasizing change as a prerequisite for growth and recognizing the existence of the social, political and economic environment describes India's position in a globalizing world.

In this study, the importance of managerial style, decision-making, environmental influence and organizational demand are explored in the context of Indian leadership behaviours. The importance of leadership behaviours for leadership excellence and the facilitating (mediating) effects of personal style and communication are then considered in the context of leadership excellence in India. Based on the above discussion, Figure 5.2 below provides the conceptual framework for this study, while also indicating the hypotheses that will be tested.

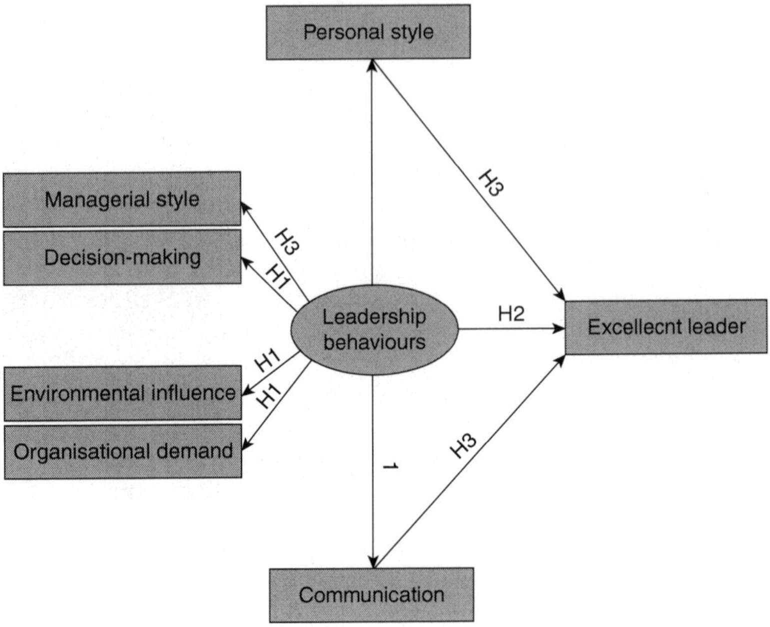

Figure 5.2 Conceptual model

Hypothesis 1. Managerial style, decision-making, Organisational demand and environmental influence are all important in terms of Leadership Behaviours.

Hypothesis 2. Leadership Behaviours define what constitutes an Excellent Leader.

Hypothesis 3. Personal Style and Communication together mediate the relationship between Leadership Behaviours and Leadership Excellence.

Hypothesis 4. Leadership dimensions are defined differently in different regions of India.

Research methodology

The data collection was carried out using the questionnaire developed by Selvarajah et al. (1995), and 539 managers from 22 Indian states completed the survey. The leadership project was coordinated by the Bharathiar School of Management and Entrepreneurship Development (BSMED) at Bharathiar University in Coimbatore in Tamil Nadu, South

India. Both national and regional organizations were contacted, questionnaires were distributed, and completed questionnaires were returned to BSMED. The Likert-type questionnaire had 94 items, and in the answer section 1 indicated no importance and 5 indicated very important. Neither the respondents nor their organizations were required to identify themselves. A total of 3500 'Asian Perspectives on Excellence in Leadership' questionnaires were distributed and 612 were returned. Of the 612 returned, 539 were useable, giving a 15.4% effective return rate. As English is the commercial language in India, there was no necessity to have the questionnaire translated into a local language.

In this research, we developed scales for constructs, using the framework for the characteristics of an excellent leader consisting of personal qualities, managerial behaviour, organizational demands and environmental influences (provided in tables below). The work of Selvarajah et al. (1995) provided the basis for these scales but certain improvements were introduced in the current structure. In particular, in order to produce discriminant validity between the scales, the statements about the excellent leader are not included in any of the other four scales, and exploratory factor analysis is used to split the managerial behaviour and personal qualities constructs into scales that relate to the hypotheses. It was found that managerial behaviour was composed of two dimensions discussed above, namely, managerial style and decision-making, and personal qualities was also composed of two dimensions, namely, personal style and communication. Organizational demand and environmental influences retained their singular structures.

The reliability of the scales was measured by Cronbach's alpha, and the internal validity of the scales was assured using confirmatory factor analysis. The results of the confirmatory factor analyses where the root mean squared error of approximation (RMSEA) is less than 0.10 (Byrne, 2001), a goodness of fit (GFI) statistic is above 0.90 and a normed chi-squared (CMIN/DF) statistic is less than 3, suggest adequate internal validity (Arbuckle & Wothke, 1999) for all the scales. All reliability scores in this study exceed 0.68, which makes all the scales at least reasonably reliable (Hair et al., 1998).

An initial correlation analysis for the scales is used to test whether the hypothesized dimensions are associated with perceptions of leadership, and structural equation modelling is then used to test first hypothesis, effectively validating the conceptual model proposed in Figure 5.1. Finally, tests of invariance are performed in order to determine whether there are age and gender differences with regard to what characteristics are perceived as being more important in an Indian leader, and whether there are significant differences between the Northern and Southern managers. In all of Selvarajah's APEL studies, a concerted effort is also made to study subpopulation effects within nations and regions. The same is done in this study. SPSS v21 and AMOS v21 are the software packages used for the above analyses.

Results

The majority of the managers (345) were located in South India, with 194 managers located in North India. Tamil Nadu in the South and Jharkhand in the North were the best-represented states, with 46% and 27% of the respondents respectively. There were 13 most commonly spoken languages, with Tamil and Konkani the most commonly spoken languages for 37% and 22% of the sample, respectively. There was a strong gender bias: 76% of the respondents were men and only 24% women. This is in line with Chhokar's (2008) observation where he stresses that although there is increasing urbanization and education, India continues to be a traditional and male-dominated society. Hinduism (74%) and Christianity (22%) were the most common religions in this study. This breakdown in the sample by religion is not representative of the Indian population. The available census data, as at census date 2001 (Census, 2011), indicates a total Indian population of 1,028 million people, with Hindus in the majority with 80.5%, followed by Muslims (13.5%) and Christians (2.3%). The majority of the respondents were employed in the banking industry (69%), with 10% in textiles, 6% in insurance and 14% in other industries. This suggests an important bias in the data in terms of religious representation and industry.

The majority of the respondents were employed in middle-management positions (59%), with 20% in senior management and 24% in line management. In addition, the majority of the respondents were at most 35 years old (52%) with 27% in the 36–45 age group and 16% in the 46–55 age group, with only 4% over 55 years of age. As expected from the industry breakdown, almost half the respondents worked in organizations employing over 1,000 people, with only 11% employed in organizations with at most 50 people, 18% in organizations with at most 100 people, 36% in organizations with at most 500 people and 51% in organizations with at most 1,000 employees. However, 34% worked in departments employing at most 10 people, with 22% in departments employing between 11 and 25 people. While 11% worked in departments with between 26 and 50 people and 10% worked in departments with between 51 and 100 employees, 23% worked in departments with more than 100 people.

The effect of regional differences on demographic

The relationships between gender, age, region and management position were investigated using a log linear analysis. Only second order interactions were found to be significant. In particular, major significant differences were found between the northern and southern samples. The northern sample was younger than the southern sample with 65% of the northern managers being at most 35 years old as opposed to only 45% for the southern sample. As a result, there was a higher percentage of senior managers in the southern sample (25%) than in the northern sample (12%). In addition, there was a higher percentage of men in the southern sample (82%) than in the northern sample (65%). There was also a very significant difference with regard to industry. Although both samples were dominated by the banking industry, the percentage of banking managers was much higher in the northern sample (97%) than in the southern sample (54%). This means that any comparison of the northern and southern samples must be treated with caution.

In addition, there was an interesting significant relationship between gender and age with females comprising 33% of the under-35 age group in the sample, but only 14% of the over-35 age group. This suggests that a major change is taking place in India as women start to enter the workforce in growing numbers. However, the relationship between management position and gender and that between management position and age show that senior management is still very much the preserve of older males. In this sample, 91% of the senior managers were male, while only 20% of the senior managers were less than 35 years old. In contrast, 76% of the middle managers were males and 49% of these managers were aged under 35. Finally, 63% of the line managers were male and 88% of these managers were less than 35 years old.

Development of measurement models for leadership excellence

Single scales were constructed for excellent leader, environmental influence and organizational demands. However, it was found that there were two constructs underpinning personal qualities – personal style and communication – and two constructs underpinning managerial behaviour – managerial style and decision-making. As shown in Table 5.1, the measurement models for excellent leader, environmental influence, organizational demand, managerial behaviour and personal qualities described the overall sample well.

Table 5.1 Goodness of fit for measurement models with complete sample

	Normed chi-squared	GFI	AGFI	TLI	CFI	RMSEA
Excellent leader (EL)	2.31	0.99	0.97	0.97	0.99	0.05
Environmental influence (EI)	2.91	0.98	0.96	0.93	0.95	0.06
Organizational demand (OD)	2.73	0.98	0.95	0.92	0.95	0.05
Managerial behaviour (MB)	2.76	0.94	0.92	0.90	0.92	0.06
Personal qualities (PQ)	1.87	0.98	0.97	0.97	0.98	0.04

As shown in Table 5.2, all seven scales had reasonable reliability for an exploratory study and the correlations between the scales were mostly of moderate strength. In particular, there were strong correlations between the managerial style, decision-making, environmental influence and organizational demands scales, suggesting that these scales together provided a good measure of leadership behaviours in India, providing support for the first hypothesis.

We now consider the issue of subsample differences. When these models were fitted separately for each demographic group (gender, age, region and management position) the fit was still acceptable according to Byrne (2001) with values for the RMSEA always less than 0.10 as shown in Table 5.3.

Using the complete data set, the postulated conceptual model could be tested using structural equation modelling, allowing the testing of the hypotheses. Structural equation modelling showed that the above conceptual model described the data well (normed chi-squared = 2.685, GFI = 0.98, AGFI = 0.96, TLI = 0.99, CFI = 0.99, RMSEA = 0.056). The model explained 72% of the variation in the excellent leader scale. In Figure 5.3, the strong loadings for management style, decision-making, organizational demand and environmental influence on the leadership behaviours construct provide further support for the first hypothesis. In support of the second hypothesis, there is a moderately strong relationship between leadership behaviours and excellent leader. However, personal style and communication partially mediated this relationship, serving to strengthen it and providing support for the third hypothesis. Indeed, only 64% of the standardized total effect size for the leadership behaviours – excellent leader link – can be attributed directly to leadership behaviours. The remaining 36% of this effect is conditional on the personal qualities of the leaders, their personal style and communication effectiveness.

Table 5.2 Descriptive statistics and correlations

	Excellent leader (1)	Managerial style (2)	Decision-making (3)	Environmental influence (4)	Organizational demand (5)	Personal style (6)	Communication (7)
Mean	4.32	4.01	3.95	3.85	4.07	4.22	4.06
SD	0.59	0.55	0.72	0.59	0.57	0.68	0.62
Cronbach Alpha	0.84	0.86	0.69	0.76	0.68	0.73	0.68
(1)	1	0.774**	0.463**	0.611**	0.703**	0.668**	0.722**
(2)	0.774**	1	0.585**	0.719**	0.758**	0.627**	0.753**
(3)	0.463**	0.585**	1	0.443**	0.470**	0.440**	0.482**
(4)	0.611**	0.719**	0.443**	1	0.663**	0.473**	0.611**
(5)	0.703**	0.758**	0.470**	0.663**	1	0.579**	0.634**
(6)	0.668**	0.627**	0.440**	0.473**	0.579**	1	0.524**
(7)	0.722**	0.753**	0.482**	0.611**	0.634**	0.524**	1

Table 5.3 Goodness of fit for measurement models for demographic groups (RMSEA)

		N	EL	EI	OD	MB	PQ
Gender	Male	409	0.054	0.058	0.062	0.066	0.052
	Female	130	0.056	0.079	0.015	0.074	0.089
Age	Under 35	282	0.043	0.051	0.047	0.064	0.017
	Over 35	256	0.079	0.072	0.082	0.086	0.046
Region	South	345	0.061	0.053	0.055	0.070	0.050
	North	194	0.030	0.093	0.084	0.063	0.038
Position	Senior	109	0.064	0.074	0.061	0.076	0.079
	Middle	301	0.060	0.074	0.061	0.073	0.057
	Line	128	0.085	0.095	0.087	0.089	0.039

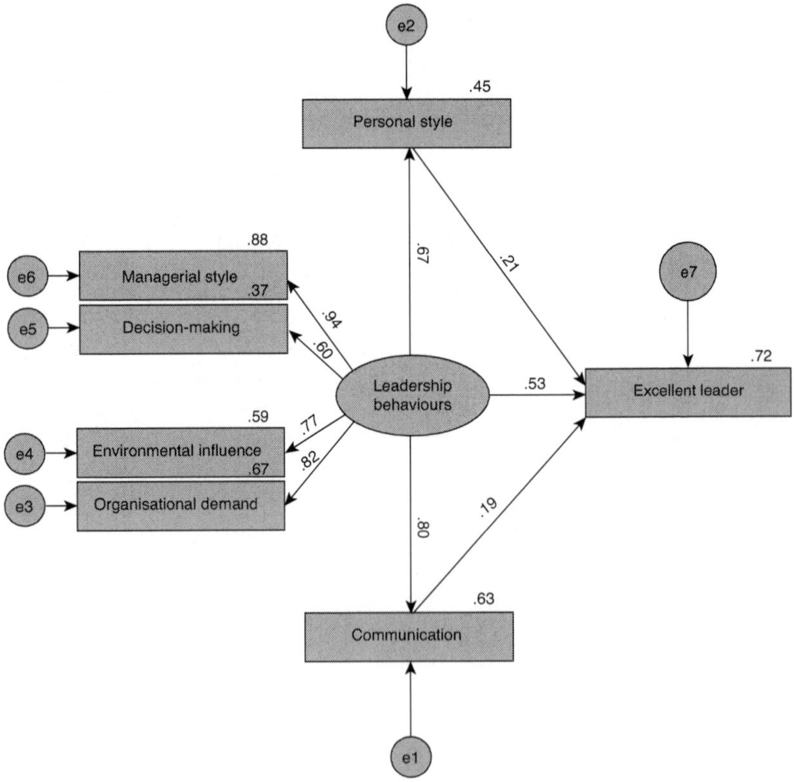

Figure 5.3 Fitted model showing beta weights and R^2 values

In Table 5.4, a test of invariance is performed for each demographic variable for each measurement model to determine whether demographic groups attach similar importance to the items used to construct each measurement model, and to test the fourth hypothesis.

The construct with the greatest demographic differences appears to be managerial behaviour. Significant gender, age, regional and positional differences were observed for this construct. However, for organizational demand there were no significant demographic differences, and in the case of personal qualities there were only differences in relation to management position. Age differences were observed for the excellent leader and environmental influence construct, but there were also regional differences for the excellent leader construct. In Tables 5.5 to 5.9, these differences are explored in greater depth. Only significant differences in the weights are highlighted in bold in these tables and are discussed below.

There are three significant differences in weights for the excellent leader construct in Table 5.5. In particular, younger managers attribute

Table 5.4 Demographic comparisons of measurement model weights

	Gender			Age			Region			Position		
	χ^2	*df*	*P*	χ^2	*df*	*P*	χ^2	*df*	*P*	χ^2	*df*	*P*
EL	12.6	6	0.050	31.8	6	>0.001	23.4	6	0.001	19.8	12	0.070
EI	13.3	7	0.065	16.3	7	0.023	4.9	7	0.677	29.0	14	0.011
MB	36.6	15	0.001	32.3	15	0.006	48.1	15	>0.001	51.8	30	0.008
OD	7.5	7	0.380	10.1	7	0.182	4.7	7	0.693	11.3	14	0.661
PQ	11.2	7	0.131	6.9	7	0.437	9.0	7	0.250	28.2	14	0.013

Table 5.5 Excellent leader standardized regression weights

		Region		Gender		Age	
	Overall	North	South	Male	Female	Under 35	Over 35
Give recognition for good work	0.748	0.674	0.763	0.702	0.837	0.724	0.775
Create a sense of purpose and enthusiasm in the workplace	0.682	0.659	0.686	0.669	0.703	0.619	0.757
Motivate employees	0.641	0.680	0.602	0.622	0.700	0.655	0.609
Continue to learn how to improve performance	0.627	0.698	0.500	0.567	0.724	**0.747**	**0.482**
Have confidence when dealing with work and with people	0.620	0.681	0.491	0.515	0.797	**0.691**	**0.513**
Have a strategic vision for the organization	0.616	0.619	0.558	0.590	0.681	0.609	0.625
Be honest	0.603	**0.721**	**0.435**	0.576	0.617	0.579	0.620

more importance to "continue to learn how to improve performance" and "have confidence when dealing with work and with people", while managers from the northern region attribute more importance to "be honest" than managers from the southern region. However, no significant gender differences emerged, although overall the gender effect was (just) significant with $P = 0.05$.

Table 5.6 also shows major demographic differences, this time in terms of perceptions regarding managerial behaviour. "Using initiative and taking risks" is relatively unimportant for young managers and for line managers. Female managers are more in favour of leaders who "trust those to whom work is delegated", "think about the specific details of any particular problem" and "try different approaches to management" than are their male colleagues. Interestingly, managers from the North think that "trust those to whom work is delegated" is more important than their southern neighbours, despite the fact that the northern sample has a higher percentage of men than the southern sample. The over-35 age group is more concerned that leaders "keep up to date on management literature", while female managers and middle managers attribute the most importance to "be consistent with making decisions". Southern managers are more concerned that leaders "select work wisely to avoid overload". In terms of decision-making, line managers are most concerned that leaders "make decisions earlier rather than later", while senior managers are least concerned that leaders "make decisions without depending too much on others". Finally, it seems that northern managers expect leaders to "make decisions earlier rather than later" to a greater extent than their southern neighbours.

No significant differences were found between demographic groups in regard to the relative importance of the organizational demand attributes. As shown in Table 5.7, the items "focus on maximizing productivity", "act as a member of the team" and "support decisions made jointly by others" were seen to be particularly important by all Indian managers.

Table 5.8 shows major differences between ages and positions in regard to the importance of environmental influence. Managers in the over-35 age bracket were more concerned that a leader should "check consistently for problems and opportunities", "use economic indicators for planning purposes" and "study laws and regulations that may have an impact on work". However, it was middle and line managers rather than senior managers who thought that "check consistently for problems and opportunities" and "be socially and environmentally responsible" was particularly important, with middle managers giving the

Table 5.6 Managerial behaviour standardized weights

		Age		Gender		Region		Position		
Managerial style	**Overall**	**Under 35**	**Over 35**	**Male**	**Female**	**North**	**South**	**Senior**	**Middle**	**Line**
Tell subordinates what to do and how to do it	0.670	0.642	0.695	0.630	0.779	0.641	0.672	0.555	0.742	0.604
Think about the specific details of any particular problem	0.666	0.685	0.652	**0.596**	**0.826**	0.720	0.616	0.603	0.688	0.646
Persuade others to do things	0.657	0.653	0.658	0.666	0.645	0.661	0.680	0.613	0.671	0.640
Listen to and understand the problems of others	0.641	0.633	0.640	0.593	0.714	0.666	0.591	0.629	0.634	0.629
Delegate	0.560	0.604	0.502	0.507	0.689	0.646	0.491	0.575	0.550	0.574
Be strict in judging the competence of employees	0.544	0.536	0.567	0.575	0.478	0.495	0.582	0.472	0.577	0.504
Be objective when dealing with work conflicts	0.528	0.531	0.494	0.527	0.581	0.560	0.489	0.395	0.515	0.601
Keep up to date on management literature	0.521	**0.455**	**0.600**	0.484	0.608	0.562	0.467	0.518	0.514	0.519
Try different approaches to management	0.518	0.591	0.455	**0.443**	**0.687**	0.603	0.459	0.599	0.489	0.592
Focus on the task in hand	0.513	0.579	0.457	0.453	0.624	0.538	0.465	0.310	0.561	0.558
Be consistent in making decisions	0.499	0.505	0.465	**0.435**	**0.600**	0.551	0.412	**0.328**	**0.531**	**0.429**
Select work wisely to avoid overload	0.491	0.484	0.511	0.479	0.492	**0.400**	**0.531**	0.575	0.461	0.529
Trust those to whom work is delegated	0.487	0.493	0.458	**0.390**	**0.696**	**0.634**	**0.333**	0.264	0.498	0.559
Use initiatives and take risks	0.453	**0.346**	**0.563**	0.439	0.458	0.356	0.490	**0.502**	**0.540**	**0.208**
Decision-making										
Make decisions earlier rather than later	0.679	0.737	0.614	0.615	0.822	**0.766**	**0.584**	**0.635**	**0.611**	**0.853**
Make work decisions quickly	0.639	0.558	0.712	0.653	0.627	0.601	0.670	0.601	0.672	0.588
Make decisions without depending too much on others	0.634	0.664	0.624	0.642	0.717	0.677	0.665	**0.381**	**0.719**	**0.630**

Table 5.7 Organizational demand standardized weights

	Overall
Focus on maximizing productivity	0.611
Act as a member of the team	0.594
Support decisions made jointly by others	0.579
Give priority to long-term goals	0.492
Adjust organizational structures and rules to the realities of practice	0.477
Adapt to changing working conditions	0.452
Share power	0.426
Sell the professional or corporate image to the public	0.283

Table 5.8 Environmental influence standardized weights

		Age		**Position**		
	Overall	**Under 35**	**Over 35**	**Senior**	**Middle**	**Line**
Identify social trends that may have an impact on work	0.653	0.692	0.636	0.613	0.700	0.606
Have a multicultural orientation and approach	0.626	0.549	0.708	0.666	0.627	0.623
Check consistently for problems and opportunities	0.610	**0.530**	**0.677**	**0.425**	**0.628**	**0.670**
Study laws and regulations that may have an impact on work	0.526	**0.449**	**0.586**	**0.320**	**0.635**	**0.438**
Foster an international perspective in the organization	0.526	0.532	0.521	0.553	0.475	0.602
Be socially and environmentally responsible	0.513	0.439	0.597	**0.280**	**0.540**	**0.557**
Use economic indicators for planning purposes	0.503	**0.391**	**0.583**	0.561	0.543	0.380
Be responsive to political realities in the environment	0.279	0.382	0.205	**0.183**	**0.210**	**0.500**

most weight to "study laws and regulations that may have an impact on work" and line managers giving the most weight to "be responsive to political realities in the environment". Overall therefore, senior managers appear to view environmental influence as less important than managers in lower positions.

Table 5.9 shows major differences in positional attitudes in regard to the importance of personal qualities, with senior managers considering "be dependable and trustworthy", "accept responsibility for mistakes" and "be informal when dealing with employees outside work"

Table 5.9 Personal qualities standardized weights

		Managerial position		
Personal style	**Overall**	**Senior**	**Middle**	**Line**
Be consistent when dealing with people	0.708	0.778	0.729	0.678
Be dependable and trustworthy	0.681	**0.428**	**0.695**	**0.679**
Accept responsibility for mistakes	0.600	**0.118**	**0.642**	**0.751**
Be an initiator – not a follower	0.584	0.484	.620	.522
Communication				
Speak clearly and concisely	0.725	0.768	.724	.701
Respect the self-esteem of others	0.700	0.544	.715	.754
Deal calmly with tense situations	0.623	0.487	.610	.716
Write clearly and concisely	0.397	0.275	.439	.390
Be informal when dealing with employees outside work	0.361	**–0.046**	**.376**	**.509**

as relatively unimportant, while middle managers and line managers found these attributes to be relatively important.

Overall, there are clearly major demographic differences in perceptions of leadership excellence as viewed in India. Only in the case of organizational demand does there appear to be consensus. However, the confounding of regional and demographic effects makes it likely that these are mostly caused by regional differences.

Discussion and conclusion

In this chapter we explored a number of assertions based on existing literature on culture and leadership in India. India is known for advancing to the world philosophies and spiritual knowledge from the Vedas and the ancient treatise based on dharma. The Eastern world, especially, has benefitted immensely from the works of the Mahabharata and the Ramayana, as the West has from the Iliad. Though the Mahabharata and the Ramayana are Hindu scriptures, the philosophical base for dharma has been secular and has influenced the mind and behaviour of Indians generally, irrespective of religious affiliation. It is from this premise that this chapter explores leadership behaviour in India.

We commenced this chapter by discussing ancient philosophical thrusts associated with dharma, the caste system, the British influence and modernization to guide our thinking about behaviour and specifically leadership behaviour in organizations in India. Dharma has evolved and influenced the secular system of India. It forms the central beliefs in all the religions that originated in the Indian subcontinent, such as Buddhism, Hinduism, Jainism and Sikhism. The philosophy was transported along the silk and spice routes to the far corners of East Asia and influences the spiritual psyche of people in the Far East, including Japan where it merges with Confucianism.

In this chapter we therefore assert that dharma influences the contextual thinking and behaviour of Indian leaders. As one studies the influence of Confucianism in East Asia, dharma from India has also influenced South East Asian thinking (see Selvarajah et al., 2012, 2013b). In this chapter we have therefore attempted to explore the societal value-base when studying the leadership phenomenon in Indian organizations.

In furthering the understanding of this phenomenon, we sought evidence from earlier researchers such as Sinha (1980) and the more recent the works of Cappelli et al. (2010a, b) and we were able to weave in the four ancient doctrines of dharma to explain the observable Indian leadership behaviours. What we are able to gauge from the results is a distinct Indian leadership behaviour model. In this study, perceptions of what makes an excellent leader in India have been examined through the lenses of the four-dimensional framework suggested by Selvarajah et al. (1995) in their exploratory research of leadership excellence in Asia. The findings suggest that the initial four APEL dimensions produced six valid dimensions unique to India to explain the cultural phenomenon of leadership excellence observed in the Indian organizations. The Indian cultural model provided the explanation of the excellent leader construct and its relationship to the six behavioural dimensions. Reliable scales have been constructed for these dimensions and the excellent leader construct – and overall ratings are high for all six dimensions – confirming their importance.

Correlation analysis showed that the four dimensions of personal qualities, managerial behaviour, environmental influence and organizational demand are all associated with the excellent leader construct, while the structural equation model showed that the model is a reflection of a social system that values a paternalistic approach to management. The leadership behaviours of importance to the Indian manager incorporate a managerial style that reflects decision-making that is swift and personal, where leadership behaviour accepts and operationalizes social trends that impact on work performance and where organizational demands (needs) are supported by workers who engage in activities that will maximize organizational prosperity. These leadership behaviours, thus, directly influence what the Indian managers perceive as an excellent leader. However, the leadership behaviours are improved and made stronger in their relationship to an excellent leader by the personal styles of the managers and the level of communication. The importance of personal style and its congruence to the Indian social system and the importance of transparent congenial communication systems in Indian organizations are highlighted in the two articles by Mathew and Jones (2012, 2013) where they explain that an foreign personal managerial style and an equally foreign communication system have been disastrous to Toyotas' performance in India. Suzuki's experience as a joint venture company with the Indian car company, Maruti, has been worse, with management staff killed by employees, of property destroyed and the eventual shut-down of the factory (Vijay Kumar, 2013).

The excellent leader in India is, therefore, one who values social interdependence in a way akin to family members and, as such, these leaders have the need to experience intense emotional interdependence. This peculiar Indian characteristic has its roots in the Indian cultural system, which is familial, purposeful and guided by a doctrine that seeks specific outcomes at an individual's life stages. The paternalistic culture identified by researchers such as Sinha (1980, 1990), which we describe as intrinsically Indian, is a culmination of virtues based on India's cultural inheritance. A view commonly shared in the literature is that paternalism combines benevolence with authority (Pellegrini et al., 2010) and the subordinate's decision-making is controlled (Martinez, 2005). This leads to respect based on societal hierarchy, though total equality is seldom evident in daily life. However, this notion of control over a subordinate's decision-making is being challenged (Cappelli et al., 2010a; Gelfand et al., 2007). This is especially so in modern Indian organizations where the Indian way of life is taking a new meaning and where the cultural traits of the Indians are harnessed to increase organizational performance. Reading *The India Way* (Cappelli et al., 2010b), we are drawn to the conclusion that the new breed of Indian business leaders have unshackled the traditional servitude of caste- and clan-based behaviours, at least in the business organizations, to accept a purely familial type of behaviour. India's Achilles heel is its strong caste-based system, and the values associated with it are deemed unsuitable for advancement of a modern society. Literature recognizes the dual systems of management – the old and the new. As Sapre (2000, p. 295) says, Indian organizations are experiencing "a kind of internal conflict, as if the nation were facing two ways simultaneously and not quite able to make up its mind". Virmani (2000) explains the dualism as a distinct hiatus between professed policies and actual practices in the Indian organizations. India, he explains, has adopted the British style of management and this is an overlay for the way Indian management is practised.

This debate and India's contribution to management and leadership has just begun, and we will be seeing more publications in this field in years to come. Even though the article and the book by Cappelli et al. (2010a, 2010b) seem to suggest that Indian management style has come of age and is an 'exportable commodity' and that the West can learn from the lessons, more empirical research is needed to support this claim.

Limitations of the study

This study is based on ratings of importance for 94 items in terms of leadership excellence collected using a single questionnaire. This means that common variance bias may have affected the results. However, as commented by Meade et al. (2007) on the basis of Confirmatory Factor Analysis CFA models applied to 24 multitrait-multimethod correlation matrices, while not trivial, common variance bias is often minor in magnitude. Also the work of Siemsen et al. (2010) with respect to multivariate linear relationships shows that common method bias generally decreases when additional independent variables suffering from common method variance are included in a regression equation. In this study the APEL dimensions were tested simultaneously, suggesting that common method variance has been addressed to some extent in the analysis itself. Podsakoff et al. (2003) have suggested several research designs that can be used to reduce the effect of common method variance, and Podsakoff et al. (2012) suggested that future research should consider some of these procedural remedies. In addition, it is suggested that items allowing the measurement of possible causes of common method variance, such as social desirability, be included in the questionnaire, enabling the use of statistical remedies for common method variance.

Admittedly, a research design that allowed an objective measure of leadership excellence as the dependent variable would have been preferable. However, this is not easily done and even well-known studies, such as House's GLOBE study, have been unable to achieve this (see Chhokar et al., 2008; House et al., 2004). In particular, several demographic differences have been identified as influencing perceptions of leadership excellence in India and these needs to be investigated further. However, what has not been explored is the way in which these differences will affect work behaviour and the consequences of ignoring these differences in an organizational setting. Also, it must be acknowledged that the current sample is biased with regard to the religious representation of the population and the over-representation of the banking industry.

References

Arbuckle, J. L. & Wothke, W. (1999). *AMOS 4.0 User's Guide.* Chicago, IL: Small Waters Corporation.

Aycan, Z. (2006). Paternalism: Towards conceptual refinement and operationalization. In Kim, U., Yang, K. S., & Hwang, K. K. (eds), *Indigenous and Cultural Psychology: Understanding People in Context.* New York: Springer: 445–466.

Aycan, Z., Kanungo, R. N., Mendonca, M., Yu, K., Deller, J., Stahl, G., & Kurshid, A. (2000). Impact of culture on human resource management practices: A 10-country comparison. *Applied Psychology: An International Review,* 49(1): 192–221.

Bhawuk, D. P. S. (2008). Toward an Indian organizational psychology: Indigenous and cross-cultural approaches to research. In Rao, K. R., Paranjpe, A. C. & Dalal, A. K. (eds), *Handbook of Indian Psychology,* New Delhi, India: Cambridge University: 471–491.

Budhwar, P. S. (2009). Human resource management in the Indian context. In Budhwar, P. S., & Bhatnagar, J. (eds), *The Changing Face of People Management in India,* Oxon: Routledge: 3–13.

Byrne, B. (2001). *Structural Equation Modeling with AMOS: Basic Concepts, Applications and Programming.* Mahwah, NJ: Lawrence Erlbaum.

Cappelli, P., Singh, H., Singh, J. V., & Useem, M. (2010a). Leadership lessons from India: How the Indian companies drive performance by investing in people. *Harvard Business Review,* 88(3): 90–97.

Cappelli, P., Singh, H., Singh, J. V., & Useem, M. (2010b). *The India Way: How India's Top Business Leaders are Revolutionizing Management,* Harvard Business Press: Boston, MA.

Census (2011). Table 21: Distribution of Population by Religion. New Delhi: Government of India, Ministry of Home Affairs, Office of the Registrar General & Census Commissioner. Available at: http://censusindia.gov.in/Census_And_You/religion.aspx.

Chandra, V. (2012). Work-life balance: Eastern and Western perspectives. *The International Journal of Human Resource Management,* 23(5): 1040–1056.

Chhokar, J. S. (2008). India: Diversity and complexity in action. In Chhokar, J. S., Brodbeck, F. C., & House, R. J. (eds), *Culture and Leadership Across the World: The GLOBE Book of In-depth studies of 25 Societies,* New York: Lawrence Erlbaum: 971–1020.

Chhokar, J. P., Brodbeck, F. C., & House, R. J. (2008). *Culture and Leadership Across the World: The Globe Book of In-depth Studies of 25 Societies.* New York: Lawrence Erlbaum.

Das, G. (2002). *India Unbound: The Social and Economic Revolution from Independence to the Global Information Age.* New York: Anchor Books.

Den Hartog, D. N., House, R. J., Hanges, P. J., Ruiz-Quintanilla, S.A., Dorfman, P. W. & other GLOBE Country Investigators (1999). Culture specific and cross-culturally generalizable implicit leadership theories: are attributes of charismatic/ transformational leadership universally endorsed? *Leadership Quarterly*, 10(2): 219–256.

Dickson, M. W., Den Hartog, D. N., & Mitchelson, J. K. (2003). Research on leadership in a cross-cultural context: Making progress, and raising new questions. *The Leadership Quarterly*, 14(6): 729–768.

Dorfman, P. W., Howell, J. P., Hibino, S., Lee, J. K., Tate, U., & Bautista, A. (1997). Leadership in Western and Asian countries: Commonalities and differences in effective leadership processes across cultures. *The Leadership Quarterly*, 8(3): 233–274.

Farh J. L. & Cheng B. S. (2000). Paternalistic leadership in Chinese organizations: A cultural analysis. *Indigenous Psychology Research in Chinese Society*, 13: 127–180.

Gelfand, M. J., Erez, M., & Aycan, Z. (2007). Cross-cultural organizational behaviour. *Annual Review of Psychology*, 58: 479–514.

Goswami, S. (2013). Strategic crisis of Indian multinational corporations: A study. *IUP Journal of Business Strategy*, 10(3): 7–18.

Hair, J. F., Anderson, R. E., Tatham, R. L., & Black, W.C. (1998). *Multivariate Data Analysis*, Englewood Cliffs, NJ: Prentice-Hall.

Herald, M. (2011). Employee perceptions of reward and recognition policy of Indian MNC BPO firms – An empirical study. *International Journal of Business Economics and Management Research*, 2(7): 19–28

Hilton, A. L. (1998). Why did I kill?: The Cambodian genocide and the dark side of face and honor. *Journal of Asian studies*, 57(1): 93–122.

House, R., Hanges, P., Javidan, M., Dorfman, P. W., & Gupta, V. (2004). *Culture, Leadership and Organizations: The GLOBE Study of 62 Societies*, Thousand Oaks, CA: Sage.

Jain, H., Mathew, M., & Bedi, A. (2012). HRM innovations by Indian and foreign MNCs operating in India: A survey of HR professionals. *The International Journal of Human Resource Management*, 23(5): 1006–1018.

James, K., Chen, D. L., & Cropanzano, R. (1996). Culture and leadership among Taiwanese and US workers: Do values influence leadership ideals? In Ruderman, M. N., Hughes-James, M. W., & Jackson, S. E. (eds), *Selected Research on Work Team Diversity*. Washington, DC: American Psychological Association/Center for Creative Leadership: 33–52.

Javidan, M., & Carl, D. E. (2004). East meets West: A cross-cultural comparison of charismatic leadership among Canadian and Iranian executives. *Journal of Management Studies*, 41(4): 665–691.

Jayakody, J. A. S. K. (2008). Charismatic leadership in Sri Lankan business organizations. *Journal of Management Development*, 27(5): 480–498.

Jong, M. G. de., Steenkamp, J. B. E. M., & Veldkamp, B. P. (2009). A model for the construction of country-specific, yet internationally comparable short-form marketing scales. *Marketing Science*, 28(4): 674–689.

Kalra, S. K. & Gupta, R. K. (1995). Patronising as an effective managerial style in the context of Indian culture, a paper presented at the Symposium on Indigenous Behaviour in Effective Management and Organisation, *Proceedings of the Asia-Pacific Regional Conference of Psychology*, Guangzhou, China, 27–30 August.

Kerlinger, F. N. (1973). *Foundations of Behavioral Research*, New York: Holt, Rinehart & Winston.

Marcoulides, G. A., Nathanael, P., Marcoulides, L. D., & Soteriou, A. (2004). Cross-national stability of a leadership model. *Psychological Reports*, 94(2): 517–522.

Martinez, P. G. (2005). Paternalism as a positive form of leadership in the Latin American context. In Elvira, M., & Davila, A. (eds), *Managing Human Resources in Latin America: An Agenda For International Leaders*, Oxon: Routledge: 75–93.

Mathew, S. K., & Jones, R. (2012). Satyagraha and employee relations: Lessons from a multinational automobile transplant in India. *Employee Relations*, 34(5): 501–517.

Mathew, S. K., & Jones, R. (2013). Toyotism and Brahminism: Employee relations difficulties in establishing lean manufacturing in India. *Employee Relations*, 35(2): 200–221.

Mathur, P., Aycan, Z., & Kanungo, R. N. (1996). Work cultures in Indian organizations: A comparison between public and private sector. *Psychology and Developing Societies*, 8(2): 199–223.

Meade, A. W., Watson, A. M. & Kroustalis, C. M. (2007). Assessing common methods bias in organizational research, unpublished paper presented at the 22nd Annual Meeting of the Society for Industrial and Organizational Psychology, New York, 27–29 April 2007.

Morrison, A. J. (2000). Developing a global leadership model. *Human Resource Management*, 39(2–3): 117–131.

Northouse, P. G. (1997). *Leadership: Theory and Practice*, Thousand Oaks, CA: Sage.

Pasa, S. F., Kabasakal, H., & Bodur, M. (2001). Society, organizations, and leadership in Turkey, *Applied Psychology: An International Review*, 50(4): 559–589.

Pellegrini, E. K., Scandura, T. A., & Jayaraman, V. (2010). Cross-cultural generalizability of paternalistic leadership: An empirical investigation. *Group & Organization Management*, 35(4): 391–420.

Pio, E. (2007). HRM and Indian epistemologies: A review and avenues for future research. *Human Resource Management Review*, 17(3): 319–335.

Podsakoff, P. M., MacKenzie, S. B., Lee, J. Y., & Podsakoff, N. P. (2003). Common method biases in behavioural research: A critical review of the literature and recommended remedies. *Journal of Applied Psychology*, 88(5): 879–903.

Podsakoff, P.M., MacKenzie, S.B. and Podsakoff, N.P. (2012). Sources of Method Bias in Social Science Research and Recommendations on How to Control It. *The Annual Review of Psychology*, 63, 539–569.

Raghavan, A. (2008). Going global and taking charge: The road ahead for the Indian manager. *The Journal for Decision Makers: Vikalpa*, 33(4): 61–68.

Ramaswami, A., & Dreher, G. F. (2010). Dynamics of mentoring relationships in India: A qualitative, exploratory study. *Human Resources Management*, 49 (3): 501–530.

Rao, S. A. (2007). Effectiveness of performance management systems: An empirical study in Indian companies. *The International Journal of Human Resource Management*, 18(10): 1812–1840.

Sanyal, S. (2008). *The Indian Renaissance: India's Rise after a Thousand Years of Decline*, New Delhi: Penguin Viking.

Sapre, P. M. (2000). Realizing the potential of management and leadership: Toward a synthesis of Western and indigenous perspectives in the modernization of non-Western societies. *International Journal in Education*, 3(3): 293–305.

Selvarajah, C., and Meyer, D. (2006). Archetypes of the Malaysian manager: Exploring dimensions that relate to leadership. *Journal of Management & Organization*, 12(3): 251–269.

Selvarajah, C., and Meyer, D. (2008a). One nation, three cultures: Exploring dimensions that relate to leadership in Malaysia. *Leadership and Organization Development Journal*, 29(8): 693–712.

Selvarajah, C., and Meyer, D. (2008b). Profiling the Chinese manager: Exploring dimensions that relate to leadership. *Leadership and Organization Development Journal*, 29(4): 359–375.

Selvarajah, C., Meyer, D., & Davuth, D. (2012). The effect of cultural modelling on leadership profiling of the Cambodian manager. *Asia Pacific Business Review*, 18(4): 649–674.

Selvarajah, C., Meyer, D., & Donovan, J. (2013b). Cultural context and its influence on managerial leadership in Thailand. *Asia Pacific Business Review*, 19(3): 356–380.

Selvarajah, C., Meyer, D., Jeyakumar, R., & Donovan, J. (2013a). Flowers in a greenhouse: Profiling excellence in leadership in Singapore. *Leadership and Organization Development Journal*, 34(8): 784–804.

Selvarajah, C., Duignan, P., Nuttman, C., Lane, T., & Suppiah C. (1995). In search of the ASEAN leader: Exploratory study of the dimensions that relate to excellence in leadership, *Management International Review: Journal of International Business*, 35(1): 29–43.

Siemsen, E., Roth, A., & Oliveira, P. (2010). Common method bias in regression models with linear, quadratic, and interaction effects. *Organizational Research Methods*, 13(3): 456–476.

Sinha, J. B. P. (1980). *The Nurturant Task Leader: A Model of the Effective Executive*, New Delhi: Concept Publishing.

Sinha, J. B. P. (1990). *Work Culture in the Indian Context*, New Delhi: Sage.

Sinha, J. B. P. (1994). Major trends in research on leadership and power. *Indian Psychological Abstracts*, 1: 385–414.

Sinha J. B. P. (1997). Indian perspectives on leadership and power in organizations. In Kao, H.S.R. & Sinha, D. (eds), *Asian Perspectives on Psychology*. Thousand Oaks, CA: Sage: 218–235.

Sinha, J. B. P., & Chowdhary, G. P. (1981). Perception of subordinate as a moderator of leadership effectiveness. *Journal of Social Psychology*, 113: 115–121.

Smith, P. B., Misumi, J., Tayeb, M., Peterson, M., & Bond, M. (1989). On the generality of leadership-style measures across cultures. *Journal of Occupational Psychology*, 62(1): 97–109.

Som, A. (2007). What drives adoption of innovative SHRM practices in Indian organizations. *The International Journal of Human Resource Management*, 18(5): 808–828.

Sparrow, P. R., & Budhwar, P. S. (1997). Competition and change: Mapping the India HRM recipe against worldwide patterns. *Journal of World Business*, 32(3): 224–43.

Taormina, R., & Selvarajah, C. (2005). Perceptions of leadership excellence in ASEAN nations. *Leadership*, 1(3): 299–322.

Vijay Kumar, T. (2013). *Labor Unrest at Maruti Suzuki India Limited*, Hyderabad: IBS Center for Management Research. Available at: www.icmrindia.org.

Virmani B R. (2000). *Managing People in Organizations – Challenges of Change*, New Delhi, Thousand Oaks and London: Response Books, Sage Publications.

Virmani, B. R., & Guptan, S. U. (1991). *The Indian Management*, New Delhi: Vision Books.

Vroom, V. H. (2000). Leadership and the decision-making process. *Organizational Dynamics*, 28(4): 82–94.

Vroom, V. H., & Yetton, P. W. (1973). *Leadership and Decision-Making*, Pittsburgh, PA: University of Pittsburgh Press.

Part II

Internationalization of Asian Firms: Perspectives and Strategies

6

Adapting to Change: The State of Singaporean Private Enterprise in China

Wilfred How and Caroline Yeoh

Introduction

One of the most affluent and developed nations in South East Asia, the city-state of Singapore relies largely on tapping global resources for economic growth to ameliorate its tiny land area and accompanying lack of natural resources. Its current prominence is to a great degree owing to an early recognition of the need for this tapping of global resources, as is observable from policy documents from the 1990s (Singapore Economic Development Board, 1993, 1995a, 1995b), and a well-documented stratagem of expanding its foreign direct investments (FDIs) as a means to stimulate economic development (Blomqvist, 2001; Huff, 1995; Murray & Pereira, 1995) and strengthen the city-state's external economy. This was a process of, in many ways, equal parts careful planning and trial and error, with the island and its firms progressing through a number of distinct phases of overseas investment initiatives, each with its own successes and, inevitably, failures, and with the city-state taking away, in each case, lessons learnt. Initial ventures in North America and Western Europe, attempting to expedite access to new technology and markets, proved largely unprofitable, suggesting efforts were best refocused elsewhere (Sitathan, 2002). A shift occurred toward regionalization, with a focus on opportunities within Asia, particularly in China, Indonesia and Vietnam (Okposin, 1999; Tan, 1995); this was embarked upon largely under the aegis of government support, through the vehicle of state-sponsored industrial townships, negotiated at the state level and managed heavily through government-linked companies (GLCs) – in effect, the state and its attendant GLCs providing a beachhead and shelter for the country's private enterprises, a pattern that would be almost characteristic of Singaporean regionalization and internationalization for the next decade and beyond (Yeung, 2000). This ultimately achieved much more positive, although yet somewhat mixed, results, as described in our older research, and provided a number of invaluable and cautionary lessons as to the exportability of Singaporean-styled business practices and systems to foreign cultures (How & Yeoh, 2007; Yeoh et al., 2006) – which, in short, was that wholesale exportability was less than tenable in the long-term.

The natural progression for the city-state was to expand its aims once more from regionalization to internationalization, with its eyes set on the cryptic Middle East region – at the time possessing a flourishing property-development market, fed by a new wave of local investment and international interest. With experiences from China, Indonesia and Vietnam in mind, Singapore's gambits in this region reflected a less dominant role of government institutions and, instead, a greater emphasis on the company, which perhaps were intended to galvanize private enterprises into a more prominent role in creating self-sustainable economic space (Yeoh et al., 2011). However, all-too-familiar elements were easily observable. GLCs were found, once again, at the spearhead of the internationalization effort; the same tactic of managing strategic cooperations and engaging with private or semi-private enterprises (a tactic that admittedly, to date, has had at least some observed success) was oft repeated; and though ostensibly different, many initial entries into the region were through methods extremely similar to those observable in the era of regionalization. Also all too familiar, were the undercurrents of tension and disconnected viewpoints over business practices, among which were the insistence on Singaporean-style working environments and the heavy concentration of decision-making authority in Singaporean managers, both onsite in the Middle East and in Singapore (Yeoh & How, 2012). Although at first these did not appear to be sufficiently major so as to be problems, they rapidly became so in the wake of the worldwide financial crisis in 2008, most notably in Dubai, one of the areas hardest hit by the crisis and one of the major centres of Singapore's internationalization efforts (Yeoh & How, 2011). By 2012, Singaporean involvement in the region, while still significant, had of necessity evolved to be more cautious, as well as more flexible toward the interests of local stakeholders, cultures and business practices – this, perhaps, being the pertinent lesson from the most recent phase of the city-state's internationalization efforts.

However, this was a lesson perhaps not as easily learnt by some. Our recent research as of 2012 points toward Singapore's GLCs in the

Middle East having made a smoother transition – and, indeed, having been more adaptable in general – than the city-state's private enterprises, contrary to common expectation (Shome, 2009; Feng et al, 2004), suggesting, possibly, that the shelter provided by GLCs might have its own costs. These findings are reinforced peripherally, but on a global scale, by official data from Singapore (International Enterprise Singapore, 2013) about the city-state's small-medium enterprises (SMEs) and non-SMEs from 2011 to 2012, from which two findings relevant to the relative adaptability of Singapore firms surface. The first, that the intention of Singaporean SMEs to venture into other economic regions dropped (sometimes sharply) across the board for every region but South East Asia, suggests a propensity to stick with safer and more familiar pastures. The second, that the percentage of SMEs identifying various major export-related challenges as significant factors remained relatively unchanged, while the percentage of non-SMEs doing so dropped by a large extent for many challenges, suggests a greater degree of adaptability on the part of Singapore's non-SMEs than on the part of SMEs. In the context of Singapore's GLCs almost completely belonging to the non-SME category, and of SMEs making up much of the private enterprise in greatest need of the economic space internationalization provides, an inferential, if not substantive, observation can be made as to the relative adaptability of Singapore's GLCs and private enterprises. While Singapore firms still generally possess a reputation for, and advantage in, systemic efficiencies and technical expertise (How & Yeoh, 2013), these advantages are diluted in the global marketplace, and further, are qualities that are at their most effective when tempered with sufficient adaptive rigour to adjust to the shifting demands of new environments and changing markets. For these firms, lacking such adaptivity hobbles these competitive advantages, which is a distinct liability when in the same arena as strong global competitors from the USA, Europe and East Asia.

Given the importance of fully private enterprise in the long-term sustainability of any internationalization effort, and Singapore's obvious recognition of this importance, the above observations may be a cause for some concern for the city-state and its internationalization strategy and, indeed, for any country seeking to actively encourage the internationalization of its firms, most especially those smaller Asian countries whose internationalization programmes are relatively recent. It is, therefore, the purpose of this study to examine a selection of Singaporean companies – in this case, Singaporean private enterprises specifically – operating in China (which features both a sizeable market attracting considerable international investment, and a highly fluid and changing business environment) so as to obtain a loosely representative impression of the extent to which Singaporean private enterprise is actually able to adapt to foreign business environments and to changes that occur therein. The reasons for, advantages of and some limitations inherent in the chosen methodology are set out in full in the following section.

Methodology

Empirical data was first obtained through a series of in-depth and, whenever possible, face-to-face interviews with top management personnel from the case study companies. The interviews took place over a number of years, from 2009 to 2013. Special emphasis was placed on the most recent interviews, from 2013, so as to increase the strength and relevance of the information gleaned. With this primary data as the main input, secondary resources, including press releases, news reports, performance indicators and even some degree of anecdotal evidence, are tapped to provide corroborating and/or contradicting data. The case studies are constructed from an analysis of this body of available data, with attention paid to the observations, inferences and conclusions that may be drawn from the abovementioned corroborations and/or contradictions between primary and secondary accounts of the case study companies' experiences in China.

For the purpose of this study, all four chosen case study companies are privately owned enterprises, not a mix of private companies and GLCs. The reason for this choice is due to the limitations of a fully comparative study. Owing partially to differences in profiles of the general Singaporean GLC and private companies – namely, that the former are generally much larger and have more resources, so much so as to be almost universally counted among non-SMEs and thus tend to be involved in distinctly different industries than many of their private counterparts – an exhaustive comparison of Singaporean GLCs and private companies in the same industries is only possible to a limited extent, and would, in all possibility, produce industry- or sector-specific results. Therefore, it is more useful in this case to examine private enterprises of various profiles, across a number of distinct industries and sectors, with pertinent comparisons to any GLC counterparts (data for which has been obtained, in most cases, in a similar fashion, via interviews as part of our body of data) of these case study companies incorporated into the construction of the case study at the secondary data level, and referred to where points of interest arise in the context of the case studies.

For a similar reason, all four case studies are based upon the operations of the chosen companies in China. This is to reduce variations in data arising from different local environments and circumstances, whether financial, geographical or sociopolitical. In this way, the strength of comparisons between the case study companies is increased. This is not to say such variations are eliminated. For a number of reasons, operations in China have been chosen for this study despite the existence of precisely the same varying local environments and circumstances across the wide area spanned by the China. First, distinct differences exist across China's various regions in consumer tastes, cultural nuances and other business-affecting minutiae – and any significant utilization of the vast economic space China has to offer must necessarily involve the expansion of operations across some of these regions, providing a useful and pertinent point of examination as to the adaptive capability of Singaporean private enterprises. Second, with its sizeable resource pool and deep economic potential, China is unquestionably a region of high interest to any internationalization effort. A study of Singaporean firms' experiences in China is therefore more likely to be of relevance both to and about Asian firms in general than one in a more minor region. Finally, China, as a yet continually developing and increasingly affluent nation, possesses a business environment that varies not just across geography, but also across time – the China of today is a very different place to do business in than it was ten or even five years ago. Many Singaporean companies are dealing with a much changed (and perhaps more importantly, *changing*) environment from when they first entered into China – the degree to which companies are making necessary adaptations being invaluable in the assessment of the adaptive capability of Singaporean private enterprise.

Theoretical considerations

In principle, for most enterprises, the internationalization process is embarked upon with circumspection, and involves risk minimization and strategic planning (UNIDO, 2009). During internationalization, some duties and tasks are centrally performed to reap integration benefits, while others are performed locally to adapt to local needs (McGee et al., 2010). An enterprise may opt to employ differing levels of integration and adaptation in its foreign operations, depending on the enterprise's priorities and expense tolerance. From our previous research, for example, many Singaporean companies in the Middle East appear to have initially defaulted to a strategy of high integration and low local adaptation.

Enterprises venture into markets that are more familiar and less risky, and commit minimal resources to gain experience before foraying deeper into relatively riskier business environments. Enterprises, depending on the conditions of the foreign countries and their level of resource commitment, employ different internationalization stratagems – which include exporting, licensing, franchising, management contracts, turnkey operations, joint ventures and full ownership. Likewise, a stages model demonstrates that an enterprise's level of commitment in its internationalization stratagem is contingent on its stage of expansion. At the onset, the enterprise often seeks to reduce its risk. Hence, it is not surprising that initially the enterprise mainly exports only its core competencies (or its existing products) into new geographic markets (Delios et al., 2010).

In time, however, as the enterprise gains experience, and as circumstances in these new geographic markets change and consequently both new opportunities and threats emerge, it must reasonably follow that the enterprise should re-evaluate its priorities and adjust its strategies and level of commitment, and thus progress onto a further stage of expansion into these new markets. While continuing in the same vein is a valid option, it is also one that generally does not represent full exploitation of available opportunities. It is at this stage, possibly, that Singaporean private enterprises do not fully exercise the options at their disposal.

Thus, the two central hypotheses that need to be examined in the following case studies are clear. First, that Singaporean private enterprises are lacking in adaptive willingness and/or capability in response to changing circumstances to the degree that they suffer in comparison to their GLC counterparts; and second, that Singaporean private enterprises do not fully exploit available opportunities in their areas of internationalization. Both of the above hypotheses, it is noted, are issues linkable to risk aversion and resource strain, factors previously observed in Singaporean companies. The degree to which these hypotheses are proven by an analysis of the case studies serves as strong, although not authoritative, evidence of the predominance and influence of these factors on Singaporean private companies.

Case studies

Company A: Property development (commercial)

One of Singapore's more venerable companies, Company A has a long and storied history as one of the city-state's major department store chains. Growing competition locally in the early 1990s led the company to hasten diversification efforts into various other sectors, and now its property development and investment arm is a more major part of Company A's business than its original retail business, contributing well over 90% of the company's profit margin since 2010. The early diversification efforts in the 1990s induced Company A's first forays into China in 1994 – a very much earlier entry than most, and one which would consequently imply all the ramifications of being, to all intents and purposes, a first mover, both in the positive and the negative. These ramifications would have been all the more influential given the company's relative lack of appropriation of available Singaporean governmental support, being neither by industry or location under the auspices of the Singaporean-styled industrial township in Suzhou, at the time the focus of the city-state's regionalization programme.

In other ways, however, Company A's entry into China was fairly typical for a Singaporean company – the company's first venture was accomplished through a joint venture with a major local developer in Shanghai with ties to the municipal government, an all-too-familiar, albeit effective, strategy, and one replicated right down to the majority of both management and technical expertise being provided by the Singaporean partner, as was the case with most Singapore ventures over in Suzhou. Building on its experience in the retail industry, Company A's initial development in Shanghai was to be a large-scale retail mall, from which the company would derive rental revenues and would establish it as a significant player in China retail space development. The company, however, chose not to import their core retail business into China – initially because of a difference in affluence and demographics, with the company's target middle- to high-income groups not yet present in sufficient numbers. Company A's presence in China is thus entirely in the retail property development industry, with major malls in the main cities of Beijing, Shanghai and Guangzhou, and similar properties on a smaller scale across a number of developing Chinese cities – a result that certainly appears to speak well for the company's performance in its new frontier.

A more contextual study, however, reveals a not-insignificant number of hints toward endemic behaviours not unusual among Singaporean private enterprises. A comparison with similar companies – in this case, Singapore government-linked companies in the same industry – finds that the government-linked companies expanded more daringly into the China market, with the most similar such company having penetrated some 40 cities by 2008, as compared to Company A's rather more limited presence. While a difference in resources and experience is a factor, for such a gap to open over 14 years is undoubtedly a sign of a more cautious and restrained approach – one that quite arguably represents less than optimal exploitation of available opportunity, supporting the second hypothesis. Signs also exist as to an insufficient degree of adaptation to differences in tastes and expectations across even the major cities in China. One of Company A's more major properties in Beijing underwent major renovations in 2009 to adapt better to local needs, having been too similar to one of its Shanghai properties. Issues such as the above are obviously vital concerns for the company, as it expands gradually into China's developing cities – with, one might note, retail malls that show a markedly lower degree of differentiation than those in the three major cities. Also, despite the changing face and markedly increased affluence of the Chinese populace in general, Company A shows no signs of importing its retail business into China – understandable, perhaps, given the vastly larger profits from the property industry, yet still curious given the company's expansion of its retail business into other, less affluent countries, and the obvious synergies between its ownership of retail malls and its retail business – especially given the opportunity its current expansion into China's developing cities would seem to offer for its retail business. Evidence points toward Company A's example also providing support for the first hypothesis.

Company B: Manufacturing and retail (health products)

A major producer and retailer in Singapore of a wide variety of health products under a stable of different labels, Company B also possesses a significant international presence, with operations across Asia, Africa, Europe and the Middle East – suggesting a wealth of experience in dealing with varying cultural and corporate norms. As a developer and manufacturer of many of its own products, Company B's methods of international expansion arguably require a greater range of considerations than some companies. It needs to juggle research and development with practical manufacturing concerns and promotion needs – a fact that makes the company's wide international expansion all the more impressive, and suggests a more voracious appetite for risk and expansion than most of its peers.

Company B's entry into China was in 1994, preceding, in fact, the company's public listing in Singapore. Somewhat atypically for Singaporean companies, perhaps owing to its status at the time as a private company, it entered in a contractual joint venture rather than attempting to reduce risk by seeking an influential local partner. In fact, it would have preferred to utilize a fully owned subsidiary, as it does in most of its international operations – and did indeed switch to full ownership when it became possible, regardless of losing previous tax incentives for partial ownership by a local firm. Nonetheless, Company B's initial approach was not without endemic Singaporean caution. It tested the waters with a single outlet in Beijing. However, following outstanding sales numbers from this and subsequent forays into Shanghai, Company B discarded its previous approach and embarked on an impressively aggressive expansion strategy, fuelled perhaps by new funding from the company's public listing, and as of the end of 2009 had a multitude of outlets in over 50 Chinese cities. Similarly, the minutiae of Company B's operations reveal no reservations about adopting new paradigms. Coherent marketing strategies include a deliberate distribution of outlets into higher-end department stores in order to appeal to a higher-income group, as opposed to a more general marketing strategy adopted in Singapore and elsewhere, and a purposeful lack of instalment plans, in light of observations as to the preferences and quixotic tendencies of well-to-do Chinese. Adaptive vigour also shows in the company's response to bootleg products. It shortened its research and development cycle in China so as to maintain the technological edge, and offered trade-in deals for not just its own older products, but also bootleg and rival products. Between Company B's swift and purposeful expansion, and its ready willingness to adopt new strategies in light of local sociocultural circumstances, it is hard to say that the company's experience supports either hypothesis, at least in the short term. Instead, it stands as a good counterexample.

This is, of course, not to say that Company B does not display some of the more typical habits of Singaporean companies in general, and Singaporean private enterprise in particular. Even with its rapid pace of expansion, its management staff is largely non-local, the majority being, unsurprisingly, Singaporean – which, like examples of the same staffing decisions in other Singaporean companies, is a potential for long-term issues, such as integration with local staff, problems with management succession and availability of importable managerial staff, as suggested by our previous research with regard to the degree of exportability of Singaporean-styled business practices, and supported by more recent experiences in the Middle East. It is worth noting, however, that anecdotal evidence suggests that, in the short term at least, this preponderance of Singaporean managerial staff actually quells potential tensions stemming from the promotion of local staff over their peers. As Company B has few concerns as to staff relations, despite the significant length of its presence in China, this may be less of an issue in China than in some other parts of the world. However, quality-control staff in China are also heavily Singaporean, and all exports from China are first shipped to Singapore for additional quality-control testing, which, while engendering greater quality assurance, also generates additional logistical costs. Improving local quality standards, one would think, would be a possible direction for future cost reduction. Some greater degree of skill- and relationship-building with local employees, perhaps, might still be on the cards for Company B.

Company C: Retail (consumer goods)

A relatively more recent addition to Singapore's stable of private enterprises, Company C is engaged in the design and retail of luxury goods and accessories, most notably shoes and bags. Incorporated in 1996, the company now has a presence in well over 20 countries in various regions across South East Asia, the Middle East and, of course, China, and has also attracted international attention and investment in recent years. Company C, it seems, appears rather more internationally minded than might be expected, an observation further supported by the company's appropriation and promotion of various international campaigns in its marketing efforts, and its embracing of the online store paradigm, which is, perhaps, evidence of the company's adaptability, given that its international expansion began only in 2004.

Company C's expansion into China, however, occurred only in 2009, long after the affluence of the average Chinese citizen had begun to climb meteorically, and when the luxury goods industry had long been established in the country. It's actual entry was a simple affair – legislation had long shifted to more business-friendly configurations, and Company C already had manufacturing and distribution centres located in China, albeit with no retail stores until this point. The most notable characteristic of Company C's initial entry, in fact, was its small scale, that is, in only Shanghai – a choice made, apparently, due to both an unsurprising measure of caution, and the need to sufficiently establish the brand name in China before embarking on a larger scale expansion. Similarly to Company B, the company's rate of expansion since its initial foray has been rapid and fierce – today 45 stores in a large number of cities bear the company's brand name, a development enabled partially by the company's already heavily China-based operational structure, with design, research and development, quality control, procurement, manufacturing and distribution all already occurring in China. So well does the company appear to be performing in China, in fact, that the question arises as to why the company chose not to tackle this vibrant market earlier. In relation to the first hypothesis, Company C is a rather mixed bag – the rapid rate of expansion arguably points against a lack of adaptive willingness, but the long delay in tackling the market appears to support a failure to swiftly adapt to changing circumstances, and in either case the relatively short span of the company's operations in China render attempts to measure the company's adaptability over time in China moot.

However, the company's odd delay in tackling the China market is not the only question to arise. Anecdotal evidence ascribes an initial reluctance on Company C's part to engage in its usual franchising strategies in the company's initial entries in Shanghai, apparently because of quality control concerns and the desire to reduce chances of replication by competitors – an understandable precaution in light of the need to establish the brand, but nonetheless rather curious given the proportion of the company's value chain already located in China at the time. The company's current preponderance of storefronts suggests that these reservations have been long allayed, but the existence of the reservations in the first place may suggest some degree of the familiar risk-averse Singaporean mindset creeping in. Taking this into consideration, together with the abovementioned delay in entering a lucrative market where much of the company's main operational activities were already located, there appears to be circumstantial, though not strong, support for the second hypothesis. As well, the company's management remains highly centralized in Singapore-based managers and executives; a phenomenon less justifiable than it is for Company B, given the multinational composition of most of the company's value-producing sectors (most significantly Singaporean, Malaysian and Chinese). While no internal pressures are as yet evident, this is no guarantee that such internal pressures may not be an issue in the future; certainly, as our previous research suggests, there have been more than a few Singaporean firms that can attest to similar staffing decisions causing problems down the road.

Company D: Manufacturing (industrial/pharmaceutical)

Engaged in the production of medical cables and assemblies, Company D, too, counts among Singapore's relatively newer private enterprises, having been incorporated in 1998, but sells its products worldwide and has a significant presence in Europe, America, Japan, and China, and counts among its clients a good number of well-known multinationals, such as Siemens AG and GE Healthcare. Company D, however, differs from its peer, Company C, in two distinct ways. The first, and more obvious, of these differences is the nature of the company: manufacturing-based and in a rather more rarefied industry than Company C. The second difference is, simply, a disparity in experience. Company D's founder was previously involved with a company in a similar industry, which spent some years with its manufacturing activities centred in Shenzhen, as far back as 1985, and which enjoyed a fair degree of success before being sold just prior to Company D's incorporation. In this context, Company D's immediate choice of Shenzhen as a manufacturing base following its incorporation is highly unsurprising.

Interestingly, the circumstances of Company D's entrance into China were, in addition to the familiar joint venture vehicle, the exact opposite of those of many other Singaporean companies. Shenzhen's status as the first Special Economic Zone of China made the region a favourable choice for Company D, with a conglomeration of locational advantages ranging from ready availability of materials, to logistical conveniences, to the various and sundry incentives extended to companies operating in Shenzhen. It was, however, the location of the founder's previous company in Shenzhen that was cited as a major factor in the decision to locate the company's manufacturing activities in the region. Specifically, it was stated that continuity of business relations with suppliers and other relevant stakeholders in the region – in effect, the eponymous *guanxi*, built through the previous company's years in the region and a partnership with a local firm – was a great, and perhaps even deciding, influence in the choice of location. Company D was, in effect, providing the locational advantages while the joint venture partner, an Australian medical technology firm, was providing the technical and technological expertise, as well as a link to the client base, which, for this industry, is rarefied and well established. Atypical as it was for a Singaporean company, the partnership proved an effective one, reaping first-mover advantages from both the cheaper costs of production in Shenzhen compared to the at the time majority production in developed countries, and a burgeoning of the medical device industry, a paradigm to which China itself contributes. Company D today holds a sizeable percentage of the market share for the products it manufactures, with as much as 80% of the market share for one type of cable, and enjoys a reputation for safety, reliability and cost effectiveness. This ability to identify potential trends and opportunities, and to capitalize on them, would seem to suggest that Company D is another counterexample as far as the first hypothesis is concerned.

For the second hypothesis, however, perhaps Company D is rather less a counterexample. Interviews and financial reports intimate that proceeds from the sale of the founder's previous company in Shenzhen provided far more capital than was actually reinvested in Company D, suggesting that the capacity existed for a larger scale of operations in Shenzhen than was actually embarked on. This is supported by two further observations as to the company's initial strategy. First, the company's initial product choice consisted of two types of cables that are used in more common health diagnostic equipment, and thus require relatively low technology bases for their production. This arguably represented a rather light tapping of the technological expertise of the Australian partner firm, which arguably proved to have consequences, as we note later. Second, the maximum monthly production capability for each cable was set by the company at half of that of the previous firm's – a decision perhaps justifiable from a risk reduction perspective, given the need to break into a new market as opposed to selling to an established market, but one that had immediate consequences as the surge in demand in the late 1990s proved larger than expected, and had Company D scrambling to keep up by increasing production capacity substantially over that same period.

The early limitations (which were likely risk-aversion-related) on product selection may arguably be now further limiting the company's future expansion. Company D expressed an intention to expand into the production of another kind of cable, one that is increasingly demanded and that the company is financially able to expand production into. However, the cable also requires a higher standard of technical and technological knowledge than its previous products, a standard enforced by major potential clients in the healthcare equipment industry – requiring a technology transfer that Company D may find difficult to negotiate from its Australian partner, given the potential for employees to leak intellectual property. This is an issue acknowledged by the company to be an ongoing problem, because it does not have much proprietary technology of its own and relies heavily on blueprints from its clients. The company itself appears to have only a limited idea of how to deal with this issue. Certainly, some degree of evidence exists in Company D's example to support the second hypothesis. The company also appears to have no intention to expand their manufacturing capabilities further than Shenzhen, despite increasing competition from less location-bound local and international competitors and constantly rising wages in Shenzhen, which already has the fourth highest minimum wage per hour in China. This apparent unwillingness to adjust operations in response to changing circumstances not only provides evidence supporting the second hypothesis, but also supports the first hypothesis, weakening the degree to which the case of Company D is a counterexample to the first hypothesis.

Analysis

An examination of the above four case studies, vis-à-vis the stated hypotheses, produces an interestingly mixed range of observations. At a glance, while Company A's case supports both hypotheses, Company B's case provides a strong counterexample against both hypotheses. The cases of both Company C and Company D provide weak-to-middling support for the second hypothesis, but Company D is also a weak counterexample to the first hypothesis, while Company C's case is inconclusive either way with regard to the first hypothesis. On a general level, it appears that not enough evidence exists to support the first hypothesis – that Singaporean private enterprise is not sufficiently adaptive in response to changing circumstances – and that, therefore, it would seem to not generally be the case, although most definitely not a non-existent issue. The second hypothesis, that Singaporean private enterprise does not fully exploit available opportunities in areas of internationalization, does in fact appear to be more generally the case, with more support for it derivable from this set of case studies, albeit with some heartening exceptions.

A comparison taking into account the demographics of the case study companies reveals a number of interesting nuances. It is not altogether surprising to find that neither Company B nor Company C, the two companies engaged in retail and thus arguably the most likely to have a hand on the pulse of the local environment, provides evidence against the first hypothesis, albeit in the case of Company C, only to a limited extent and only after actual entry into the market, while Company A, despite (or perhaps because of) its long presence in and experience with China, proved less dextrous with respect to adjusting to the changing local environment. Company D's case is slightly more complicated, with mixed signals from the company's past, largely accurate foresight and from its current issues. However, Company D's picture possibly becomes clearer when considered in the context of the company's predecessor, which was in partnership with a local Chinese firm, and said predecessor from which Company D derived many of its locational advantages. The implication is that Company D was initially well appraised of changing conditions and opportunities in China because of its predecessor's connection with a local firm, and later became dissociated from the local environment, being in partnership with an Australian firm with little local input. Peripheral support for this theory emerges when one considers that none of the other three companies – not even Company A, arguably the most similar to its government-linked peers in industry and in strategy – identified any particular issues with personnel, while Company D's issues with possible employee breaches of confidentiality in relation to intellectual property appear to be a major limiting factor in its future plans. The counterargument, of course, is that Company D is more vulnerable to intellectual property breaches than the other companies – however, considering Company B's actual possession of proprietary technologies, that argument proves less than convincing. These findings appear to reinforce the need for any firm to maintain a local connection – not at all a new concept (Prahalad & Doz, 1987). Whether through local partners, local managerial staff or simply efforts in continuous communication, a need certainly exists to establish such a connection to keep in tandem with a fast-changing business environment, even for firms from an Asian country with some degree of shared ethnicity. Naturally, firms engaged in more detached industries, such as Companies A and D, might need to go to greater lengths to establish such a connection than those in, say, retail industries.

It must be acknowledged that the full exploitation of available opportunity alluded to in the second hypothesis is, in fact, reasonably subjective with respect to risk concerns. The case of Company D illustrates this. While the company's initial risk-reducing strategies do appear to have complicated or even limited the company's current avenues for growth, the company's current reputation is for safety, reliability and cost-effectiveness, the first two of which, logically, are of critical importance in the healthcare industry and would potentially have suffered had the company initially overextended itself either in terms of production capacity or in technological expertise. Certainly, this is an industry-specific concern, one that the other three companies in this study would find much less a factor, if at all; but it must be noted that it is specific conditions, whether specific to an industry or to a specific company, that must be considered by an individual firm in the formulation of its strategy. It is also a fact that, given Singapore's small size, many Singaporean private enterprises do in fact tend to suffer resource constraints, an observation alluded to and supported by our previous research on Singaporean firms in China, and a limitation shared, if not more heavily felt, by firms from up-and-coming smaller Asian nations. In this context, a balance does often have to be struck with risk management. That being noted, the apparent affirmation of the second hypothesis by this study does suggest that, on a more holistic level, Singaporean private enterprises could stand to be somewhat less risk averse and be bolder in their internationalizing strides than they currently appear to be – especially, one would imagine, in the midst of the continually burgeoning market that China provides. The lesson for other similarly sized Asian firms is the need to reconcile risk management and the taste for opportunity, which is a balancing act heavily reliant on the individual firm's industry and available resources, and that, taking into account the need for continuous adaptation highlighted by the first hypothesis, the metaphor of the balancing act only becomes all the more apt.

Conclusion

China's rate of hyper-development shows few signs of abating significantly as of 2013 – even while slowing it outpaces many other regions of the world. As the affluence of the Chinese populace in general and the metropolitan populace in particular continues to rise, there remains a wealth of opportunities for the daring company to seize. The observations in this chapter provide a somewhat positive, but still uncertain, picture when attempting to frame the Singaporean private enterprise in the silhouette of such a daring company. Also, unlike what our previous research centring on the Singaporean firms in the Middle East suggests, Singaporean firms in China do not appear to suffer overmuch from adaptive sluggishness, though they do generally appear to be lacking on the "daring" front. At a time when both international and local competition is on the rise a hypothetical daring company would need to expand at a rapid pace to not be left in the dust, and any lack of daring should be a reason for concern.

Of the two main probable causes for this lack of daring, the relative resource constraints of Singaporean companies vis-à-vis their international counterparts (most especially those from the United States, Japan and Korea) and a groundswell of local Chinese firms is alluded to, in our previous research, as being at least partially due to the spreading of resources across various high-development regions, such as China and the Middle East. A more concentrated approach, as some of the companies in this study have taken, might be a more practical solution for the company with more limited resources, such as firms from smaller and developing Asian countries. Indeed, the latest IE Singapore Internationalisation Survey finds that many Singaporean non-SMEs appear to be consolidating their resources on selective markets with higher potential. Perhaps smaller private enterprises, likely to suffer even more from resource constraints, might be well advised to follow suit. The other main probable cause – the endemic Singaporean risk-averse mindset – is unfortunately a stickier issue, with less clear potential solutions. While there is much that rising Asian firms might learn from the Singaporean examples, they might be advised to not emulate this aspect of the Singaporean experience.

It is clear that there is still much room for improvement for Singaporean private enterprise as a whole to become the carrier of the city-state's sustainable international development, even in China. It is a fact that the face of China – its business environment, demographics and financial influence on the countries around it – has changed remarkably in less than a decade, and will continue to do so as the country attempts to further improve and expand its economy. A possible interesting direction for future research would be to track over time the experiences of, measures taken by and successes and failures of Singaporean companies. Alternatively, more specific studies might be undertaken to compare the experiences of Singaporean companies in particular regions of China. More specific to the risk aversion and caution question, a specific and in-depth comparison might be drawn between some otherwise sufficiently similar companies that occupy different spots on the risk-appetite spectrum, should we identify companies of such similar profiles in the course of our data collection. However, it appears clear that adaptation will remain the keyword for Singaporean companies in China – successful, or otherwise – and is, as a matter of course, also likely to be the keyword for any other firms looking to China to expand their economic horizons.

References

Blomqvist, H. (2001). State and development policy: The case of Singapore, Asian Profile, 29. *ERN APS*, 7(2): 01162002.

Delios, A., Beamish, P. W., & Lu. J. W. (2010). *International Business: An Asia Pacific Perspective*. Singapore: Pearson.

Feng, F., Sun, Q., & Tong, W. H. S. (2004). Do government-linked companies underperform? *Journal of Banking And Finance*, 28(10): 2461–2492.

How, W. & Yeoh, C. (2007). The internationalization of Singapore's state-enterprise networks in the context of Asia's transborder industrialization: further evidence from Indonesia, Vietnam and China. *Journal of Asian Business*, 23(1): 1–25.

How, W. & Yeoh, C. (2013). The state-enterprise experience in the GCC: Whither Singapore Inc. *Research Journal of Economics & Business Studies*, 2(9): 62–70.

Huff, W. (1995). The development state, Singapore, and Singapore's economic development since 1960. *World Development*, 23(8): 1421–1438.

International Enterprise Singapore (2013). *IE Singapore Internationalisation Survey 2012/13: Corporate Sentiments Towards Internationalization*. Available at: http://www.iesingapore.gov.sg/~/media/IE%20Singapore/Files/Publications/IE%20Internationalisation%20Survey/Internationalisation20Survey202013.pdf.

McGee, J., Thomas, H., & Wilson, D. (2010). *Strategy: Analysis and Practice*. Berkshire: McGraw-Hill.

Murray, G. & Pereira, A. (1995). *Singapore: The Global City-State*. London: Heinemann.

Okposin, S. B. (1999). *The Extent of Singapore's Investment Abroad*. Aldershot, UK: Ashgate.

Prahalad, C. K. & Doz, Y. L. (1987). *The Multinational Mission, Balancing Global Integration with Local Responsiveness*, New York: Free Press and London: Collier Macmillan.

Shome, A. (2009) Singapore's state-guided entrepreneurship: A model for transitional economies? *New Zealand Journal of Asian Studies*, 11(1): 318–336.

Sitathan, T. (2002) Singapore's regionalization challenge? *Asia Times*, 26 July. Available at: http://www.atimes.com/atimes/Southeast_Asia/DG27Ae02.html

Singapore Economic Development Board (1993) Regionalization forum proceedings, Singapore, 21–23 May.

Singapore Economic Development Board (1995a). *Regionalization 2000*. Singapore: Singapore Economic Development Board.

Singapore Economic Development Board (1995b). *Singapore Unlimited*. Singapore: Singapore Economic Development Board.

Tan, C. H. (1995). *Venturing Overseas: Singapore's External Wing*. Singapore: McGraw-Hill.

United Nations Industrial Development Organization (UNIDO) (2009). *Patterns of Internationalization for Developing Country Enterprises – Alliances and Joint Ventures*. New York: United Nations.

Yeoh, C., Cai, J. L., & Koh, C. S. (2004). Singapore's regionalization blueprint: A case of strategic management, state enterprise network and selective intervention. *Journal of Transnational Management Development*, 9(4):13–36.

Yeoh, C., & How, W. (2011). The internationalization of Singapore's state enterprise network: Notes from Singapore's gambits in the Gulf Region. *World Journal of Management*, 3(1): 134–145.

Yeoh, C., & How, W. (2012). Singapore business in the GLC: Un tour d'horizon. *World Review of Business Research*, 3(1): 103–114.

Yeoh, C., How, W., & Sim, V. (2006). Re-engineering economic space: The case of Singapore's transborder industrialization 'gambits' in Asia. *Journal of Asia Business Studies*, 1(1): 34–45.

Yeoh, C., How, W., & Wong, J. (2011). Singapore's venture into the Gulf: Undiscovered treasure or empty pot? *Journal of Economics and Behavioural Studies*, 3(5): 317–325.

Yeung, H. W. C. (2000). State intervention and neoliberalism in the globalizing world economy: Lessons from Singapore's regionalization programme. *The Pacific Review*, 13(1): 133–162.

7
Perspectives on Chinese Foreign Direct Investment in Australia

Robert Graham Jack and Lijun (Karl) Qin

Introduction

China's rapid economic growth has increasingly drawn the attention of international business researchers to the international investment activities of its firms (Buckley, 2008; Buckley et al., 2007; Cui & Jiang, 2010; Kang & Jiang, 2012; Liu et al., 2005; Rui & Yip, 2008; Voss et al., 2008; Yang et al., 2009; Zeng et al., 2012). More broadly, China's expanding outward foreign direct investment (OFDI) is in line with its increasing global trading presence. Together, they strengthen China's growing global influence and, therefore, have implications extending beyond issues of trade and economics.

Specifically, Chinese firm internationalization into the Australian market has received coverage in the business media, although reported on a piecemeal basis, but little academic work has been done to date to analyse firm strategies and their implications for established theories and conceptual frameworks of firm internationalization (Fan et al., 2012). The decision by any organization to internationalize requires a significant commitment of financial and human resources. Selecting the right markets is critical for the international success of Chinese organizations, and understanding the risks and uncertainties associated with operating in overseas markets is an important element of assuring this success.

The investment phenomenon of firm internationalization from developing economies has prompted researchers (notably Buckley et al., 2007; Buckley, 2008; Child & Rodrigues, 2005) to propose that new theory may need to be developed specifically for emerging market firm-based investment. Theoretical guidelines regarding the process of this form of internationalization from emerging economies are sparse and the implications of entry strategies are difficult to determine. The aim of our chapter, therefore, is to contribute to the emerging literature in this field by adopting an exploratory, case study research design focusing on the internationalization process and local (Australian) operations of four Chinese multinational firms.

Our chapter begins with an overview of the background to the topic, which includes a review of the key concepts and relevant literature. We then propose two research questions related to Chinese firm internationalization in the Australian market – namely (i) market selection, and (ii) the operational challenges each firm faces. Our research method is then explained and the qualitative case study data presented and analysed. Finally, we conclude with the limitations of the study and provide suggestions for future research.

Background

Chinese OFDI: an overview of the literature

Since China adopted its "go global" policy in 2001, Chinese OFDI flows have grown rapidly, reaching US$84 billion in 2012 (Sauvant, 2013). By 2012, China was both the largest user, and one of the most important suppliers, of foreign direct investment (FDI) (Qiang, 2013). Indeed, China's OFDI has reached commercially and geo-economically significant levels and has begun to challenge international investment norms and affect international relations (Rosen & Hanemann, 2009). Such rising FDI outflows has been fuelled by high economic growth, rapid accumulation of foreign currency reserves as a result of trade surpluses, supportive government policies and, more fundamentally, an increasing degree of competitiveness between firms based in China (UNCTAD, 2009). Moreover, exchange-rate fluctuations and falling share prices abroad have created opportunities for Chinese firms to purchase "bargain" assets (UNCTAD, 2009).

More specifically, in terms of the current research, the focus of China's growing levels of OFDI has increasingly been devoted to the characteristics of its indigenous firms. Rugman (2010) has stated that FDI allows firms to exploit their existing firm-specific advantages. An issue that has drawn a significant amount of attention from international business researchers is the question posed by Rugman – namely, can Chinese firms develop their own firm-specific advantages (FSAs) (which can then be exploited in select overseas markets) or must they reply on their country-specific advantages (CSAs) – in the form of institutional support and low labour costs – as the basis for their international expansion?

Although studies have analysed Chinese OFDI motivations utilizing the classifications of resource seeking, market seeking, strategic asset seeking and efficiency seeking, an emerging focus considers motivations from more specific perspectives such as different investors, locations and incentives from the Chinese government. Zhang et al. (2013) categorize the locational determinants for Chinese OFDI and cite six: (i) investment in countries rich in natural resources; (ii) investment in political high-risk environments; (iii) investment in countries with significant strategic assets; (iv) investment in developed markets; (v) investment in countries with large markets and (vi) investment in geographically close markets.

As a complement to this approach, a number of studies utilized Dunning's (1979, 2001) eclectic paradigm of international production (the ownership, location and internalization, OLI, framework) to determine the internationalization of emerging market firms by FDI (see Cuervo-Cazurra, 2007; Ge & Ding, 2011; Mathews, 2006). These studies have specifically focused on the ability of Chinese firms to develop an ownership advantage (usually derived from a combination of resources and capabilities) in their home market, which can then be transferred abroad. When this advantage is combined with the locational advantages of a host country market (mainly in the form of access to factors of production), and the requirement to internalize these advantages within the firm, FDI is the outcome. However, the view that OFDI enables firms to exploit their existing FSAs or ownership advantage may have limited traction when analysing the internationalization activities of firms from China, as research has highlighted that these firms have only limited ownership advantages to exploit (Child & Rodrigues, 2005; Luo & Tung, 2007; Mathews, 2002, 2006). Without significant ownership advantages over foreign competitors, internationalization can be challenging for Chinese firms. As Child & Rodrigues (2005) note, OFDI from China is not based on using ownership advantages to exploit assets abroad, but on redressing ownership disadvantages by augmenting assets overseas (Cui & Jiang, 2010). More recent research (see Lu et al., 2011) questions this assumption and explains that having built technology-based competitive advantages (which can be classified as ownership advantages) in their home market, Chinese firms do have strong incentives to invest abroad to exploit these advantages.

As a complement to the OLI paradigm, Mathews (2002, 2006) established the LLL (linkage, leverage and learning) framework, based on the 'new stream' of latecomer firms in the knowledge-intensive industries from the Asia-Pacific region. *Linkage* involves firms exploring resources and advantages that can be acquired externally, and is often characterized by joint ventures. *Leverage* is the development of links so that resources can be leveraged or exploited. *Learning* is the repeated application of the linkage and leverage processes (Horner, 2008).

Regardless, the process of going global is assumed to be fraught with environmental uncertainty, and not characteristic of operations in one's own domestic market (Brouthers et al., 2000; Ghoshal, 1987; Miller, 1992). These uncertainties create risk to the achievement of corporate objectives and should, therefore, be evaluated and integrated into an organization's strategic responses so as to allow for the potential optimization of returns from any investment (Brouthers et al., 2000; Miller, 1992). A number of key authors (Andersen, 1993; Cavusgil, 1980; Edvardsson et al., 1993; Johanson & Vahlne, 1977, 1990; Johanson & Wiedershiem-Paul, 1975; Miller, 1992) stress that successful internationalization involves:

- choosing the right cultural environment in which to cultivate a business concept;
- adapting to the local business culture by carefully matching international markets with a firm's strategic concepts; and
- understanding and incorporating local political factors into business operations.

Because of the risk and uncertainty associated with any firm's international growth, a significant amount of research has developed around the process or sequence of internationalization. A dominant field of research has been the incremental and staged approaches to international market expansion, developed from the work of Cavusgil (1980), Johanson and Vahlne (1977, 1990) and Johanson and Wiedershiem-Paul (1975). The relevance of incremental and staged approaches to the internationalization of Chinese firms has been analysed (Cuervo-Cazurra 2007; Luo & Tung 2007). Cuervo-Cazurra's (2007) research on the internationalization of firms from developing countries revealed three distinct approaches to the sequence of market entry: (i) the establishment of sales and marketing subsidiaries in all countries first; (ii) production subsidiaries in all countries first; and (iii) marketing subsidiaries first in some markets and productive subsidiaries first in others. In fact, there are numerous types of foreign affiliates defined in law, which have differing levels of legal status, risk and responsibility – a branch office, a representative office, a branch and a subsidiary company (Zhang et al., 2013).

Luo and Tung (2007) proposed that emerging market firms may actually "springboard" into international markets, as a way to overcome their "latecomer" status. This approach provides an opportunity for these firms to acquire the strategic assets necessary to compete on an equal footing with their more established international counterparts. Indeed, Ge and Ding's (2011) findings confirmed that Chinese firms do not always follow a sequential path to internationalization.

Trends in Chinese OFDI in Australia

China is Australia's largest trading partner, having recently supplanted Japan's long-standing dominance in this area. Australia's firm-based investment in China is limited and Australia is not a significant source of FDI inflow to China. By contrast, Australia was the highest-ranked destination for China's OFDI, excluding Hong Kong and established tax havens (Larum, 2010, 2011; Larum & Qin, 2012). This ranking is primarily the result of individual investor (mainly states, but also some private) decisions about the attractiveness of individual projects and countries, rather than any policy-directed targeting of particular countries. According to Larum (2011), the view in the Chinese government is that there is no official ranking of target countries. That said, however, there is little doubt that official policy differs across industry sectors. Obviously, government policy objectives aimed at securing a consistent resource supply have played an important role in the ranking of Australia, Canada and some developing countries. Australia's top ranking as an *intended* investment destination is also confirmed by the Heritage Foundation's (2011) tracking of Chinese attempted transactions, both successful and failed.

However, some contradictions exist in official assessments of Australia's attractiveness as a destination for OFDI. For example, an official survey by the China Council for the Promotion of International Trade (CCPIT, 2010) showed that Asia was the most favoured investment destination, followed by Europe and North America, with a much smaller proportion of respondents favouring Australia (actually ranked below Africa). The CCPIT survey of Chinese investment intentions also suggested that, in terms of general openness to Chinese investment, the United States was ranked most highly, with Australia ranking second, followed by South Africa. This compares with the Organisation for Economic Co-operation and Development's (OECD) measure of FDI restrictions, where Australia was ranked as more restrictive than both the average for OECD countries and for all countries in the survey (Kalinova et al., 2010).

An overview of these issues, specific to the Australian market, provides the basis for our first research question:

RQ1: Why do Chinese multinational corporations (MNCs) target the Australian market?

Official guidance from China's Ministry of Commerce (MOFCOM) provides some indication of the issues faced by Chinese investors looking to invest in Australia. MOFCOM (2011) regards Australia as a safe and very low-risk country for foreign investment. However, it also sets out a number of problems faced when investing in Australia, such as increasingly stringent verification and approval processes, difficulty obtaining work permits, challenges of the different business operating environments, laws and regulations, and the lack of Chinese international talent. MOFCOM (2011) also emphasizes the need for Chinese companies operating in Australia to obey rules and regulations and to protect the reputation of the company.

Again, while not specific to Australia, surveys of Chinese investors highlight problems in going offshore. The CCPIT (2010) survey emphasized the difficulty of obtaining finance, the lack of understanding of Chinese brands by foreign consumers, the concerns about the quality and safety of Chinese products and a lack of international business and management personnel. Interestingly, and in contrast to other evidence, the survey reported that cultural barriers and negative responses by governments to Chinese investment were *not* significant challenges.

Considering that official surveys highlight the potential problems that Chinese firms may encounter in the Australian market, as well as some of the key challenges for Chinese firms in general when they internationalize, we propose a second research question:

RQ2: What are the operational challenges Chinese MNCs face in the Australian market?

Research methods

When the aim of a study is to gain insights to provide a better understanding of specific factors, as well as to describe a phenomenon, the qualitative approach is deemed appropriate (Yin, 2009). Qualitative methods are characterized by a "first-handedness" (Birkinshaw et al.,

2011). The detailed observations enable the study of many different aspects, which are then examined in relation to each other. The circumstances of the study are important here. The qualitative method allows researchers to understand the context-specific depth of a phenomenon. Therefore, it is likely to provide a better understanding of the dynamics of the internationalization strategy pursued by Chinese firms. It is a complex phenomenon. Understanding such an intricate relationship calls for direct contact with the respondents. The cultural context is also significant. As Ahlstrom et al. (2008) emphasize, "sensitive" data about Chinese firm policies and strategies are best obtained through face-to-face interviews.

In order to conduct an exploratory, inductive investigation, we employ a multiple case study methodology. The case study method used accords with those of prominent authors in the field, specifically Eisenhardt's (1989) and Yin's (2009) approaches. The unit of analysis will be the firm, and multiple cases will be used rather than a single case study. Such a design is especially appropriate in "new" topic areas for the development of novel, testable and empirically valid theories (Eisenhardt, 1989). Qualitative interview-based case research allows the interviewer to explore complex, strategic decision-making in detail (Denzin & Lincoln, 2005). A qualitative, case study-based research technique using in-depth, face-to-face interviews can provide a rich, focused and realistic account of the internationalization of the firm. In addition, comparisons across cases allow the researcher to suggest explanations for possible patterns, trends or linkages. The methodology is particularly apt for the current research, which seeks to understand the factors that influence a firm's market selection and to understand of their operational challenges in a foreign market.

Selecting organizations to be studied is one of the most difficult steps in case study research (Ghauri, 2004). According to Fan et al. (2012), there are approximately 200 Chinese companies and registered agencies in Australia, of which 30–40 conduct significant operations. As the case study method of theory-building relies on theoretical sampling, it is important that comparative cases likely to replicate or extend the emergent theory should be chosen (Stake, 1995; Yin, 2009). Although there is no set rule on the ideal number of cases in this type of research, a number between four and ten is usually considered appropriate (Eisenhardt, 1989). Contacts in Austrade and representative bodies, such as the Australia China Business Council (ACBC) and the Australia-China Council (ACC), assisted in identifying prospective firms, which were investigated by the researcher. All firms initially investigated had an established presence in the Australian market. A total of 30 Chinese firms were individually approached. The CEO (or equivalent) of each firm was contacted and was provided with the objectives of the research and the requirements considered essential for participation. Four firms subsequently agreed to participate.

The key details of each firm, including their initial entry mode and current operations in the Australian market, are listed in Table 7.1.

The four firms are large, with significant global operations in the form of manufacturing subsidiaries in key markets across Asia, Europe and Africa. Their initial entry into the Australian market was via exporting, through local agents and distributors. This is consistent with the first phase of international expansion into a foreign market, where the uncertainties of the market drive the firm to make use of an external market via agents and distributors (Dunning & Lundan, 2008).

For each of the four firms the evolution to the second phase was relatively rapid – two years. In this second phase each firm established a representative office. A company establishes a representative office to conduct sales, marketing and other non-transactional operations and is used where a branch office or full subsidiary is not required (Zhang et al., 2013).

Table 7.1 Firm characteristics and details of Australian market operations

Firm categorization	Ownership classification	Location of manufacturing subsidiaries	First year of entry into Australian market	Current entry mode and year of establishment
Firm 1 Electronics manufacturer	Government is the majority shareholder	Indonesia Russia Czech Republic Algeria Ukraine	(1998) Agent and distributor	Representative office (sales and distribution) (2000)
Firm 2 Industrial manufacturer	Privately owned	Vietnam Algeria Brazil	(2005) Agent and distributor	Representative office (sales, distribution and product support services) (2007)
Firm 3 Electronics manufacturer	Government is the majority shareholder	South Africa Hungary	(2006) Agent and distributor	Representative office (sales and distribution) (2008)
Firm 4 Industrial manufacturer	Privately owned	India Brazil	(2005) Agent and distributor	Representative office (sales, distribution and product support services) (2008)

Sources of information

Interviews were the primary source of information and were undertaken with founders, CEO's and general and senior managers (normally the Chief Financial Officer) of each firm. These individuals were seen as ideal candidates for providing information for in-depth analysis because of their strong ties to the firm, as well as their knowledge of the firm's approach to internationalization. The exploratory nature of the research required that a range of different types of question – closed (bivariate), rank-order and open ended – be used to allow unexpected answers and perspectives to emerge. It also allowed the inclusion of 'how and why' questions and, as a consequence, a rich information set was accumulated.

The chief investigator was responsible for the conduct of the interviews with CEOs and senior managers of each case study firm. Semi-structured interviews were undertaken with two senior managers of each firm from May to September 2011. The characteristics of each respondent are detailed in Table 7.2.

Each interview was face-to-face, took place at the workplace of the respondent and lasted for 1.5 hours. As well as the relatively structured interview guide, prompts were used during each interview to explore a number of relevant issues. To achieve construct validity, ensure a well-rounded analysis and minimize misinterpretation, a combined use of multiple secondary sources of information was utilized to allow for the triangulation of data (Stake, 2000). This included internal documentation provided by the company, the company website, product and firm brochures and any bibliographies authored by the founders of the firms.

Analysis of information

To ensure the reliability of findings, manual analysis was utilized. We began our analysis with all transcriptions being prepared and typed

Table 7.2 Key details of respondents

Firm	Respondents	Interview dates
1	Chief Executive Officer of Australian operations	May 2011
	Chief Financial Officer of Australian operations	June 2011
2	Founder	June 2011
	General Manager of Australian operations	July 2011
3	General Manager of Australian operations	July 2011
	Chief Financial Officer of Australian operations	August 2011
4	Chief Executive Officer of Australian operations	August 2011
	Chief Financial Officer of Australian operations	September 2011

by the primary researcher, enabling him to immerse himself in the data, an experience that is important as it produces emergent insights (Patton, 2002). Once this was completed, the transcript was proofread and emailed as an attachment to each interviewee with a request to check the document for its accuracy as a record of the interview. This normally occurred within one week of the interview. Any suggested changes were incorporated and further cross-checks were made for accuracy. This type of 'member check' increases the validity and reliability of data by avoiding possible interpretation errors (Flick, 2008). The research questions were used to guide the interviews as well as the investigation. This aided in structuring, gathering and analysing the empirical data (Yin, 2009). Initially, each case was analysed independently to help gain familiarity with each firm before cross-case-study analysis was implemented. This involved a detailed case write-up for each firm. Although these were largely descriptive they were essential for the generation of insight. Categories were then selected based on detailed examination of the transcripts.

After this, a cross-case-synthesis technique was employed. As similarities between answers began to emerge, categories of responses could be determined, allowing the data to be classified and sorted accordingly. Once data had been clustered, findings were summarized in conceptually clustered matrices to compare several categories at once. This promoted pattern matching and the effective categorization of data (Miles & Huberman, 1994), as well as enabling for comparisons to be made by studying factors using key dimensions in a systematic way. This also increased the opportunity to identify deviations and new factors within the body of research (Ghauri, 2004; Strauss & Corbin, 1990). The emergent findings were then tied to the extant literature, thereby enhancing internal validity and generalizability (Eisenhardt, 1989).

Analysis of results

Our research objectives detailed two key questions related to the entry of Chinese multinationals into the Australian market. Each of these questions will be discussed below.

RQ1: Why do Chinese MNCs target the Australian market?

All respondents emphasized that the value of the Australian market in two key respects: its ability to act as a test market and its attractiveness as a market for product testing. Both of these issues will be discussed below.

Australia as a test market

Significantly, all respondents highlighted the importance of the Australian market as a "test" market for their firms. The characteristics of Australia, as a Western, developed market, were considered its most attractive features as an investment destination. The CEO of Firm 1 explained:

> Australia is a "'western market" – by operating in Australia, we can get the experience in products, marketing and technology etc. It is good for the preparation in entering into other large markets in Europe and North America.

To some degree, market selection was driven by a recognition that these firms were still somewhat deficient in the development of their "softer" strategic assets, particularly in the form of product branding and marketing. As the General Manager of Firm 3 stated:

> The reason we picked it (Australia) was because it is a developed country; (we are) an emerging brand, (and) to get experience in marketing an emerging brand in a developed country, Australia is a very good choice for "testing the water".

A key finding in relation to the targeting of the Australian market was its role in each firm's global strategy. The nature of country-based risk for Chinese multinationals has been the subject of a significant amount of research. The results have been somewhat contradictory. Buckley (2008) found that evidence indicates that most Chinese private firms and non-state-owned enterprises are risk averse rather than opportunity seeking when internationalizing. However, Buckley et al. (2007) found that Chinese outward direct investors had a paradoxical attitude to risk and that risk aversion could not be assumed. An analysis of the case studies reveals that one of the key reasons for these firms to target the Australian market was each firm's desire to gain valuable international experience in a market that, although developed, was perceived to be less risky to enter and operate in compared to larger regions. This was emphasized by the General Manager of Firm 4:

> Even if we failed, for whatever reason, the consequence will not be too "bitter to chew". If we made mistakes in (a) large market, such as USA or Europe, it will make our (global) operations much more difficult.

The CEO of Firm 1 also explained:

> We made mistakes in operating in Australia. (But) the cost of making mistakes in Australia is smaller than America.

Product testing in the Australian market

In a similar manner to the previous issue, all the case study firms found Australia to be an ideal market for product testing their output for use across their global network. The quality and high-grade technical specifications of the Australian market were stressed by all the respondents. The General Manager of Firm 2 explained:

> The Australian market is very small; the requirement on quality and service is very high in Australia.

This Australia provided each firm with the unique opportunity to use the Australian market as a test market for their global product range. This was best explained by the General Manager of Firm 4:

> We test the product in Australia first. As the requirements from Australia are very similar to the requirements from Europe and USA, it is more feasible to test the product in Australia. The product can be manufactured in Europe or USA, only after it has been tested and passed in the Australian market

RQ2: What are the operational challenges they face in the Australian market?

Two key issues were raised in relation to the operational issues that each subsidiary faced in the Australian market.

Building brand awareness

This was a significant marketing problem for all the case study firms and was constantly stressed as such by respondents. All mentioned the dominance of Japanese and, particularly, Korean brands in their particular product categories. All recognized the difficulty of building brand preference. This was consistent across those case firms that were operating largely in consumer markets (Firms 1 and 3) and those operating in business-to-business markets (Firms 2 and 4). The problem was best summed up by the General Manager of Firm 4:

> In their [Australian] eyes, Chinese products are cheap and lower in quality. This is the single largest barrier we are facing. To change

> their preference from the brands they have been used for many years to our product is very difficult.

There was a definite awareness on the part of the respondents that this was a problem that would only be resolved over the long term. The CEO of Firm 1 explained:

> There is a process to Australian consumers, from know nothing to aware, understand, familiar with until acceptance or even preference. This process takes time especially from aware to understand. This is the biggest challenge we are facing in Australia.

Logistics and service delivery

The unique logistics of the Australian market represented significant challenges to each firm. All respondents complained of a large and logistically difficult land mass containing a small (albeit developed) market. The General Manager of Firm 2 encapsulated this situation:

> Australia is like a chicken rib [has some taste but not much meat]. Because it has a large land, it is very difficult to deliver the product and the after service is very difficult to manage... the repairing cost is much higher than the price of the product itself.

All case study firms had significant service components (largely after-sales services) as part of their product packages. Respondents were aware of the broader strategic implications of these logistical issues on local perceptions of efficiency and effectiveness. The General Manager of Firm 4 stressed:

> The requirement in Australia is very different from the Chinese market. We are only new to Australia, we cannot build a well operated service network and, therefore, our customers are not very satisfied with our company. We have to improve it.

Although logistical issues and their impact on the cost of service delivery were at the fore, specific instances of consumer protection in the Australian market were also rated as significant. This posed, for all respondents, a frustrating situation as product returns and subsequent refunds were based on retail-enforced consumer preferences and not related to product-based deficiencies. The CEO of Firm 1 stated:

> The challenge is the cost of the after sale service. Australia gives more protection to the consumers. We call it an after sale service cost without [being] related to our product[s].

This represented a particular problem for Firms 1 and 3, which are selling into the Australian consumer market via established retailers, each with their own competitive sale return policies. Each product return adds to warehousing and transportation overheads.

Discussion and conclusion

Our research questions aim to enhance our understanding of: (i) the reasons why Chinese manufacturing firms target the Australian market and (ii) the challenges they face in operating in Australia. Official surveys in China (CCPIT, 2010; MOFCOM, 2011) paint a mixed picture of Australia's attractiveness as an investment destination, despite its reputation as a relatively safe and low-risk FDI location. Our data analysis revealed that the case study firms primarily saw the attractiveness of the market from two perspectives: its ability to act as a test market for future expansion into larger, more complex developed markets such as the USA and Europe (some of which – i.e., by Firms 1, 3 and 4 – has already taken place), and its usefulness as a test market for new product development.

The use of the Australian market for product development testing was the result of leveraging, the high product quality and service standards/levels required to operate in this market. Evidence of each firm learning, leveraging and linking this experience in the Australian market to their global operations was evident.

Each firm's entry mode choice in the Australian market was undertaken in an evolutionary manner. The establishment of a representative office was, in all cases, preceded by exporting to Australia. The scale of each firm's market entry into Australia was small, with no plans to increase the size of their current operations. The concentration of each firm's productive activities in the Australian market was consistent in all cases. Post-productive activities in the form of sales, marketing (mainly brand related) and after-sales service requirements were the extent of each firm's commitment. The high labour costs in the Australian market, combined with low tariffs and duties on Chinese imports, made local manufacturing inappropriate.

The global strategy pursued by all case study firms (see Table 7.1) seems to accord with Cuervo-Cazurra's (2007) classification category of multinationalizing with marketing subsidiaries in some markets and production subsidiaries in others. Manufacturing operations outside China were largely confined to low-cost locations (such as Indonesia – Firm 1; Vietnam – Firm 2; South Africa – Firm 3; India – Firm 4). The international dispersal of their manufacturing operations provides the necessary cost advantages, while the establishment of representative offices builds additional advantages in terms of developing knowledge about the conditions of foreign markets and how to more effectively serve clients. Indeed, the dispersal seems to reflect the unique characteristics of individual host country markets. Regardless, all firms evolved relatively rapidly from the first phase of their entry into the Australian market (exporting via agents and distributors) to the establishment of a representative office.

Not surprisingly, all interviewees stressed the technical superiority of their products. There was no doubt that all assessed their products as equal in quality to their more established international competitors. Similarly, all stressed the significant long-term challenge in building brand preferences for Chinese-made products in developed markets. The deficiency is cited, even in China, as one of the key challenges for Chinese multinationals in developed markets. Although building brand awareness is a challenge across other developed markets, the logistical difficulties of operating in Australia were unique. To some degree, this was more prevalent in Firms 2 and 4 as the provision of after-sales service support was assessed as a key factor in the future sustainability of their operations.

Managerial relevance, limitations and future research

We trust that the results of our research will make a contribution to the current debate among international business researchers regarding the internationalization of Chinese firms. The findings presented in this chapter have important implications for practitioners. Chinese firms, or firms from emerging economies that intend to enter developed markets with a substantially different institutional and cultural environment, can consider starting with a small but challenging market. Furthermore, our findings are also relevant to established multinational corporations from developed economies. The increasing strategic focus of Chinese firms' internationalization would result in greater challenges for established multinational corporations (MNCs) from developed economies. Therefore, managers of multinational corporations from developed countries should carefully evaluate this cohort as potential competitors and be mindful of competitive threats they may pose in international markets.

The study presented in this chapter is somewhat constrained by a sample size of four MNCs – hence its generalizability is limited.

However, the richness of the data collected from multiple case studies has provided an opportunity to provide insights into the internationalization of Chinese firms. Some limitations of the study need to be highlighted. One of the major limitations is that the data collection primarily focuses on subsidiary managers perceptions. Future studies could be more inclusive of senior managers from head office, as well as comparisons with subsidiary managers in other countries.

Further analysis of this under-researched sector will contribute to theories of emerging market firm-based investment and highlight potential qualifications, modifications or consistencies with existing paradigms originally tested on Western multinational firms, explicitly in the manufacturing sector. Therefore, it will have the potential to provide insight into internationalization developments in other emerging economies. Although this research does not include the policy implications of its findings, it has the potential to contribute to more informed federal and state policies relevant to Australia's trade and investment with China and, potentially, other developing markets.

References

Ahlstrom, D., Bruton, G. D., & Yeh, K. S. (2008). Private firms in China: Building legitimacy in an emerging economy. *Journal of World Business*, 43(4): 385–399.

Andersen, O. (1993). On the international process of firms: A critical analysis. *Journal of International Business Studies*, 24(2): 209–231.

Birkinshaw, J., Brannen, M. Y., & Tung, R. L. (2011). From a distance and generalizable to up close and grounded: Reclaimining a place for qualitative methods in international business research. *Journal of International Business Studies*, 42(5): 573–581.

Brouthers, K., Brouthers, L. E., & Werner, S. (2000). Perceived environmental uncertainty, entry mode choice and satisfaction with EC-MNC performance. *British Journal of Management*, 11(3): 183–195.

Buckley, P. J. (2008). Do we need a special theory of foreign direct investment for extractive industries? *Journal of Chinese Economic and Foreign Trade Studies*, 1(2): 93–104.

Buckley, P. J., Clegg, L. J., Cross, A. R., Liu, X., Voss, H., & Zeng, P. (2007). The determinants of Chinese outward foreign direct investment. *Journal of International Business Studies*, 38(4): 499–518.

Cavusgil, S. Tamer (1980). On the internationalisation process of firms. *European Research*, 8(6): 273–281.

China Council for the Promotion of International Trade (CCPIT) (2010). *Survey on Current Conditions of and Intention for Outbound Investment by Chinese Enterprises*. Available at: http://www.ccpit.org/yewu/docs/Survey_on_Current_Conditions_and_Intention_of_Outbound_Investment_by_Chinese_Enterprises_2011.en.pdf.

Child, J., & Rodrigues, S. B. (2005). The internationalization of Chinese firms: A case for theoretical extension? *Management and Organization Review*, 1(3): 381–410.

Cuervo-Cazurra, A. (2007). Sequence of value-added activities in the multinationalization of developing country firms. *Journal of International Management*, 13(3): 258–277.

Cui, L. & Jiang, F. (2010). Behind ownership decision of Chinese outward FDI: Resources and institutions. *Asia Pacific Journal of Management*, 27(4): 751–74.

Denzin, N. K. & Lincoln, Y. S. (2005). *The Sage Handbook of Qualitative Research* (3rd edn), Thousand Oaks, CA: Sage Publications.

Dunning, J. H. (1979). Explaining changing patterns of international production: In defence of the eclectic theory. *Oxford Bulletin of Economics and Statistics*, 41(4): 69–95.

Dunning, J. H. (2001). The eclectic (OLI) paradigm of international production: Past, present and future. *International Journal of the Economics of Business*, 8(2): 173–190.

Dunning, J. & Lundan, S. M. (2008). *Multinational Enterprises and the Global Economy* (2nd edn), Cheltenham, UK: Edward Elgar Publishing Limited.

Edvardsson, B., Edvinsson, L., & Nystrom, H. (1993). Internationalisation in service companies. *The Service Industries Journal*, 13(1): 80–97.

Eisenhardt, K. M. (1989). Building theories from case study research. *Academy of Management Review*, 14(4): 532–550.

Fan, D., Zhu, C., & Nyland, C. (2012). Factors affecting global integration of Chinese multinationals in Australia: A qualitative analysis. *International Business Review*, 21(1): 13–26.

Flick, U. (2008). *Managing Quality in Qualitative Research*, Thousand Oaks, CA: Sage Publications

Ge, G. & Ding, D. (2011). Determinants of internationalisation strategies: A study of Chinese multinational enterprises. *International Journal of Business and Emerging Markets*, 3(2): 137–157.

Ghauri, P. (2004). Designing and conducting case studies in international business. In Marschan-Piekkariand, R., & Welch, C. (eds), *Handbook of Qualitative Research Methods for International Business*, Cheltenham: Edward Elgar Publishing: 109–124

Ghoshal, S. (1987). Global strategy: An organizing framework. *Strategic Management Journal*, 8(5): 425–40.

Heritage Foundation (2011). *China Global Investment Tracker*. Available at: http://www.heritage.org/research/projects/china-global-investment-tracker-interactive-map.

Horner, R. (2008). The intra-and inter-firm geography of emerging multinationals: India's pharmaceuticals. Unpublished paper presented at Emerging Multinationals: Outward Foreign Direct Investment from Emerging and Developing Economies conference, Copenhagen Business School, 9–10 October.

Johanson, J. & Vahlne, J. E. (1977). The internationalisation process of the firm – a model of knowledge development and increasing foreign market commitment. *Journal of International Business Studies*, 8(1): 23–32.

Johanson, J. & Vahlne, J. E. (1990). The mechanism of internationalisation. *International Marketing Review*, 7(4): 11–24.

Johanson J. J. & Wiedershiem-Paul F. (1975). The internationalisation of the firm: Four Swedish cases. *Journal of Management*, 12(3): 305–322.

Kalinova, B., Palerm, A., & Thomsen, S. (2010). OECD's FDI Restrictiveness Index: 2010 Update. *OECD Working Papers on International Investment, No. 2010/3*, Paris, France: OECD Investment Division. Available at: www.oecd.org/daf/investment.

Kang, Y. & Jiang, F. (2012). FDI location choice of Chinese multinationals in East and South East Asia: Traditional economic factors and institutional perspective. *Journal of World Business*, 47(1): 45–53.

Larum, J. (2010). *Into the Dragon's Den: Australian Investment into China*, Sydney: Lowy Institute for International Policy.

Larum, J. (2011). *Chinese Perspectives on Investing in Australia*, Sydney: Lowy Institute for International Policy.

Larum, J. & Qin, J. (2012). *A Long March: The Australia-China Investment Relationship*, Sydney: Australia China Business Council.

Liu, X., Buck, T., & Shu, C. (2005). Chinese economic development, the next stage: outward FDI? *International Business Review*, 14(1): 97–115.

Lu, J., Liu, X., & Wang, H. (2011). Motives for outward FDI of Chinese private firms: Firm resources, industry dynamics, and Government policies. *Management and Organization, Review*, 7(2): 223–248.

Luo, Y. & Tung, R. (2007). International expansion of emerging market enterprises: A springboard perspective. *Journal of International Business Studies*, 38(4): 481–498.

Mathews, J. A. (2002). Competitive advantages of the latecomer firm: A resource-based account of industrial catch-up strategies. *Asia Pacific Journal of Management*, 19(4): 467–88.

Mathews, J. (2006). Dragon multinationals: New players in 21st century globalization. *Asia-Pacific Journal of Management*, 23(1): 5–27.

Miles, M. B. & Huberman, A. M. (1994). *Qualitative Data Analysis: An Expanded Sourcebook*, Newbury Park: Sage Publications.

Miller, K. (1992). A framework for integrated risk management in international business. *Journal of International Business Studies*, 2(2): 311–331.

Ministry of Commerce (MOFCOM) (2011). 2010 Statistical bulletin of China's outward foreign direct investment. Available at: http://hzs.mofcom.gov.cn/accessory/201109/1316069658609.pdf.

Patton, M. Q. (2002). *Qualitative Research and Evaluation Methods*, London: Sage Publications.

Qiang, Y. (2013). How does OFDI affect trade development in developing countries? *Journal of Chinese Economic and Foreign Trade Studies*, 6(2): 85–90.

Rosen, D. H. & Hanemann, T. (2009). China's changing outbound foreign direct investment profile: Drivers and policy implicaitons. *Peterson Institute for International Economics*, Washington DC, USA. Available at http://www.iie.com/publications/pb/pb09–14.pdf .

Rugman, A. (2010). Globalization, regional multinationals and Asian economic development. *Asian Business and Management*, 9(3): 299–317.

Rui, H. & Yip, G. S. (2008). Foreign acquisitions by Chinese firms: A strategic intent perspective. *Journal of World Business*, 43(2): 213–226.

Sauvant, K. (2013). Three challenges for China's outward FDI policy. In Sauvant, K. (ed.), *Columbia FDI Perspectives*. New York, Shanghai: Vale Columbia Center on Sustainable International Investment: 1–3.

Stake, R. (1995). *The Art of Case Study Research*, Thousand Oaks, CA: Sage Publications.

Stake, R. (2000). Case Studies. In Denzin, N., & Lincoln, Y. (eds), *Handbook of Qualitative Research*, Thousand Oaks, CA: Sage Publications: 435–454.

Strauss, A. L. & Corbin, J. M. (1990). *Basics of Qualitative Research: Grounded Theory Procedures and Techniques*, Newbury Park, CA: Sage Publications

United Nations Conference on Trade and Development (UNCTAD) (2009) *World Investment Report 2009: Transnational Corporations, Agricultural Production and Development*, New York: United Nations Conference on Trade and Development.

Voss, H., Buckley, P. J., & Cross, A. R, (2008). Thirty years of Chinese outward foreign direct investment. Unpublished paper given at the CEA (UK) conference Three Decades of Economic Reform (1978–2008), Cambridge University, Cambridge, UK, 1–2 April 2008.

Yang, X., Jiang, Y., Kang, R., & Ke, Y. (2009). A comparative analysis of the internationalization of Chinese and Japanese firms. *Asia Pacific Journal of Management*, 26(1): 141–162.

Yin, R. (2009). *Case Study Research: Design and Methods*, Thousand Oaks, CA: Sage Publications.

Zeng, R., Zeng, S., Xie, X., Tam, C., & Wan, T. (2012). What motivates firms from emerging economies to go internationalization? *Technological and Economic Development of Economy*, 18(2): 280–98.

Zhang, J., Wei, W., & Liu, Z. (2013). Strategic entry and determinants of Chinese private enterprises into Africa. *Journal of African Business*, 14(2): 96–105.

8
Acquisition versus Greenfield: The Strategy of Chinese Privately Owned Investors in Developing Countries

Wiboon Kittilaksanawong, Xudong Chen and Shanshan Xie

Introduction

A substantial body of literature has developed on the prominence of China's position as a source of foreign direct investments (FDI) and its consequences on the global economy (e.g., Buckley et al., 2007, 2008; Child & Rodrigues, 2005; Luo & Tung, 2007; Peng, 2012; Peng et al., 2008). Although the composition of Chinese outward foreign direct investments (OFDIs) is still biased toward state-owned enterprises (SOEs), the continuing reforms of the public sector in the 1990s and more recently the launch of the 'go global' policy by the Chinese government have reduced many constraints to overseas investments by privately owned enterprises (POEs) (Luo et al., 2010). Such reforms and policy incentives at home have resulted in the significant rise of Chinese POEs in the global marketplace.

For Chinese POEs, which are mostly small- and medium-sized enterprises (SMEs), capital is a major constraint on their internationalization (Kittilaksanawong et al., 2013; Sutherland & Ning, 2011). Their state-owned counterparts, however, are likely to exploit the monopolistic market position at home, as well as privileged access to strategic resources such as political support, and capital from state-owned banks to invest abroad (Song et al., 2011). Many Chinese POEs are pushed to invest overseas due to the difficulties of raising capital at home (Luo & Tung 2007). OFDIs have therefore become an important strategic alternative for Chinese POEs to use to overcome such unique institutional disadvantage at home and to remedy their limited resources and experience necessary to compete more effectively at home and on the global stage.

Most of the literature has focused on OFDIs made by large Chinese firms, including Chinese SOEs, in Western developed countries in order to acquire strategic technology or marketing resources. Developing countries, however, are characterized a lack of institutional and market supporting mechanisms, and thus impose a greater challenge for Chinese privately owned investors. Therefore, the research on drivers, contingencies and development paths of the emerging overseas investments made by Chinese POEs in other developing countries has the potential to contribute to the theories and practices of FDI. This chapter is based on multiple case studies of eight representative Chinese POEs from Zhejiang and Guangdong province, two of the most developed private economies in China. OFDIs from these two provinces to other developing countries, particularly in South East Asia, South America and Africa have started to rise at an accelerated speed (MOFCOM, 2010).

Outward foreign direct investments from developing countries

Many scholars have found that the traditional theories of FDI may not completely explain overseas investments made by developing economy firms (e.g., Child & Rodrigues, 2005; Deng, 2013; Luo & Tung, 2007; Mathews, 2006; Peng et al., 2008). These firms have to overcome a variety of challenges by exploiting their existing limited resources and experience, or by acquiring necessary resources and experience from others (e.g., via acquisitions or collaborations) (Mathews, 2006). These efforts however may not be realized without support from the government in their home countries and the country of destination (Kittilaksanawong et al., 2013; Peng, 2012; Peng et al., 2008). For example, since the global financial crisis in 2008, the China economy has not experienced a severe loss as its counterparts in the West due to a variety of remedial measures implemented by the Chinese governments at national and provincial level. The crisis has even offered Chinese enterprises more acquisition targets in many countries because of weakened overseas competitors and more attractive prices of assets in these countries (Buckley et al., 2008). Through these acquisitions, many Chinese firms have strengthened their resources and capabilities to compete more effectively at home and on the global stage.

The pattern of Chinese OFDIs also differs between SOEs and POEs. While the latter follow a pattern of OFDI that the traditional theories predict, the formers' pattern is based on strategic needs that are usually linked to the Chinese government (Amighinia et al., 2013). In particular, Chinese POEs are mainly attracted by host countries with large markets, strategic assets and relatively stable economic and political environments, while their state-owned counterparts are generally more interested in natural resources and indifferent to the political and economic risks in the host countries (Duanmu, 2012; Ramasamy et al., 2012). For SOEs, this is not because of their risk preferences but rather because of the political relations that reduce such risks (Li & Liang, 2012). Investment decisions made by SOEs often reflect the political agendas rather than the profit-maximizing objectives of private companies (Child & Rodrigues, 2005).

Many POEs in China have grown significantly not only as a result of rapid economic development in the country, but also due to the relaxation of national policy on OFDIs and particularly the 'go global' policy that provides a variety of incentives for overseas investment (Peng, 2012). While the domestic institutional environment is the facilitator of Chinese OFDIs, the dynamics in international markets also increasingly raises many uncertainties and challenges that these POEs with limited resources and international management experience have to deal with. Therefore, OFDIs made by Chinese POEs in other developing economies where the institutional environments are not fully developed provide an enormous opportunity for academics to revisit and complement the traditional theories on FDIs and for practitioners to learn the new rules of the game in the competitive world economy.

Profile of company cases and overseas investments

The methodology used for the multiple case studies is based on Yin (2003) and Eisenhardt (1989). Only POEs are included in the study to ensure that strategic decisions related to their OFDIs are indeed made by the focal firm. To trace the motivations and the development paths of OFDIs, only firms with long-term visions and ongoing business operations are included. These firms are drawn from different industries to increase the generalizability of the results. To ensure reliability of the data, data of case companies and their business activities are drawn from published articles, government offices, business and trade associations or other transparent public media, including the companies' websites. Based on these criteria, eight representative POEs based in Zhejiang and Guangdong are included. Tables 8.1 and 8.2 summarize these company

Table 8.1 Cases of Chinese privately owned investments in developing countries via acquisitions

Cases	Longsheng	Seduno	Market Union	Midea
Main industry	Chemical dyes	Garments and knitwear	General trading	Home electrical appliances
Firm size	Assets of RMB 5.2 billion, 5,200 employees, 39 subsidiaries worldwide	Sales revenue of RMB 2.97 billion, assets of RMB 250 million, 5,000 employees	Export value of US$200 million, 900 employees	Sales revenue of RMB 140 billion, assets of RMB 100 billion, 22 production bases at home and abroad, 150,000 employees
Year & location of establishment	1970 – Shangyu, Zhejiang	1994 – Ningbo, Zhejiang	2004 – Ningbo, Zhejiang	1968-Shunde, Guangdong
Internationalization & major OFDIs	• Established a satellite office in Hong Kong for investments and trade • Collaborated with Japan Itochu on advanced heat-rcovery system • Joint ventured with Kiri in India for chemical dye manufacturing • Acquired Kiri's chemical dyes business in India • Acquired the German company Dystar, the world's largest supplier of dyes	• Acquired Ming Union Garments in Cambodia and built on its foundations, further expanding the production capacity	• Acquired First Cape Town, the largest hypermarket in Cape Town, South Africa to be a major outlet of product exports from China.	• Collaborated with Carrier in Latin America for market development. • Acquired air conditioning business of Carrier in Latin America as a wholly owned subsidiary. • Acquired Miraco, an exclusive distributor of Carrier in Egypt.

Table 8.2 Cases of Chinese privately owned investments in developing countries via greenfield investments

Cases	Nanyuan	Xinglong Vehicle	Shenzhou Knitting	Apache Footwear
Main industry	Hotel management and real estate development	Bicycles and mining	Garments and knitwear	Footwear
Firm size	Ranked among ten largest investors in domestic tourism and among the 500 largest enterprises in domestic service industry	Sales revenue of RMB 100 million, 350 employees, annual production of 1 million vehicles	Total assets of RMB 1.6 billion, 17,000 employees, daily production of 300,000 pieces	Registered capital of US$30 million, 400-acre modern production base in Taiping Industrial Park, an average monthly production of 1.2 million pairs, over 17,000 employees
Year and location of establishment	1990 – Ningbo, Zhejiang	1997 – Ningbo, Zhejiang	2004 – Shenzhou, Zhejiang	2000 – Guangzhou, Guangdong
Internationalization & major OFDIs	• Established a wholly owned subsidiary in Cambodia and secured forest concessions from the local government to exploit natural forestry resources	• Diversified from bicycle manufacturing to mining in Congo, Africa	• Invested in Cambodia to construct the textile production plants.	• Invested in India to construct footwear production plants.

cases based on their main industry, size of assets, year and location of establishment, as well as major OFDIs in developing countries.

Zhejiang Longsheng Group

The Longsheng Group had grown at home through continuously improving product standardization and production technologies for dye additives. The company began internationalization by first establishing a satellite office in Hong Kong for investment and trade. Thereafter, through collaboration with the world-class enterprises like Japan Itochu Corporation, the company learned and adopted the international advanced heat-recovery system. Building on the accumulated resources and experience, the company then entered a joint venture with Kiri, the largest Indian dye manufacturer, to implement the largest active dye construction project in India. The annual overseas production capacity since this joint venture positioned the company as the largest manufacturer of chemical dyes in India. After a year of collaboration with Kiri, in January 2010, the company acquired the entire joint venture and other subsidiaries of Kiri in Singapore and India. Via Kiri's Singaporean subsidiary, the company also acquired the German company Dystar, the world's largest supplier of dyes in all key markets. This acquisition allowed the company to gain significant control over the world's dye industry.

Ningbo Seduno Group

The Seduno Group grew at home and abroad through a world-class garment production system. The company exported mostly through collaboration as a contract manufacturer for internationally renowned sportswear brands. The continuing introduction of new and innovative products not only increased the value added, but also the efficiency of production processes. In response to the rising labour costs at home, the company acquired Ming Union Garments in Cambodia and built on its existing production facilities to expand further. The acquisition not only shortened the approval processes by the local authorities and accelerated the production capacity overseas, but also positioned the company in the networks of the global supply chain.

Ningbo Market Union

Market Union aspired to be the global hub for trade services. Because of the contracted market demands after the global financial crisis, together with the increased price of materials and the strengthening Chinese currency, the company decided to acquire First Cape Town, a hypermarket in the commercial centre of Cape Town in South Africa as another distribution outlet for products exported from China into the region. Before the acquisition, the company had been its supplier and earned a very small profit. However, after the acquisition, the reduction on a number of intermediary costs had greatly increased the profit.

Midea Group

Midea collaborated with the world's air conditioning expert, Carrier in Latin America, to penetrate the air conditioning markets in the region. Through years of cooperation, Midea had realized the combined benefits between Carrier's distribution networks in Latin America and Midea's strong manufacturing capability in China. The company later acquired Carrier and Miraco, an exclusive distributor of Carrier in Egypt. The acquisition was not only to promote the Midea brand in the region, but also to expedite the market entry and to mitigate various trade barriers in these markets.

Zhejiang Nanyuan Group

The company grew rapidly in the related hotel and real estate industries. Because the domestic price of seedlings continued to rise, the company conducted an in-depth study of woodland projects in Cambodia and decided to enter an agreement on the joint development of these projects with the Cambodian government. In March 2011, the company registered a local subsidiary company in Cambodia, which was the first exploratory step into internationalization. The Cambodian economy relies mainly on agriculture. The country also has abundant forestry resources with significant forest coverage.

Ningbo Xinglong Vehicle

Xinglong Vehicle was a manufacturer of professional bicycles for foreign renowned brands. After visiting Congo in Africa to study the market potential for bicycles, the company found that Congo was very rich in valuable mineral resources. Particularly interestingly, the local government allowed foreign investors to apply for extraction rights. The company then decided in 2004 to diversify into this industry. Based on this emergent opportunity, the company made significant revenue from selling extracted copper and cobalt in China.

Ningbo Shenzhou Knitting

Shenzhou Knitting owned world-class production equipment. Products were exported all over the world, including to Japan and Europe. After the financial crisis in 2008, many textile enterprises in Europe and the United States increasingly safeguarded their local businesses from the export of textiles from China by implementing a variety of anti-dumping measures, as well as other tariff and non-tariff trade barriers. Because Europe and the United States did not strictly impose tariff and non-tariff measures on imports from other developing countries, by establishing the production subsidiary in Cambodia, the company was able to export indirectly via Cambodia to these Western developed markets.

Guangzhou Apache Footwear

Apache Footwear is a manufacturer of sports shoes for a world-renowned Adidas brand. The company has a world-class technology development centre. Through years of cooperation with Adidas, the company built up the capability necessary to fulfil global requirements. The company constructed factories in India in response to the increase in international trade barriers to imports from China and rising production costs in China. That investment led to Adidas quickly increasing its order to the subsidiary in India.

Motivations for OFDIs and modes of entry in developing countries

The motivations for OFDIs made by Chinese POEs are based on the four basic impetuses for foreign-owned production identified by Dunning (1993). These impetuses are market seeking, strategic asset seeking, efficiency seeking and natural resource seeking. Because the home and host countries of FDIs made by all eight firms are developing countries where the governments play a vital role in the economic development, this study includes government interventions as another driver for these OFDIs. Built on transaction cost theory (Hennart, 1982), mergers and acquisitions theory (Caves, 1982) and theory of the growth of the firm (Penrose, 1959), this study identifies five contingencies that potentially moderate the modes of entry between acquisitions and greenfield investments. These moderators include size of the investor and its FDIs, experience of the investor in host country, competition and entry barriers of the target industry, degree of diversification of the investor and speed of overseas expansion.

Market seeking

Due to increasing competitive pressure by large incumbents at home, including state-owned counterparts, many Chinese POEs have looked for new markets overseas. Although China has entered the World Trade Organization, the ongoing imposition of tariff and non-tariff protectionism in the USA, Latin America and Europe has increasingly affected the Chinese OFDIs going to these regions (Buckley et al., 2008; Peng et al., 2008). Many Chinese enterprises have therefore relocated manufacturing plants in countries where the nations in these Western industrialized regions set few import quotas and other anti-dumping measures (Buckley et al., 2008; Taylor, 2002). Developing countries are often given preferential policy incentives in terms of trade and investment by nations in these Western industrialized regions. The market-seeking FDI is also a response of Chinese firms to deepening regional economic integration in some parts of the world. For example, a number of Chinese investments have gone to Latin America and Asia to benefit from free trade agreements and preferential treatments within those regions (Buckley et al., 2008).

By acquiring Kiri, an Indian global leader in the chemical dyes industry, Longsheng was able to bypass entry barriers imposed on Chinese exports in European markets and leverage Kiri's existing marketing networks of in these markets. Similarly, Midea acquired the air-conditioning business of Carrier in Latin America and Miraco in Egypt to penetrate those markets. By acquiring Ming Union Garments in Cambodia and then exporting products manufactured from this subsidiary (instead of exporting directly from China), Seduno was able to mitigate threat from trade barriers imposed on import by the Western industrialized markets. Instead of entering Cambodia by making acquisitions, Shenzhou Knitting constructed a textile factory there to export products to markets in the West. In response to the contraction of Western markets as a result of the financial crisis in 2008, Market Union acquired First Cape Town, the largest hypermarket in the second largest city of Cape Town in South Africa, as an additional outlet for its exports from China.

> **Proposition 1:** Chinese POEs are likely to invest in other developing countries via acquisitions or greenfield investments to expand markets there or to mitigate protectionisms in developed countries.

Strategic asset seeking

There are few cases of investment in developing countries to acquire strategic assets. However, Longsheng, Market Union and Midea are exceptions. Acquisitions are chosen when the required complementary strategic resources are less costly to acquire and bundle in a going concern than to purchase them in a disaggregated form via the market

(Caves, 1982; Hennart, 1982, 1988; Wilson, 1980). Such strategic resources are, for example, product- or industry-specific knowledge and general knowledge of the local markets held by the personnel of the acquired units, as well as their business networks. Therefore, Chinese investors seeking strategic assets in other developing markets will prefer acquisitions as a mode of entry in these markets.

The financial crisis in 2008 gave Kiri in India an opportunity to acquire Dystar, one of the world leaders in the chemical dyes industry, which had a number of technology patents and extensive marketing networks. After Longsheng acquired Kiri in India, the company became the largest shareholder and gained access to strategic assets of both Kiri and Dystar. The general manager of Longsheng mentioned that Indian companies were much more experienced than Chinese companies in international collaboration and acquisitions, not only in terms of English language communication, but also in international financial and legal affairs. Similarly, to access to strategic marketing networks, Market Union acquired First Cape Town, the largest hypermarket in Cape Town, while Midea acquired the air-conditioning business and related technologies of Carrier in Latin America. These acquisition cases emphasize a gap in technology and management expertise in developing countries that attract OFDIs for strategic asset seeking.

> **Proposition 2:** Chinese POEs are likely to invest in other developing countries via acquisitions (rather than greenfield investments) to acquire strategic assets (e.g., technology or marketing network).

Efficiency seeking

Increasing regional economic integration and international division of labour provide firms with more opportunity to internationalize for efficiency seeking by taking advantage of comparatively different factor endowments (Dunning, 1993). Because labour, land and other factor inputs such as raw materials in domestic markets are increasingly more costly, Chinese POEs have an incentive to enhance their production efficiencies by relocating manufacturing facilities abroad. The policy incentives derived from the regional economic integrations such as the North American Free Trade Agreement (NAFTA) and various economic agreements among nations in South East Asia not only shape investment strategies of Chinese POEs for market seeking, but also for efficiency seeking (Buckley et al., 2008).

Apache Footwear and other shoe manufacturers and exporters in Guangdong province had increasingly suffered from rising labour costs and prices of raw material, as well as the strengthening of the Chinese currency, after the financial crisis in 2008. Many companies in the province were also adversely impacted by changes in the local government's policy on export tax rebates. The number of companies in the shoe industry in Guangdong decreased significantly as a result of the crisis. International buyers had also shifted their orders to manufacturers in countries with lower labour and material costs, including Vietnam, India, Cambodia and Bangladesh. In response to the crisis, Apache Footwear decided to significantly reduce the shoe production in Guangdong and establish the main production base in India. Similarly, Seduno and Shenzhou Knitting also relocated their production to Cambodia via acquisitions and greenfield investments, respectively, with strong support from the local government in Cambodia. Both companies were able to significantly reduce the labour and material costs through local procurement in Cambodia.

Proposition 3: Chinese POEs are likely to invest in other developing countries via acquisitions or greenfield investments to reduce operating costs (e.g., labour or material).

Natural resource seeking

The high level of economic growth in China has always driven Chinese investors in many sectors to look for raw materials and other inputs in resource-rich countries. With strong support from the government and their own abundant organizational resources, Chinese SOEs have invested in natural resources extraction across a broad range of resource-rich countries (Buckley et al., 2008). These SOEs are largely indifferent to the political and economic conditions in the host countries. The support from the Chinese government is not only in the form of direct financial assistance, but also in the form of the negotiation of bilateral investment treaties and trade agreements with host countries (Li et al., 2013). In particular, the provision of official development aid by the Chinese government to many developing resource-rich countries in Africa may have facilitated negotiations and agreements for the extraction rights granted to Chinese investors in the region (Li et al., 2013).

Like their state-owned counterparts, Chinese POEs are also interested in countries with abundant natural resources that can provide them with related products and services. However, Chinese POEs are generally subject to limitations in organizational resources and management capability. POEs are more averse to economic and political risks than SOEs when choosing investment locations and modes of entry abroad.

Their investments in other developing markets are, thus, relatively smaller when compared to those made by SOEs. Therefore Chinese POEs are likely to invest in natural resources overseas mostly via greenfield investments while their state-owned counterparts do so via acquisitions. For example, Nanyuan and Xinglong Vehicle made greenfield investments in forestry in Cambodia and mining in Congo, respectively. These Asian and African countries, like as other developing countries, are generally rich in natural resources demanded in China markets.

> **Proposition 4:** Chinese POEs are likely to invest in other developing countries via greenfield investments (rather than acquisitions) to seek for natural resources.

Government policy

Since the reform and opening-up policy, particularly after 1999, the Chinese government has used a variety of incentives via the 'go global' policy, to encourage Chinese enterprises to make overseas investments (Kittilaksanawong et al., 2013; Peng, 2012). In the natural resource sector, most investors, particularly SOEs, benefit from strong government support in the form of direct financial assistance or the negotiation of bilateral investment treaties and trade agreements with the host country government for preferential extraction rights in exchange for official Chinese development aid (Buckley et al., 2008; Li et al., 2013). In other sectors, FDIs are also highly welcomed in most developing countries as investments are an important element in their economic development. The Chinese government and the government of host developing countries indeed play a vital role in the development of Chinese POEs' OFDIs in many industrial sectors.

In the case of Xinglong Vehicle, the company initially intended to visit Congo to explore the market opportunity for its bicycles, but later found that Congo had abundant rare mineral resources that are in high demand and command high prices in China. Meanwhile, the government in Congo had relaxed restrictions on natural resource extraction made by foreign investors. The company was able to secure extraction rights for copper and cobalt in 2005. The company then decided to diversify its investments from bicycles into these natural resources. The company shipped these mineral resources back to China by sea, via Durban, South Africa. Similarly, Nanyuan signed an agreement for a joint woodland project directly with the Cambodian government agency, highlighting the interest of the Cambodian government in the exploitation of natural resources in the country.

Many Chinese exporters relocate their production to other developing countries to mitigate trade and investment barriers in sectors that the governments in many developed countries have imposed on the direct imports from China. The acquisition of Kiri allowed Longsheng not only to leverage the critical technology and marketing networks of Kiri and its subsidiary, Dystar, but also to bypass tariff and non-tariff protectionism and export its products via India to other Western industrialized countries. Governments in these Western industrialized countries generally imposed few restrictions on imports from developing countries. In addition, the acquisition strategy also helped Longsheng to overcome the hurdles of complicated procedures involved in creating a new entity in India. Similarly, in the acquisition case of Seduno and the greenfield investment case of Shenzhou Knitting in Cambodia, both companies were able to export their products directly from Cambodia to many developed countries without encountering the trade barriers. In particular, the European governments and the United States government generally gave preferential treatment to products imported from Cambodia, while at the same time they implemented stringent trade barriers, including anti-dumping, countervailing, anti-trust, and intellectual property investigations, and other restrictions on textile imports from China (Peng et al., 2008).

> **Proposition 5:** Chinese POEs are likely to invest in other developing countries via acquisitions or greenfield investments to gain preferential treatments from the governments at home and in host countries.

Size of firm and overseas investments

The size of the assets that a firm holds indicates a certain level of resource slack. Resource slack is the level of availability of a resource. Resource slack thus gives firms the ability to take advantage of opportunities and to withstand turbulence in the economic environment (Thompson, 1967). Acquisitions allow investors to quickly take advantage of opportunities in the target businesses and countries. However, this mode of entry not only requires that the investor pay an upfront full value for the target, but also gives the investor little time and opportunity to learn about the target business. Compared with greenfield investments, acquisitions therefore involve a higher level of risk as a result of upfront payments and post-acquisition integration.

For Chinese POEs, the risks from acquisitions are likely to be high because of their limited resources and international management experience. These risks are likely to be even more pronounced when the acquisitions are made in other developing countries because the information about the target business and economic environment in these countries is often not sufficiently transparent. Accordingly, acquisitions are more likely to be used by the larger POEs, rather than the smaller ones, to enter other developing countries. This argument is supported by all eight cases. In particular, Longsheng, Seduno, Market Union and Midea are all much larger in terms of total assets than Nanyuan, Xinglong Vehicle, Shenzhou Knitting and Apache Footwear. The four larger companies entered other developing markets via acquisitions, while the four smaller companies entered these markets via greenfield investments.

> **Proposition 6.1:** Size of Chinese POEs moderates the relationship between motivations of OFDIs in other developing countries and modes of entry in such a way that larger firm size favors acquisitions (rather than greenfield investments).

A firm may not without limitation, recruit and train managers to facilitate its expansion (Penrose, 1959). The limitations on recruitment and training are even more pronounced in Chinese POEs, which are mostly SMEs lacking in international management experience. When investments are large, expansion via greenfield investments may be limited by the availability of managerial resources in the parent company (Caves & Mehra, 1986). Particularly in developing countries, in spite of their large populations, Chinese POEs may have trouble in recruiting managers and other skilled workers to facilitate greenfield investments (Khanna et al., 2005). An acquisition is therefore more likely to relieve these constraints because the acquired firm comes with its own ready-to-use management talents. Accordingly, the larger the investments in other developing countries, the more likely it is that the entry will be through acquisitions. This argument is supported by the evidence in all eight cases. In particular, the size of investments made by Longsheng, Seduno, Market Union and Midea via acquisitions is larger than that made by Nanyuan, Xinglong Vehicle, Shenzhou Knitting and Apache Footwear via greenfield investments.

> **Proposition 6.2:** Size of investments in other developing countries made by Chinese POEs moderates the relationship between motivations of these OFDIs and modes of entry in such a way that larger size of investments favors acquisitions (rather than greenfield investments).

Experience in host developing countries

Inspection and interaction are two major challenges in mergers and acquisition (Ravenscraft & Scherer, 1987). The inspection problem arises from the fact that the target firm usually has better information than the acquirer firm (Ackerlof, 1970). The presence of such information asymmetry may not bias the choice between acquisitions and greenfield investments. Further, acquisitions are much more difficult to manage than greenfield investments due to the interaction problem arising from integrating the new unit into the acquirer's existing businesses. An acquired unit has its own culture that may be difficult to assimilate with that of the acquirer. These two challenges are likely to be more pronounced in developing countries where market information is less transparent than in developed countries. Especially in relation to post-acquisition integration, as stated by the general manager of Longsheng, Chinese POEs were much less experienced in international collaboration and acquisitions than Indian firms. Therefore, the experience of Chinese POEs in their target businesses in developing countries not only mitigates the information asymmetry during the process of due diligence, but also contributes to the successful restructuring and integration after the acquisition.

The acquisition of Carrier's air-conditioning business in Latin America by Midea was not the first business deal between the two companies. Both companies had previously closely collaborated through equity and non-equity deals for market development of home and commercial air-conditioning business. The collaboration had benefited both companies and enabled Midea to access essential technologies and market knowledge in Latin America. In 2010, before the acquisition, Midea also learned from the acquisition of an air-conditioning business from Miraco in Egypt. In the Longsheng case, the general manager of the company said that the acquisition of Kiri in India was not a difficult deal because both companies were in the dye industry and knew each other very well. In the case of Market Union, the acquisition in First Cape Town was also not the first deal between the two companies. Market Union had been a supplier to First Cape Town for many years before the acquisition.

> **Proposition 7:** Experience of Chinese POEs in target businesses in host developing countries moderates the relationship between motivations of OFDIs in other developing countries and modes of entry in such a way that more experienced firms favor acquisitions (rather than greenfield investments).

Industry competition and entry barriers

By acquiring a rival, a foreign entrant may reduce competition and increase market power. Acquisitions do not add capacity to the market supply; therefore, the market prices are less likely to fall (Yip, 1982). Through greenfield investments, however, the investor not only creates a new competitor and additional capacity, but the investor also has to compete with the incumbents, which requires a considerable amount of time and resources. In addition, in developing countries, the possibility of being scrutinized by the local government on the acquisitions for reducing market competition and increasing market power may not be as high as that in developed countries. This is evidenced by the Midea and Longsheng cases.

Although Midea had experience in Latin America, the high level of competition in the air-conditioning business meant that there was a particular entry barrier. By acquiring Carrier, the market leader in Latin America, the company was not only able to mitigate the level of competition barrier, but was also able to position itself as a market leader. Although China has entered World Trade Organization and implemented a variety of policies liberalizing the country's trade and investment, a variety of tariff and non-tariff barriers still exist in many of its counterparts, particularly in Europe and United States. Such barriers are less practised against entrants from other developing countries. By acquiring Kiri, an Indian global leader in the chemical dyes industry, Longsheng was able to mitigate entry barriers in Western developed markets by leveraging the existing technologies and marketing networks of Kiri in these Western markets.

> **Proposition 8:** Industry competition and entry barriers in target businesses of Chinese POEs moderates the relationship between motivations of OFDIs in other developing countries and modes of entry in such a way that higher levels of industry competition and entry barriers encourage the use acquisitions (rather than greenfield investments).

Degree of diversification

Firms making an overseas investment exploit some of their firm-specific advantages developed at home and combine them with other assets available in the host country at lower marginal costs (Hennart & Park, 1993). Highly diversified firms are likely to have sophisticated technical expertise or organizational capability. Highly diversified investor firms are likely to have sophisticated technical expertise or organizational capability. Their embedded firm-specific advantages may be compatible with and successfully combine with those in the prospective subsidiaries through acquisitions (Caves & Mehra 1986; Yip, 1982; Zejan, 1990). Less-diversified investor firms, however, are likely to be more narrowly specialized. The firm-specific advantages embedded in these less-diversified firms may be incompatible with those in the prospective subsidiaries. In particular, their firm-specific advantages may be highly tacit (rather than explicit) and tightly bound to their organization in such a way that is difficult for those firm-specific advantages to be assimilated into going concerns in the target subsidiaries through acquisitions.

To minimize the post-acquisition interaction problems and enhance organizational control, less-diversified firms are likely to exploit their firm-specific advantages by recreating in the host market a duplicate of their parent firm via greenfield investments. Greenfield investments enable the parent firms to efficiently transfer their firm-specific advantages to their subsidiaries by installing their own managerial practices from the outset. In particular, while firms making acquisitions inherit the acquired firm's labour force and corporate culture, firms making greenfield investments are able to mould the affiliates by hiring their own labour force (Jemison & Sitkin 1986). This is evidenced in all eight cases. Longsheng, Seduno and Midea, which entered other developing markets via acquisitions, are relatively more diversified than Nanyuan, Xinglong Vehicle, Shenzhou Knitting and Apache Footwear, which entered these markets via greenfield investments.

> **Proposition 9:** Diversification degree of Chinese POEs moderates the relationship between motivations of OFDIs in other developing countries and modes of entry in such a way that firms with greater degrees of diversification favor acquisitions (rather than greenfield investments).

Speed of globalization and new market development

Many Chinese POEs encounter intense competition at home (Luo & Tung, 2007). Going global and looking for new markets has become a priority mission. In the case of Midea, the company occupied a leading market position in home electrical appliances in China with a well-recognized Midea brand. Because of increasing competition and saturated home markets, the company found it very difficult to expand at home. For example, although the company gained the largest market share at home as a result of newly launched air-conditioning products with a variable DC inverter in 2012, the overall financial performance was still significantly lower than the year before because of thin competitive margins in the home market. To improve its performance, the company acquired Carrier's air-conditioning business in Latin America. Through acquisition of this air-conditioning world leader, Midea was able to control the distribution networks in Latin America and gain rapid access to markets in Brazil, Argentina and Chile under the Midea brand. This success enabled Midea to grow quickly to become the largest manufacturer and distributor of air-conditioning products in the region.

Similarly, following the financial crisis in Europe and the continuing recession in the Japanese economy, many export trading companies in Ningbo, including Market Union, were looking for new markets to counter the market contraction in Europe and Japan. Market Union acquired First Cape Town, the largest hypermarket in Cape Town, the second largest city in South Africa, to open up new markets in South Africa. Market Union significantly increased sales in the first year after the acquisition of the hypermarket. The success in South Africa enhanced the company's aspiration to be the world's product and material sourcing destination. These cases demonstrate that Chinese POEs chose acquisitions as a way to a speedy entry in overseas developing markets. Building a subsidiary from scratch via greenfield investments takes more time than buying a going concern in a host market (Caves, 1982). Therefore, an investor chooses an acquisition if the opportunity cost of delaying the investment in the host country is high (Hennart & Park, 1993).

Proposition 10: New market development speed of Chinese POEs in host developing countries moderates the relationship between motivations of OFDIs in other developing countries and modes of entry in such a way that firms looking for a faster new market development favor acquisitions (rather than greenfield investments).

Conclusions and implications

This study highlights the rise of Chinese multinationals, and Chinese POEs in particular, in the global marketplace. Chinese POEs invest overseas not only because of policy incentives from the government, but also because of their institutional disadvantages, when compared to their state-owned counterparts, in accessing critical resources, and the lack of resources and experience at home. OFDIs are an important strategic alternative for Chinese POEs to use to overcome their institutional disadvantages at home and to remedy their limited resources and increase the experience necessary to compete more effectively at home and on the global stage.

Based on case studies of eight representative Chinese POEs, this study finds that their motivation to invest in other developing countries is not only to seek markets, strategic assets, efficiency and natural resources (Dunning, 1993), but is also to respond to policy incentives of the Chinese government and the governments of host countries. When Chinese POEs are motivated to pursue OFDIs for market seeking and efficiency seeking and for preferential treatment by governments, they are likely to use acquisitions or greenfield investments as the mode of entry. However, when they are motivated to do so for strategic asset seeking and natural resource seeking, they are likely to use acquisitions and greenfield investments, respectively.

For strategic asset seeking, acquisitions are chosen to gain complementary resources that are less costly to acquire and bundle in a going concern than to purchase them in a disintegrated form via the open market. Acquisitions facilitate the bundling of tacit (rather than explicit) strategic resources that are often subject to high transaction costs when purchasing them in a disintegrated form via the open market (Hennart 1982, 1988). This study also finds that developing countries can also be a potential source of strategic assets that attract OFDIs from other developing countries. For natural resource seeking, greenfield investments are preferred because most Chinese POEs are SMEs and subject to constraints in relation to organizational resources and management capability.

Built on transaction cost theory (Hennart, 1982), mergers and acquisitions theory (Caves, 1982) and the theory of the growth of the firm (Penrose, 1959), this study identifies contingencies that potentially moderate the modes of entry between acquisitions and greenfield investments. In particular, larger and more diversified Chinese POEs with greater investment power and more experience in the host country, as well as those POEs that invest in industries with higher levels of competition and barriers and that look for quicker development in new markets, are likely to invest in other developing countries through acquisitions rather than greenfield investments.

Larger Chinese POEs are likely to possess more abundant resources and have more management capability, which may buffer them from investment risks while allowing them to exploit emergent opportunities in developing countries (Thompson, 1967). When investments are large, Chinese POEs are likely to face constraints from their limited professional personnel to manage overseas expansion (Penrose, 1959). Expansions via acquisitions may thus relieve these constraints because the acquired firm comes with ready-to-use management talents. Experience in the host country is likely to reduce the information asymmetry that facilitates the effective due diligence and the integration of the new entity (Ravenscraft & Scherer, 1987). Highly diversified firms are likely to hold firm-specific advantages that are compatible with, and able to be combined with, those in the prospective subsidiaries via acquisitions (Caves & Mehra 1986; Yip, 1982; Zejan, 1990). In industries with higher levels of competition and entry barriers, acquisitions may reduce competition and increase market power. Because acquisitions do not add capacity to the market supply, threats from price competition may be reduced (Yip, 1982). Particularly in developing countries, the possibility of being scrutinized by the local authorities on the acquisitions for reducing market competition and increasing market power may not be very high. Lastly, acquisitions allow an instant access to the target businesses without having to risk time and resources creating the businesses from scratch.

To enhance the competitiveness at home and abroad, Chinese POEs may consider partnership opportunities or look for ways to compete with their state-owned counterparts. By collaborating with SOEs, POEs may be able to work in industries that would otherwise be restricted, apply for special government-related projects and enjoy preferential policy incentives. Working with SOEs also allows POEs a greater opportunity to access critical resources such as capital, land and natural resources. Because manufacturing and resource-seeking OFDIs by Chinese SOEs go mostly to developing or lower-income countries (Amighinia et al., 2013), partnering with SOEs could serve as a platform for POEs to access other developing markets more effectively. However, POEs should be aware that an SOE's priorities might be largely linked to a particular central or local government agency and, as a result, constrain their long-term company development or profitability. To compete with SOEs, POEs may have to avoid monopoly industries and industries where SOEs have preferential access to tax incentives, subsidies and other special funds, as well as to government procurement procedures. SOEs have special advantages, including subsidies and easy access to bank loans for competition inside and outside of China. POEs may need new strategies to compete with SOEs outside of China as they move to other developing countries such as Africa, India and South America. Because Chinese SOEs will only become stronger in the future, POEs should consider how to interact with them, not only as competitors, but also as partners.

This study is not without limitations. Chinese POEs are mostly not large and publicly listed enterprises. Their internal in-depth information is thus difficult or even impossible to obtain. While OFDIs made by these firms in other developing countries has increased significantly in recent years, the number of firms that pursue acquisitions overseas is still very limited. Therefore, the eight company cases in this study may not reflect a complete understanding of overseas investments made by Chinese POEs. Future research should verify various propositions developed in this study with a larger set of company data. In addition, future research should also explore the operations and management of Chinese POEs in the host countries following their investments via acquisitions or greenfield investments, because most of them have little or no prior experience in cross-border management and operations.

Acknowledgements

This research project was supported by the grant from European Union's Erasmus Mundus (Grant No. FIIR2011/14) and Zhejiang Provincial Natural Science Foundation of China (Grant No. LY12G02011).

References

Ackerlof, G. (1970). The market for 'lemons': Quality uncertainty and the market mechanism. *Quarterly Journal of Economics*, 84(3): 488–500.

Amighinia, A. A., Rabellottic, R., & Sanfilippob, M. (2013). Do Chinese state-owned and private enterprises differ in their internationalization strategies? *China Economic Review*, 27(C): 312–325.

Buckley, P. J., Clegg, L. J., Cross, A. R., Liu, X., Voss, H., & Zheng, P. (2007). The determinants of Chinese outward foreign direct investment. *Journal of International Business Studies*, 38(4): 499–518.

Buckley, P. J., Cross, A. R., Tan, H., Liu, X., & Voss, H. (2008). Historic and emergent trends in Chinese outward direct investment. *Management International Review*, 48(6): 715–748.

Caves, R. (1982). *Multinational Enterprise and Economic Analysis*, New York: Cambridge University Press.

Caves, R. & Mehra, S. (1986). Entry of foreign multinationals into US manufacturing industries. In M. Porter (ed.), *Competition in Global industries*, Boston: Harvard Business School Press: 449–481.

Child, J. & Rodrigues, S. B. (2005). The internationalization of Chinese firms: A case for theoretical extension. *Management and Organization Review*, 1(3): 381–410.

Deng, P. (2013). Chinese outward direct investment research: Theoretical integration and recommendations. *Management and Organization Review*, 9(3): 513–539.

Dunning, J. H. (1993). *Multinational Enterprises and the Global Economy*. Wokingham: Addison Wesley.

Duanmu, J. L. (2012). Firm heterogeneity and location choice of Chinese multinational enterprises. *Journal of World Business*, 47(1): 64–72

Eisenhardt, K. M. (1989). Building theories from case study research. *Academy of Management Review*, 14(4): 532–550.

Hennart, J. F. (1982). *A Theory of Multinational Enterprise*. Ann Arbor, MI: University of Michigan Press.

Hennart, J. F. (1988). A transaction costs theory of equity joint ventures. *Strategic Management Journal*, 9(4): 361–374.

Hennart, J. F. & Park, Y. R. (1993). Greenfield vs acquisition: The strategy of Japanese investors in the United States. *Management Science*, 39(9): 1054–1070.

Jemison, D. B. & Sitkin, S. B. (1986). Corporate acquisition: A process perspective. *Academy of Management Review*, 11(1): 145–163.

Khanna, T., Palepu, K. G., & Sinha, J. (2005). Strategies that fit emerging markets. *Harvard Business Review*, 83(6): 63–76.

Kittilaksanawong, W., Chen, X. D., & Duan, C. Q. (2013). What drives the strategic alliance formation of transition-economy small- and medium-sized enterprises? The moderating role of intermediary organizations. In T. S. Chan and G. Cui (eds), *Multinationals and Global Consumers: Tension, Potential and Competition*, New York: Palgrave Macmillan: 40–57.

Li, Q. & Liang, G. (2012). Political relations and Chinese outbound direct investment: Evidence from firm- and dyadic-level tests. *RCCPB Working Paper 19*, Bloomington, IN: Research Center for Chinese Politics and Business, Indiana University.

Li, J., Newenham-Kahind, A., Shapiro, D. M., & Chen, V. Z. (2013). The two-tier bargaining model revisited: Theory and evidence from China's natural resource investments in Africa. *Global Strategy Journal*, 3(4): 300–321.

Luo Y. & Tung R. L. (2007). International expansion of emerging market enterprises: A springboard perspective. *Journal of International Business Studies*, 38(4): 481–498.

Luo, Y., Xue, Q., & Han, B. (2010). How emerging market governments promote outward FDI: Experience from China. *Journal of World Business*, 45(1): 68–79.

Mathews, J. A. (2006). Dragon multinationals: New players in 21st century globalization. *Asia Pacific Journal of Management*, 23(1): 5–27.

Ministry of Commerce (MOFCOM) (2010). 2010 *Statistical Bulletin of China's Outward Foreign Direct Investment*. Beijing: MOFCOM.

Peng, M. W. (2012). The global strategy of emerging multinationals from China. *Global Strategy Journal*, 2(2): 97–107.

Peng, M. W., Wang, D. Y. L., & Jiang, Y. (2008). An institution-based view of international business strategy: A focus on emerging economies. *Journal of International Business Studies*, 39(5): 920–936.

Penrose, E. (1959). *The Theory of the Growth of the Firm*. Oxford: Blackwell.

Ramasamy, B., Yeung, M., & Laforet, S. (2012). China's outward foreign direct investment: Location choice and firm ownership. *Journal of World Business*, 47(1): 17–25.

Ravenscraft, D. & Scherer, F. M. (1987). *Mergers, Sell-Offs, and Economic Efficiency*. Washington, DC: Brookings.

Song, L., Yang, J., & Zhang, Y. (2011). State-owned enterprises' outward investment and the structural reform in China. *China & the World Economy*, 19(4): 38–53.

Taylor, R. (2002). Globalization strategies of Chinese companies: Current developments and future prospects. *Asian Business and Management*, 1(2): 209–225.

Sutherland, D., & Ning, L. (2011). Exploring "onward-journey" ODI strategies in China's private sector businesses. *Journal of Chinese Economic and Business Studies*, 9(1): 43–65.

Thompson, J. D. (1967). *Organizations in Action*. New York: McGraw-Hill.

Wilson, B. (1980). The propensity of multinational companies to expand through acquisitions. *Journal of International Business Studies*, 11(1): 59–65.

Yin, R. K. (2003). *Case Study Research: Design and Method*. Thousand Oaks, CA: Sage Publication.

Yip, G. (1982). Diversification entry: Internal development versus acquisition. *Strategic Management Journal*, 3(4): 331–345.

Zejan, M. (1990). New ventures or acquisitions: The choice of Swedish multinational enterprises. *Journal of Industrial Economics*, 38(3): 349–355.

9

Different Roads to Rome? Patterns of Internationalization in Chinese Firms

Geng Cui, T. S. Chan, Hua Zhang and Ling Peng

Introduction

Existing findings on the internationalization of firms have largely been based on studies of firms from developed economies, following the knowledge-development process model of increasing commitment from export to foreign direct investment, and emphasizing firm-specific advantages and outward activities (Johanson & Wiedersheim-Paul, 1975). Such studies are, however, less informative about how firms generate competitive advantages in the first place. Studies that have examined the role of inward activities in firms' internationalization suggest that firms can be integrated into the global economy through inward activities (Loustarinen & Welch, 1997; Welch & Loustarinen, 1993) or upstream internationalization (Kuada & Sørensen, 2000). Inward activities play an important role in the internationalization process of firms, particularly for firms from emerging market economies, such as China, where many firms start the internationalization process by becoming customers or joint venture partners of foreign multinationals. Thus, inward activities provide an alternative approach to beginning the internationalization process.

Although studies have explored the effect of inward activities on the outward internationalization process, they have not yet provided a coherent framework to explain how inward activities lead to outward activities and eventually to the internationalization of firms. How inward activities help firms to develop the prerequisite capability and knowledge to operate overseas remains elusive. Moreover, among the firms that have engaged in inward activities, some have taken a gradual, generic approach to internationalization while others have been more aggressive in overseas expansion (Child & Rodrigues, 2005). What are the firm and environmental factors that drive the internationalization efforts and result in different patterns? This study attempts to achieve the following objectives. First, we furnish a brief review of the literature on the internationalization of firms. Second, we adopt the resource-based view (RBV) to examine how inward activities facilitate outward activities and the internationalization process. We also explore how entry strategies and environmental factors affect patterns of internationalization. Based on case studies of four Chinese enterprises, Haier, TCL, Lenovo and Founder, we find that by engaging in inward activities, firms can acquire the prerequisite knowledge and critical resources and enhance their export and manufacturing capability for internationalization. The extent of their success is conditional upon the entry strategies taken, the degree of industry internationalization, and government support. Finally, we discuss the role of inward activities and firm and environmental factors in the internationalization of firms from emerging markets, and identify directions for future research.

Literature review

Internationalization of firms

In recent decades, multinational companies have expanded rapidly in different parts of the world, accounting for an increasing portion of global economy activity. The process through which firms become internationalized has attracted much attention from researchers. A number of theories have been put forward to explain how a firm expands beyond its home market, including the international product-life-cycle theory (Vernon, 1966) and the so-called process or knowledge development model (Johanson & Vahlne, 1977).

A leading theory of international expansion is the eclectic paradigm, which posits that firms will choose the most appropriate entry modes into foreign markets based on their ownership (O), locational (L), and internalization (I) advantages (Dunning, 2003). Thus, the existence of multinational firms is based on the assumption that firms have the ability to internalize market transactions given market imperfections. This approach specifies the appropriate mode of entry based on the types of advantages that firms enjoy, and has dominated international business research for recent decades (Peng, 2003). These theoretical perspectives are largely based on considerations of transaction costs and studies of Western multinationals, and assume that firms develop their capabilities and competitive advantages before embarking on the internationalization process (Sim & Pandian, 2003).

Alternative approaches to internationalization

Since the 1980s, the international markets have undergone dramatic changes, marked by modern transportation and logistics systems and new information technologies such as the Internet. The breaking down of trade barriers and globalization of the world's economies have made it much easier for firms to acquire knowledge about foreign markets and conduct business across national boundaries. New theoretical frameworks have emerged to explain the internationalization of firms, such as the role of communication technologies and networks theory (Freeman et al., 2006). Recent studies have also explored the internationalization of small- and medium-sized enterprises (SMEs), born-global companies and third world multinationals (Wells, 1983).

Previous research on the internationalization of firms has emphasized outward activities. A number of authors have pointed out an equivalent process of knowledge development via inward activities, which cover a multiplicity of forms, such as the importing of products, finance and technology, learning through franchising, licensing and alliance agreements, and joint ventures and partnerships with foreign firms (Luostarinen & Welch, 1997). Several researchers have explored the role of inward activities in the internationalization of firms and their findings suggest that domestic firms can begin the knowledge development process by engaging in inward activities, such as by becoming a distributor of foreign products or forming a joint venture with a foreign company *(Bjorkman & Kock, 1997; Welch & Luostarinen, 1993)*. Firms can be integrated into the global economy through such inward activities (Loustarinen & Welch, 1997) or upstream internationalization by moving up the value chain (Kuada & Sørensen, 2000).

International expansion of Chinese firms

At the end of the 1970s, China instituted its opening up and reform policies because of its low level of economic development and lack of technology, capital and modern management practices among domestic firms. Subsequently, almost all industries were gradually opened up for foreign participation. Many Chinese firms formed joint ventures with foreign partners to explore new technologies and manufacturing processes. By importing products, machinery and capital from foreign countries, Chinese enterprises developed rapidly, and China's export market experienced exponential growth, resulting in a huge trade surplus. In the meantime, China's domestic markets had become saturated and some industries, such as household appliances, experienced serious over-capacity. Chinese firms began to explore overseas markets by exporting products or establishing overseas subsidiaries via outward foreign direct investment (OFDI) or through mergers and acquisitions (M&As). An increasing number of Chinese companies have become major players in their respective industries or product categories.

Clearly, these inward activities facilitated the rapid development of Chinese firms and the saturation of the domestic market. Inward activities, including the purchasing of machinery and equipment and acquisition of technical and management know-how via joint ventures, facilitate technological upgrading and the development of critical capabilities, which lead to outward activities (Young et al., 1996). Firms that have enhanced their competitive capability through inward activities have begun exporting to international markets and setting up overseas subsidiaries. Although researchers have proposed inward activities as an alternative approach to the internationalization of firms, a systematic framework is needed to explain why some domestic firms have expanded overseas and experienced rapid internationalization while others have not. The entry strategies and environmental factors of internationalized firms may help to shed light on the underlying mechanism of this process, elucidate the role of inward activities and provide coherent explanations for the divergent patterns of internationalization among Chinese firms.

Research framework

In the international business literature, researchers have adopted the RBV to explain the international expansion of firms and to establish a connection between inward and outward activities (Anderson, 1997; Elango, 2001). They propose that by engaging in inward activities, firms can acquire the critical resources that cannot be accessed in the local market or developed within a short period. These can be acquired through various inward activities, such as by becoming a distributor of foreign products, importing equipment and technology, or forming a joint venture with a foreign company (Karlsen et al., 2003). For Chinese firms, these resources are rare and valuable during the early stages of the transition to a market economy. Thus, the inward activities of Chinese enterprises constitute a process of organizational learning and resource acquisition. Inward activities provide knowledge about international business fields, including foreign markets, overseas operations, international trade and cross-cultural management. Over time, firms may integrate these resources and develop their own capabilities, which consequently help them to become fierce competitors in the domestic market and prepare them for expansion overseas. By drawing from the resource theory, we posit that the resources acquired from inward activities influence the outward activities and internationalization of firms.

> **Proposition 1**: Inward activities have a positive effect on firms' development of the resources and knowledge that are required to operate in overseas markets.

The RBV suggests that whether the resources acquired by a firm can deliver competitive advantages depends on several factors, because rent-generating resources may be influenced by firm and environmental factors (Pfeffer & Salancik, 1978). A firm's other resources can provide complementary assets for it to develop stronger capabilities. These resources also form the basis of firms' strategies and are critical in the implementation of their internationalization strategies (e.g., Barney, 1991). In other words, firm resources and strategies interact to produce competitive advantages and positive returns (Hitt et al., 2001). Moreover, firms from emerging countries often expand overseas to secure new resources and complementary assets. Mathews (2006) suggests that multinational companies from emerging markets not only need to access resources through external linkages and learning through internationalization, but also to leverage different resources. The incremental process of knowledge development from inward activities partially explains the link between inward and outward activities. Learning from firms in other countries through various inward activities, such as exporting, original equipment manufacturing or joint ventures, provides a good opportunity for firms to learn foreign trade and overseas operations, thus placing them in a better position for outward activities. Thus, organizations with such learning experiences are more likely to leverage the experiences gained from inward activities to facilitate overseas expansion (Cohen & Levinthal, 1990). Firms can apply their acquired knowledge to implement similar strategies in terms of entry mode and location when they expand overseas.

> **Proposition 2**: Firms that have performed various inward activities are more likely to enact similar strategies in terms of entry mode and location choice in overseas expansion.

Environmental factors such as industry structure and growth may influence the availability and cost of such resources. These factors make certain resources more valuable in certain conditions, under which they become the sources of competitive advantages. First, the degree of industry internationalization puts considerable pressure on firms to internationalize, which makes the acquired resources more valuable for these firms. Firms facing a higher degree of internationalization in their industries are more motivated to compete in the international market and more proactive in transferring the acquired resources learned from inward activities overseas markets. Second, a firm's home institutional environment, such as the level of government support, plays an important role in supporting its internationalization. Many governments have policies and programmes to assist internationalization (Chaudhry & Crick, 2002; Taylor, 2002). Since the early 2000s, under the Chinese government's "Going Global" policy, Chinese firms have been encouraged to invest overseas and become more competitive in the international market (Child & Rodrigues, 2005). The "Going Global" policy reinforces the government's efforts to support the rapid development of technological skills, management know-how and marketing strategies, and the building of global brands for Chinese firms. Thus, government support can be a critical factor in firms' outward internationalization (Young et al., 1996). Based on these arguments, we propose the following propositions.

> **Proposition 3**: The degree of industry internationalization propels firms in such industries to face the pressure of globalization and actively pursue internationalization.
>
> **Proposition 4**: Home government support has a positive influence on firms in their pursuit of internationalization.

Method and results

Although there has been much publicity on the international expansion of Chinese firms and their overseas business activities, systematic firm-level data on the international activities of Chinese firms are scarce. There are no official sources of such information from the government or research organizations. Given the exploratory nature of our research, we adopted the case study approach. After an extensive search for information on the internationalization activities of firms, we finally chose four Chinese firms for our study: Haier, Lenovo, TCL and Founder. These are well-known companies in the home appliance and IT industries in China. Even so, detailed information on the international activities of these firms was difficult to locate. The international activities of firms are often related to their overseas subsidiaries and thus not reported in detail in their annual reports. We used the following secondary sources to collect data on these companies: (1) the Internet, including industry and firm websites, in both Chinese and English, (2) the Proquest, Ebscohost and LexisNexis databases, (3) the reports of other researchers who have studied Chinese firms, and (4) reports from government agencies in China.

Interviews with the top level management (such as the CEOs) of these companies published in prestigious business magazines and newspapers were another important source of information. For instance, Chuanzhi Liu of Lenovo and Ruimin Zhang of Haier have both appeared in prominent business magazines, such as *Fortune, Harvard Business Review, Business Week, Time* and many Chinese publications. Because such interviews invariably focused on the development of these companies, including their internationalization efforts, they were very relevant to our study and provided insight into the growth and operations of these firms.

Firms and their industries

When China's household appliance industry began to develop in the 1980s, the world household appliance industry was already in the mature stage with intensive competition. Before the mid-1990s, the demand for household appliances in the Chinese domestic market could not be satisfied. In 1985, for instance, China imported 4.99 million colour TV sets. In the following two decades, the Chinese household appliance industry developed rapidly and improved its production capability and efficiency. Some firms began to expand overseas. Haier and TCL are the leading Chinese home appliance manufacturers. They have invested overseas aggressively and achieved a significant market share in a number of developed and developing countries (Liu & Li, 2002). In comparison, although the information technology (IT) industry in China has developed very rapidly, it is still very young. While some crucial technologies are controlled by foreign firms, many IT companies in China have grown rapidly to become powerful competitors. Lenovo and Founder are just two of the Chinese IT firms that have achieved remarkable success in internationalization. The basic data on the four firms and the degree of their internationalization are presented in Table 9.1. In the following sections, we discuss the four companies and their inward and outward activities in the internationalization process.

Based on Table 9.1, we can assess the extent and success of internationalization among these four firms. All four firms are active exporters and

Table 9.1 Profiles of the four companies and their degree of internationalization

Company	Hair	TCL	Lenovo	Founder
Established	1984	1981	1984	1986
Location of HQ	Qingdao	Huizhou	US	Beijing
Core business	home appliances	TV & PC	PC& software	laser typesetting
Turnover (2012)*	163.1	69.6	198.0	61.8
Export (2012)**	8.9	24.6	16.9	2.5
Export % (2012)	5.47%	38%	8.56%	4.0%
No. of countries exported to	over 160	over 100	over 100	over 30
No. of overseas subsidiaries	over 30	over 8	over 100	over 6
% revenue from overseas*	10.5	36.3	57.0	12.4
Global resource integration	√	√	√	
Leading product quality	√	√	√	√
Capability of world-class R&D	√		√	√
Have well-known brand(s)	√	√	√	

Notes: *in billion RMB, from the annual reports of companies. ** in billion RMB from the data released by the China Ministry of Commerce and estimated from the report of Founder.

have direct investments in foreign countries. Both TCL and Lenovo have resorted to M&As and have achieved a very high percentage of foreign sales. Although Haier's percentage of foreign sales is lower, it is ranked among the top ten appliance manufacturers in the world. As for other indicators of internationalization, the first three firms have demonstrated the ability to integrate resources from various countries, including human resources, financing and raw materials or supplies. Both Haier and Lenovo have established research and development (R&D) centres in overseas countries. More importantly, the first three firms have achieved leading quality and established well-known brands for their products. In contrast, Founder has achieved limited success in these areas.

The role of inward activities

A brief history of each of these companies, including their inward and outward activities, is provided in Boxes 9.1, 9.2, 9.3 and 9.4. Based on the firms' inward and outward activities, we adopt the pattern-matching method to identify the key inward and outward activities, compare the four firms' internationalization efforts and attempt to answer the research propositions. The results are summarized in Table 9.2.

All four firms engaged in various inward activities, including acting as agents or distributors of foreign products (TCL and Lenovo), importing machinery (Haier and TCL) and acquiring foreign technology and capital through joint ventures (all four firms). They all formed R&D centres with large multinationals to develop products for the Chinese market. Initially, all of these inward activities focused on the domestic market. Through these inward activities, the firms acquired and upgraded key technologies and learned modern product standards and manufacturing processes. As a result, the firms have become highly successful and emerged as leaders in their respective industries and product categories in the Chinese domestic market.

Haier

Box 9.1 Haier Group

Introduction

Haier began in 1984 as a collectively owned enterprise – Qingdao Refrigerator Factory. Over the past 30 years, it has grown into a multinational company with over 50,000 employees throughout the world. It now manufactures 96 different models of household appliances, exports to more than 160 countries and regions, and owns 13 plants outside China (SinoCast, 2006). Haier is China's largest household appliance manufacturer (Liu & Li, 2002) and ranked ninth in the world in the home appliance industry .

Inward activities

In 1984, Haier bought an assembly line from a Germany company, Liebherr, to access the company's technology and equipment, and cooperated with Liebherr in manufacturing refrigerators.

In 1992, Haier obtained ISO9001 certification, which laid a solid foundation for further expansion.

In 1993, Haier became listed on the Shanghai Stock Exchange (SHA: 600690).

In 1995, Haier began producing microwave ovens and washing machines, completed a merger with Qingdao Red-Star Appliance Co., Ltd, and began exporting to the US, initially through original equipment manufacturing (OEM) and later with Haier branded products.

In 2000, Haier formed a joint venture with CCT Telecom Holdings to make mobile phones, and became listed on the Hong Kong Stock Exchange.

In 2002, Haier formed a joint venture with Sanyo and diversified its product portfolio by acquiring a number of local firms in China: Qingdao General Refrigerator Factory and Qingdao Air Conditioner General Factory.

In 2007, Haier formed a strategic alliance with Cisco and INTEL to make computers for China and overseas markets.

In 2009, Haier and the International Electrotechnical Commission (IEC) jointly established the Haier–IEC Standard Innovation Base.

In 2010, Haier and Hewlett-Packard (HP) signed a strategic agreement to support HP's expansion in China with the support of Haier's Goodaymart network. Haier and FramTech, Norway's leading provider of green technology, signed an agreement to develop green technology in China. Haier signed a collaboration agreement with the Japanese Lixil Group to develop integrated design solutions for residential units.

In August 2011, Haier and Carlyle signed a Memorandum of Understanding (MOU) for a strategic partnership in which the Carlyle Group agreed to invest US$137 million in Haier through convertible bonds.

Outward activities

In the early 1990s, Haier started to export its products to Asia, Europe, Japan and the US.

In 1996, Haier established its first overseas joint venture in Indonesia.

In 2001, Haier purchased a refrigerator factory in Italy (Meneghetti) and established its overseas industrial park in Pakistan (Bengal), and set up a refrigerator plant in the US.

In 2004, Haier began to export notebooks and computers to France.

In 2005, it established a design centre in Los Angeles and a trader centre in New York.

In 2005, Haier submitted a bid to purchase Maytag.

In 2006, the National Basketball Association from the U.S. and Haier announced a strategic partnership.

In 2009, Haier purchased 90% of Fisher & Paykel of New Zealand

In 2012, Haier purchased Sanyo Electric's home appliance business and began to market the new AQUA brand.

In 2013, Haier formed a joint venture with Fagor in Poland.

Since 1996, Haier has set up 30 overseas plants and developed a network of 58,800 sales agents worldwide.

TCL

Box 9.2 TCL Corporation

Introduction

Founded in 1981, TCL is one of the biggest consumer electronics firms in China, making televisions, PCs and mobile phones. It has more than 63,000 employees in 145 countries. By 2005, TCL had exported 5.64 million colour TV sets. The domestic market accounts for only 36% of its total profit from colour TVs, with foreign markets accounting for 64% (European market:

27%, US market: 24%, the remaining 13% from other countries). TCL has set up a dozen research and development centres in China, the US, France and Singapore. It has over 20 manufacturing and processing plants located in various countries including China, Poland, Mexico, Thailand and Vietnam.

Inward activities

In 1981, TTK Household Electronic Appliance, a joint venture with Hong Kong investors, was one of the first 12 joint ventures in China to manufacture cassette players.

In 1985, TCL Telecommunication Equipment Co., a joint venture with a Hong Kong investor, began to make touchtone phones.

In 1990, TCL began making TVs by importing semi-finished products and being an OEM supplier.

In 1992, TCL launched its own brand of big-screen colour TV in the domestic market.

In 1998, another joint venture between TCL and GVC Computer Technology Co., Ltd. was formed. The Import and Export Bank of China granted a credit line of RMB 2 billion to TCL in support of its expansion.

In 2001, TLC formed a joint venture with Taiwan's Richy Stock Co. to make air compressors.

In 2003, the Intel-TCL 3C Joint Laboratory was established.

In 2004, TLC formed joint ventures with Toshiba and Alcatel.

In 2005, Walt Disney granted a licence to TCL to use its brand and cartoon images in China.

In 2008, TCL and Intel signed an agreement to develop the next-generation Internet television.

In 2012, TCL partnered with IKEA on the development of its new living-room concept with complete TV solutions integrating TV, sound and furniture.

In 2013, the partnership between TCL and Marvel for Marvel's Iron Man 3 included brand integration and a tie-in promotion at the 2013 Consumer Electronics Show. TCL and Hong Kong's Applied Science and Technology Research Institute announced a long-term strategic partnership on wireless technology and product development.

Outward activities

In 1993, TCL Electronics (Hong Kong) Co., Ltd was established.

In 1996, TLC acquired Hong Kong Luk's Enterprise, which made colour television projectors.

In 1997, TCL started expanding overseas, including plants and subsidiaries in Vietnam, Singapore, Indonesia, Philippines, India, Thailand and Russia.

In 1999, TCL started exporting its brand-name products to emerging markets.

In 2002, TCL acquired Schneider, a famous TV maker in Germany, and "Go-video" in the US.

In 2004, TCL merged with Thomson of France and became the biggest global TV manufacturer, with its headquarters in Shenzhen, China.

In 2005, TCL merged three manufacturing operations in Mexico.

In 2006, TCL Thomson Electronics forged a strategic alliance with Philips to grow the LCD TV business. TCL began to sell its brand-name TVs through Carrefour stores in Europe.

In 2010, TCL was the official sponsor of the 16th Asian Games in Guangzhou, joined the 43rd Consumer Electronics Show (CES), and signed up India's NOVA to sell its air conditioners in India.

In 2011, TCL signed a series of contracts worth €300 million with Italian manufacturers and distributors, covering colour TVs, mobile phones and home appliances.

In 2013, TCL entered a joint venture agreement with IMAX and moved into the premium private-theatre-systems market, integrating hardware, software, services and content. TCL also purchased the naming rights to the China Theatre in Hollywood.

Lenovo

Box 9.3 Lenovo Group Ltd

Introduction

In 1984, with US$25,000 of seed money from the Chinese Academy of Sciences, 11 engineers and researchers founded a company named Legend, which provided computer maintenance and training services in Beijing. In the early 1990s, Legend began to sell own-brand computers. By 1996, Legend accounted for 9.4% of the PC market in the mainland and outranked IBM (8.4%). Since then the firm, now named Lenovo, has achieved the largest computer market share in China. It has 19,000 employees and its business covers the 3C areas: computers, communications and consumer electronics. Lenovo has transformed itself from a local company into a global player and became the third-largest PC maker in the world with an annual revenue of US$13 billion by the end of 2005.

Inward activities

In 1987, Legend became the distributor for HP and AST in China and accumulated a wealth of experiences in marketing computing products.

From 1990 to 1996, Legend was the agent distributor for PC, CAD and other products.

In 1997, sales of Toshiba notebook computers by Legend accounted for 24.7% of the Chinese market. Legend established a joint venture with Computing Associates in the US to enter the software market. In the same year, Legend signed an intellectual property agreement with Microsoft.

In 2006, Lenovo Group Ltd and Microsoft signed a global agreement and deepened their strategic cooperation through joint sales, marketing and training programmes in China and around the world.

In 2012, Lenovo appointed Gianfranco Lanci from ACER as its Senior Vice President (SVP) and the President of Lenovo of Europe, Middle East, and Africa (EMEA) to lead the rapid growth of Lenovo's business. Lenovo and EMC announced a partnership in industry standard servers and network storage solutions, while significantly expanding EMC's reach in China and other key high-growth markets.

Outward activities

In 1988, Legend established its first overseas sales branch in Hong Kong and became listed on the Hong Kong Stock Exchange in 1994.

In 2003, Legend changed its brand name to Lenovo.

In 2004, Lenovo became an Olympic worldwide partner. As a result, Lenovo became the first Chinese company to become a computer technology equipment partner of the International Olympic Commission (IOC), which helped the company to gain global brand recognition.

In 2005, Lenovo paid $1.75 billion to acquire the PC and ThinkPad divisions from IBM and established its new headquarters in Purchase, New York. Lenovo also set up research centres, in Japan, China and the US, and four sales headquarters worldwide.

In 2006, the National Basketball Association and Lenovo announced a multi-year global marketing partnership to expand Lenovo's international brand recognition.

In 2007, Lenovo announced its multi-year support for the National Engineers Week Foundation and the Global Marathon. Lenovo opened plants in Mexico and India in an effort to take on rivals HP and Dell in key markets outside China.

In 2008, the Dow Chemical Company deployed more than 44,000 ThinkPad notebooks and ThinkCentre desktops throughout its offices worldwide to support increased productivity, flexibility and computing reliability.

In 2009, Lenovo was a sponsor of the World Expo 2010 in Shanghai.

In 2011, Lenovo acquired Medion AG in a deal that took 14% of the German PC market and a 7.5% share of the overall computer market in Western Europe.

In 2012, Lenovo acquired US-based Stoneware to expand its cloud computing solutions, started up a US personal computer production line in Whitsett, North Carolina, and acquired MEDION in Germany to fuel continued growth in Europe.

In 2014, Lenovo announced its plans to acquire IBM's x86 server business. Lenovo and Google signed an agreement to acquire the Motorola Mobility smartphone business.

Founder

Box 9.4 Founder Group

Introduction

Founded in 1986 with investment from Peking University, Founder is now one of the most successful software enterprises in China. It has five listed public companies. In 2006, Founder was ranked tenth in the top 100 state electronic and information enterprises in China. With its world-class laser typesetting technology, Founder has 85% of the domestic market, and exports its products to more than 30 countries in Asia, Europe and the Americas. With over 20 subsidiaries and joint ventures, Founder has over 20,000 employees worldwide (www.founder.com).

Inward activities

In 1989, Founder cooperated with Hong Kong's Kingsoft to develop the Chinese Character Board.

In 2004, Founder cooperated with Japan's Omron Corporation to set up an R&D centre.

In 2005, Founder and Omron jointly built the Automatic Fare Collection System.

In 2006, Founder signed an Intellectual Property Rights (IPR) agreement with Microsoft.

In 2007, Founder formed a joint venture with Credit Swiss in Beijing. Founder partnered with Océ N.V. to market Océ's digital printing systems in the high-volume printing and graphic arts markets.

In 2008, Founder signed an agreement with Intel on equipment sales and technology transfer.

In 2010, Founder formed a joint venture with the Bank of East Asia of Hong Kong in Wuhan to market financial services.

In 2010, Founder signed a collaboration agreement with Taiwan's E Ink Holdings Inc. in a move into the global e-paper industry.

In 2010, Founder signed an MOU with Acer to design IT products including notebooks, netbooks and mobile Internet devices for the Chinese market.

In 2011, Founder cooperated with Hitachi to develop solutions for industrial distribution, financial industries, cloud computing and medical diagnostic instruments. Founder Fubon Fund Management Co., Ltd opened in Beijing, marking mainland China's first fund management joint venture with Taiwan.

In 2013, Founder formed a joint venture with Norway-based Odfjell Group to purchase 50% of the equity interest in Fangtong Port.

Outward activities

In 1992, Founder opened an office in Hong Kong and began to expand overseas.

In 1997, Founder entered the Japanese market, making it the first Chinese enterprise to export software with independent intellectual property rights and its own brand. By 2003, 300 Japanese newspapers used Founder's software.

In 2000, Founder and Yahoo! acquired the Hong Kong listed Rongwen Technologies Co. and renamed it the Founder Digital Co., Ltd.

In 2004, its subsidiary in Malaysia, Founder MSC, was listed on the Malaysian stock exchange. Founder RIP has more than 100 global cooperative partners.

In 2005, Founder Easiprint chain store entered the Canadian market.

In 2010, Founder International sold packaging software PaSharp to Italy Scatolificio del, representing a breakthrough for PaSharp in the European market.

In 2012, Founder Properties registered four subsidiaries in Hong Kong and Singapore.

In 2013, the Founder Pharmaceutical Research Institute signed an agreement with SKBP and Shanghai Medicilon, moving into the pharmaceutical markets in China, the United States and Europe. Founder Technology signed an agreement with AVAYA on business, technical support and solutions.

Today, Founder runs five listed public companies in China, Malaysia and Hong Kong, and over 20 wholly owned and joint ventures worldwide, including six overseas subsidiaries in Hong Kong, Japan, Canada, Malaysia and Taiwan. Its laser typesetting technology has over 90% of the Chinese language market overseas. It has also applied its technology to other languages, including Japanese, Arabic, French, Spanish and German. Its RIP technology has close to 100 distributors worldwide. Founder has since diversified into pharmaceuticals, steel making and consumer electronics.

Most notably, the four firms all formed joint ventures with foreign firms, and some with multiple joint ventures (TCL and Lenovo) that injected foreign capital and technology. Apart from accessing technology and capital, the firms have learned to apply modern practices in operations, management and quality control. Thus, their inward activities to some extent represent an equivalent process of knowledge development as prescribed by the process model (Johanson and Wiedersheim-Paul, 1975). Although they began focusing on the domestic market, Haier and TCL also engaged in OEM operations for foreign firms. While some of their foreign joint venture partners were from other Chinese economies, such as Hong Kong and Taiwan, others were large Western multinationals that were leaders in their respective industries. These activities gave the Chinese firms indirect access to the international market and opportunities for learning the ropes of international trade and global operations (see Table 9.2).

Furthermore, firms can integrate their acquired knowledge with their own resources to develop their export and manufacturing

Table 9.2 Firms' inward and outward activities and environmental factors

Dimension/Company	Haier	TCL	Lenovo	Founder
1. Inward activities				
Agent/distributor of foreign products			√	
Importing technology/ equipment	√	√		
Joint ventures with foreign firms	√	√	√	√
Joint R&D	√	√	√	√
Contract manufacturing/OEM	√	√		√
2. Outward activities				
Direct exporting	√	√		√
OFDI	√	√	√	√
M&As	√	√	√	
Strategic alliances	√	√		
Overseas R&D	√			
Acquired foreign brands	√	√	√	
Early OFDI entry locations	Indonesia, Pakistan, USA, Italy, New Zealand, Poland	Vietnam, Singapore, Indonesia, Philippines, India, Thailand, Russia.	USA, Mexico, India, Germany	Malaysia, Hong Kong, Japan, Canada, Taiwan
3. Environment/ institution				
Industry internationalization	M	M	H	L
Government support	H	M	H	M

Note: √ = yes, considered a major factor; L = low; M = medium; H = high

capabilities. These firms have fared quite well in the application and integration of acquired resources, as they all engaged in R&D with foreign firms and make products based on standard technologies in their product areas. By acquiring technology, manufacturing operations and management practices from their overseas partners, they developed capabilities that are largely transferable to overseas markets. Founder, in contrast, although operating in a high-tech industry, focuses on making software for the domestic market, thus the transferability of its capabilities is rather limited except for Chinese newspaper publishers overseas and those in Japan. However, Founder has diversified its portfolios into other industries, including real estate and financial services. Overall, these inward activities create a base for potential outward movement, with the chance of fortuitous foreign contacts leading to foreign orders, better knowledge of foreign markets and a stronger international outlook (Welch & Luostarinen, 1993). These results provide support for the first proposition that inward activities help firms acquire and develop the resources and knowledge for overseas operations.

Outward activities, strategies and environmental factors

In terms of outward activities, firms that gain experience with joint ventures in the inward process tend to form joint ventures or engage in OEM operations in their outward expansion. Firms with joint ventures with partners from advanced economies, such as Haier and Lenovo, also tend to make their initial entry into foreign markets in the advanced economies. In contrast, TCL had joint venture partners in Taiwan and Hong Kong, and thus started its OFDI in South East Asia before moving to Europe. These patterns seem to support the linkage, learning and leverage model proposed by Mathews (2006).

One noticeable difference is that Lenovo and Haier have taken a more aggressive approach to overseas expansion by investing first in advanced economies (e.g., the US and Europe) via OFDI and merger and acquisition to enhance their brand image and distributional and R&D capabilities. Haier has mainly focused on direct exports and direct investment in overseas markets, starting in advanced economies such as the US and then expanding to less developed economies. Lenovo seems to have taken a similar approach, as it acquired the PC division of IBM to gain a foothold in the US and other key markets. In contrast, TCL and Founder have taken a more generic and gradual approach. TCL first moved into less developed economies, such as Vietnam and other countries in Southeast Asia, and moved on to more developed markets, thus taking a more generic approach to internationalization (Child & Rodrigues, 2005). In terms of both entry mode and location choice, it is not difficult to see the link between the firms' inward and outward activities. Together, these findings support our second proposition that firms with previous experiences in certain activities tend to adopt a similar approach in their entry-mode strategies and location choices when expanding overseas.

Inward activities alone do not lead to outward activities or to the same degree of internationalization. The industry environment, such as the degree of internationalization, and the institutional environment, such as home government support, play a major role in the outward expansion of these firms. Clearly, the degree of industry internationalization provides the momentum for firms to expand overseas. In comparison with Founder, the other three firms operate in industries with a high degree of internationalization. The appliances industry in China was opened up to foreign competition early on and followed international practices in both product and manufacturing technologies, although some local adaptations were required. From the beginning, the IT industry in China faced even greater competition from foreign counterparts. In fact, the IT industry in China is one of the industries in which technology and operations are as standardized as those across the globe. Thus, while the pressure of globalization on these firms is different, the acquired resources for firms in certain industries are more valuable to their internationalization efforts. Firms facing a higher degree of internationalization in their industries, such as Lenovo, Haier and TCL, are more motivated to compete in the international market and keener to transfer the resources they have acquired from inward activities and apply them to exploring overseas markets. Thus, our third proposition is largely supported.

It is apparent that government support plays a critical role in the internationalization of firms, especially firms from emerging market economies such as China (Deng, 2004). Both Haier and Lenovo are large corporations that have received a lot of support from the government, which wants to set up examples for firms in the same industry. Haier, previously a collectively owned company, has benefited from both financial and policy support from the Chinese government. In the early 1990s, Haier raised funds from state-owned banks and government agencies to restructure and acquire other domestic firms to become one of the largest home appliances firms in China (Child & Rodrigues, 2005). The Chinese government's stake in Lenovo gave the firm certain advantages, including privileged access to domestic government and educational markets, which made the company a more attractive partner for IBM (Child & Rodrigues, 2005). Under the "Going Global" policy announced by former president Jiang Zemin in March 2001, the Chinese government has supported 22 companies with global potential, including both Lenovo and Haier, and removed some of the roadblocks in their path, such as tedious project approval processes, stringent foreign-exchange controls and a state monopoly over exports (Zeng & Williamson, 2003).

TCL and Founder also received government support to a certain degree, especially from local government agencies. In August 2005, TCL secured a loan of RMB8 billion from the China Development Bank for overseas expansion projects involving multimedia, mobile communications and home appliances (Comtex News Network, 2005). Founder has drawn on several technologies produced by state-funded research projects at Beijing University (Zeng & Williamson, 2003). However, both TCL and Founder have been more conservative in their overseas expansion, typically starting in developing countries before moving into the more advanced economies. The different degree of government support for these firms perhaps helps to explain the patterns of their internationalization strategies, furnishing support for the fourth proposition.

Discussion and implications

This study examines the role of inward activities in the internationalization of firms from China and to do so proposed a framework using the resource theory to examine the effect of firm strategies and environmental factors. Based on case studies of Chinese enterprises, our findings show that by engaging in inward activities, firms may acquire the critical resources that can lead to outward activities and the process of internationalization. By analysing the history and operational data of these Chinese firms, we demonstrate how these enterprises have acquired the necessary resources by engaging in inward activities to embark on the path to internationalization. Meanwhile, firm strategies for entry mode and location choice, the level of internationalization in the industry, and government support have greatly affected their patterns of internalization.

The present study has several implications for research on the internationalization of firms. While the traditional process model of internationalization may be relevant for Western multinationals, inward activities play a significant role in the internationalization of enterprises from transitional economies such as China. They are less likely to follow a linear pattern of organic growth toward internationalization. Through these inward activities, the process of internationalization in the four firms started some time before they began overseas expansion. While inward activities can help firms to acquire the necessary resources for engaging in outward activities, this approach is not inconsistent with the traditional process model of internationalization. In fact, these inward activities simply speed up the process of resource acquisition and knowledge development and accelerate the pace of outward activities and internationalization. These findings help to advance the development of theories of internationalization.

By adopting the resource perspective, we provide a coherent framework to explain how inward activities can lead to outward activities and internationalization. First, we elaborate how inward activities help firms to acquire the prerequisite resources and knowledge for internationalization, which affect their subsequent entry mode and location choice in the outward process. Combined with the contingency variables of industry internationalization and home government support, we can see why these firms have been successful in their outward activities and internationalization, perhaps more so than others that have also engaged in inward activities. Clearly, industry internationalization and government support provided an important impetus for these firms to expand outward. These findings suggest that both government agencies and firms can use inward activities more strategically and productively to promote outward internationalization.

Limitations and directions for future research

The propositions and findings notwithstanding, readers need to be aware of the limitations of the study. It is rather exploratory in nature as it is based on only four case studies and limited data from secondary sources. These cases represent only a small number of Chinese companies and a few industries. Furthermore, this approach did not allow us to objectively measure certain key factors in a systematic fashion. Thus, a larger-scale study using quantitative measures of the key theoretical variables is needed to test the hypotheses in a more rigorous manner. Comparisons with firms from other emerging market economies would help to validate the research findings.

Both theory development and empirical studies in this area can potentially furnish stronger evidence and support for firms' inward activities. The effect of institutional embeddedness, or the influence of home institutional factors, on the outward activities of multinationals from transitional economies warrants systematic investigation. Internationalization strategies, in terms of market selection and entry mode, for aspiring emerging market multinationals present a fruitful area for future research. How these companies, which are latecomers to the international marketplace and clearly limited in resources and capabilities, can overcome the disadvantages and devise viable strategies for overseas expansion demands priority attention from researchers.

References

Anderson, O. (1997). Internationalization and market entry mode: A review of theories and conceptual frameworks. *Management International Review*, 37(2): 27–42.

Barney, J (1991). Firm resources and sustained competitive advantage. *Journal of Management*, 17: 99–120

Bjorkman, I. & Kock, S. (1997). Inward international activities in service firms – illustrated by three cases from the tourism industry. *International Journal of Service Industry management, 8(5): 362–376.*

Child, J. & Rodrigues, S. B. (2005). The internationalization of Chinese firms: A case for theoretical extension? *Management and Organization Review*, 1(3): 381–410.

Chaudhry, S. & Crick, D. (2002). A research policy note on UK government support and small firms' internationalization using the Internet: The Use of www.tradeuk.com. *Strategic Change*, 11(2): 95–104.

Cohen, W. M. & Levinthal, D. A. (1990). Absorptive capacity: A new perspective on learning and innovation. *Administrative Science Quarterly, Special Issue: Technology, Organizations and Innovation*, 35(1): 128–152.

Comtex News Network (2005). TCL to Expand Overseas Market with CNY8bn Loans from CDB, Inc. 10 August. www.comtex.com.

Deng, P. (2004). Outward investment by Chinese MNCs: Motivations and implications. *Business Horizons*, 47(3): 8–16.

Dunning, J. H. (2003). Some antecedents of internalization theory. *Journal of International Business Studies*, 34(2): 108–115.

Elango, B. (2001). An exploratory study into the linkages between corporate resources and the extent and form of internationalization of US firms. *American Business Review*, 18(2): 12–26.

Freeman, S., Edwards, R., & Schroder, B. (2006). How smaller born-global firms use networks and alliances to overcome constraints to rapid internationalization. *Journal of International Marketing*, 14(3): 33–63.

Hitt, M. A., Bierman, L., Shimizu, K., & Kochhar, R. (2001). Direct and moderating effects of human capital on strategy and performance in professional service firms: A resource-based perspective. *Academy of Management Journal*, 44(1): 13–28.

Johanson, J., & Vahlne, J.-E. (1977). The internationalization process of the firms – A model of knowledge development and increasing foreign market commitments. *Journal of International Business Studies*, 8(1): 23–32.

Johanson, J., & Wiedersheim-Paul, F. (1975). The internationalization of the firm: Four Swedish cases. *Journal of Management Studies*, 12(3): 305–322

Karlsen, T., Silseth, P. R., Benito, G. R. G., & Welch, L. S. (2003). Knowledge, internationalization of the firm, and inward-outward connections. *Industrial Marketing Management*, 32(5): 385–396.

Kuada, J., & Sørensen, O. J. (2000). *Internationalisation of Companies from Developing Countries*. New York: The Haworth Press Inc.

Liu, H. & Li, K. (2002). Strategic implications of emerging Chinese multinationals: The Haier case study. *European Management Journal*, 20(6): 699–709.

Luostarinen, R. & Welch, L (1997). *International Business Operations*. Helsinki: Helsinki School of Economics, 3rd ed.

Mathews, J. A. (2006). Dragon multinationals: New players in the 21st century globalization. *Asia Pacific Journal of Management*, 23(1): 5–27.
Peng, M. W. (2003). Institutional transitions and strategic choices. *The Academy of Management Review*, 28(2): 275–296.
Pfeffer, J. M. & Salancik, G. R. (1978). *The External Control of Organizations: A Resource Dependence Perspective*. New York: Harper & Row.
Sim, A. B. & Pandian, J. R. (2003). Emerging Asian MNEs and their Internationalization strategies – Case study evidence on Taiwanese and Singaporean firms. *Asia Pacific Journal of Management*, 20(1): 27–50.
SinoCast China IT Watch (2006). Haier met losses in several sectors last year. 6 January. www. SinoCast.com.
Taylor, R. (2002). Globalization strategies of Chinese companies: Current development and future prospects. *Asian Business & Management*, 1(2): 209–225.
Vernon, R. (1966). International investment and international trade in the product cycle. *Quarterly Journal of Economics*, 80(2): 190–207.
Welch, L. S. & Luostarinen, R. K. (1993). Inward-outward connections in internationalization. *Journal of International Marketing*, 1(1): 44–56.
Wells, L. T., Jr. (1983). *Third World Multinationals*, Cambridge, MA: MIT Press.
Young, S., Huang, C.-H. & McDermott, M. (1996). Internationalization and competitive catch-up processes: Case study evidence on Chinese multinational enterprises. *Management International Review*, 36(4): 295–314.
Zeng, M. & Williamson, P. J. (2003). The hidden dragons. *Harvard Business Review*, 81(10): 92–99.

10
An Exposition of Indian Overseas Investments in Germany: Trends, Motivations and Challenges

Ritam Garg

Introduction

Firms from emerging markets, especially China and India, have emerged as important players in the world economy, stamping their authority on the global business environment, through bold and large acquisitions in the developed markets, and this has led to increased interest in their behaviour by academics and policymakers alike who are beginning to realize the important analytical and policy issues that affect the world economy due to these firms. Also, there has been a significant increase in the foreign direct investment (FDI) flows from these emerging markets owing to the overseas activities of their firms. According to Ramamurti (2012, p. 42), in 2010, emerging markets accounted for 25% of global FDI flows, compared to only 6% in 2001. Furthermore, it is estimated by the McKinsey Global Institute that by 2025, 45% of Fortune 500 firms will be based in emerging markets (MGI, 2013).

Firms from emerging markets had already started to expand overseas during the 1980s and 1990s (Jormanainen & Koveshnikov, 2012). Of all the emerging markets, China and India have clearly emerged as the most prominent actors in the global arena (De Beule & Van Den Bulcke, 2012). The announcement of the "Go Global" policy in 2001 marked a significant change in the development of Chinese outward foreign direct investment (OFDI). Once the policy was in place, the pace of Chinese OFDI began to rise significantly (Berning & Holtbrügge, 2012). Similarly, the economic reforms of 1991 and, subsequently, the guidelines for Indian firms to invest abroad, provided for automatic approval of OFDI proposals up to US$100 million by July 2002, and by 2004, Indian firms were allowed to invest abroad up to 100% of their net worth (Kumar, 2007). With few exceptions, the limit of India OFDI has been increased to 400% since then (Holtbrügge et al., 2013). The magnitude, as well as the number, of OFDI flows from both these countries has grown considerably over the past few years, signalling an impressive growth of the two economies, even though most of rest of the world was in economic turmoil, thereby strengthening the notion that firms from these countries will emerge as the drivers of the global economy in the next decade (Jormanainen & Koveshnikov, 2012).

Scholars agree that this notion is not too farfetched, as it is evidenced by the ambitions and the actions of firms from these markets. In addition, firms from India have become very active in their overseas endeavours post-liberalization of the Indian economy. Acquisitions of larger firms bigger by Indian firms in the last decade have strongly established the position of Indian firms as serious business contenders and India as a global economic power. Indian firms have also proven that they are capable of turning around the fortunes of acquired firms, for example, Tata Motor's acquisition of UK-based Jaguar Land Rover led to one of the most successful cases of post-acquisition turnaround. As a result of considerable outward investments by Indian firms, India became the world's 21st largest outward investor and stands among the giants in today's global economy. The following sections present consolidated accounts of Indian OFDI, in general, and German OFDI, in particular, and show the position of India as an emerging global power.

Indian OFDI

Although OFDI from India has accelerated since 1991, it is not a new phenomenon. In fact, Indian OFDI can be traced as far back as pre-independent India (Morris, 1987; Nayyar, 2008). One of the Indian conglomerates of the time, Mafatlal, invested in a cotton-spinning operation in Uganda in the 1920s (Hansen, 2007). India's first overseas venture was Indo Ethiopian Textile Share Company, established by the Birla Group in 1959 (Athukorala, 2009). In the early 1960s, the Tata group expanded its activities abroad, and the pharmaceutical company Ranbaxy set up its first joint venture in Nigeria in 1977 (Hansen, 2007). Although Indian firms made overseas investments from post-independence era until the mid-1960s (Lall, 1983), the official figures about these investments are largely unknown because concrete data for Indian OFDI is only available post-1980 (Verma & Brennan, 2011). However, nearly three decades of India's illiberal and restrictive policies limited OFDI to small, minority joint ventures in developing countries, which left India's economic growth drastically low levels (Verma & Brennan,

2011). Also, most OFDIs of the time were geographically concentrated in West and East Africa, the Middle East and Southeast Asia because of India's historical linkages and a shared colonial heritage with these regions (Holtbrügge et al., 2013).

India's OFDI can be broadly classified into three phases. The first phase, from the 1970s to the 1980s, was mainly led by modest investments in joint ventures in Asia and Africa and was shaped by political and regulatory constraints. OFDI was particularly manufacturing-driven, and the investing firms were mostly from the private sector and had a greater geographical and sectoral profile (Kumar, 2007). The second phase, in the 1990s and early 2000s, was characterized by a more liberal government stance (Sauvant & Pradhan, 2010). In contrast to China, however, the capability of Indian firms to invest abroad was still limited. In the third phase, which began in the early 2000s, Indian OFDI did not only grow significantly, but exhibited a diversification in terms of industrial composition, motives and destinations (Kumar, 2007; Sauvant & Pradhan, 2010).

An important characteristic of post-liberalization OFDI was the increase of cross-border mergers and acquisitions (M&As), which have emerged as a preferred mode of expansion by Indian firms in the global market (Pradhan, 2007). Around 37 M&As were registered during 2001, which increased to 170 by 2006 (Bhutani, 2007). And, by 2007 onwards, Indian firms were foraying into large-scale cross-border ventures by acquiring bigger firms bigger. Table 10.1 shows some of the major acquisitions by Indian firms, and most notable during this post-2007 period were the acquisition of the Anglo-Dutch company Corus by Tata Steel for US$12 billion, Bharti Airtel's acquisition of Zain Africa for US$10 billion and Aditya Birla Group's acquisition of Atlanta based

Table 10.1 Major Indian acquisitions

No.	Indian firm	Acquired entity	Country	Year of acquisition	Deal amount (billion)
1	Tata Steel	Corus Group plc	UK	2007	US$ 12
2	Bharti Airtel	Zain Africa	15 African Countries	2010	US$ 10
3	Adity Birla group	Novellis Inc	USA	2007	US$ 6
4	ONGC	Imperial Energy	UK	2008	US$ 2.5
5	Tata Motors	Jaguar Land Rover	UK	2008	US$ 2.3

Source: UNCTAD, 2012; author's own research

company Novellis for US$6 billion. As a result of these and other large cross-border M&As, India became the 21st largest investor with the highest OFDI flows in 2010, while among the emerging markets, it ranks in second after China (Chowdhury, 2011).

Additionally, OFDI from India was increasingly invested in greenfield projects. Table 10.2 shows the most notable greenfield investments by Indian firms. Apart from Jindal's US$3 billion greenfield investment in fossil fuel and power in Mozambique and Essar Group's US$4 billion greenfield project in iron ore and mining in Zimbabwe (UNCTAD, 2012), other major greenfield projects were the investment of US$4 billion in Africa's mining sector by Vedanta Resources, India's largest mining and non-ferrous metals company, and Tata Group's US$1.7 billion investment in automobile and hospitality businesses, also in the African continent (Krishnan, 2013). Indian firms focus on M&As for investments in developed markets and prefer greenfield investments for projects in other emerging markets. Of the total value of Indian cross-border M&As between 2000 and 2009, developed markets accounted for 83% (Sauvant & Pradhan, 2010). In recent years, firms in service industries have also become increasingly active in overseas markets, particularly in developed markets. For example, in early 2012, the State Bank of India started offering mortgages in the UK. In Russia, the State Bank of India and Canara Bank set up the Commercial Bank of India to facilitate trade and economic activities between the two countries. ICICI, another Indian bank, with a strong presence in Germany, helps to facilitate financing of cross-border Indian–German deals. Further OFDI in the services sector has been directed into business services, data processing, financial services, architecture and engineering, and other technical consultancy activities. OFDI in the manufacturing sector includes agriculture machinery and

Table 10.2 Major Indian greenfield projects

No.	Indian firm	Country	Acquired entity	Year of investment	Amount (billion)
1	Jindal Group (Jindal Steel & Power Ltd)	Mozambique	Jindal Coal Operations	2012	US$3
2	Essar Group (Essar Africa Holdings)	Zimbabwe	Zimbabwe Iron & Steel Company (ZICOSteel)	2012	US$4

Source: UNCTAD, 2012

equipment, basic organic chemicals, drugs, medicines and allied products and refined petroleum products (Holtbrügge et al., 2013).

OFDI flows from India reached US$14,752 million in 2011 and OFDI stock accounted for US$111,257 million (UNCTAD, 2012). In 2012, however, there was a slight dip in the figures as shown in Table 10.3 and Table 10.4. However, according to an estimate by the Reserve Bank of India (RBI), 472 major outward investments were made by Indian firms by the end of December 2012 (RBI, 2013).

In 2013, overseas investments by Indian firms again picked up, and overseas direct investments by Indian companies stood at US$3.24 billion in July 2013, registering an increase of 89.5% from June 2013 (RBI, 2013), and by the end of 2013, the overall OFDI flow from India for 2012–2013 stood at US$7.1 billion (RBI, 2014). Figure 10.1 shows the

Table 10.3 FDI outflows, inflows and ratio (in US$ million)

		2004	2005	2006	2007	2008	2009	2010	2011	2012
India	Outflow	2,179	2,978	14,344	17,281	17,685	15,927	13,151	14,752	8,583
	Inflow	5,771	7,606	20,336	25,127	41,554	35,596	24,159	31,554	25,543
	Ratio	0.38	0.39	0.71	0.69	0.43	0.45	0.54	0.47	0.33

Source: UNCTAD, 2013

Table 10.4 OFDI stock (in US$ million)

	1980	1990	2000	2010	2011	2012
India	78	124	1,859	96,421	111,257	118,167

Source: UNCTAD, 2013

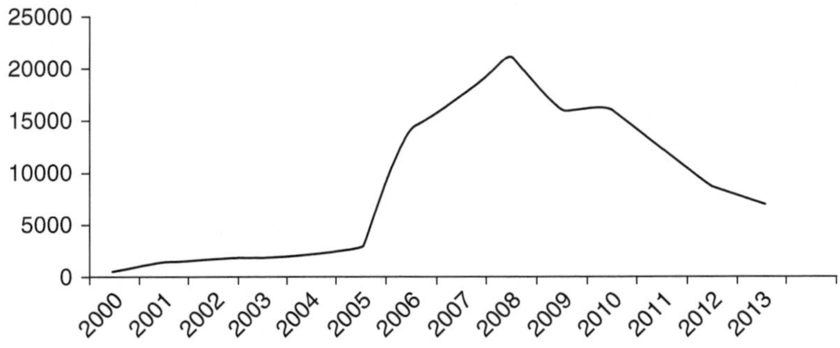

Figure 10.1 Indian OFDI flows (in US$ million)
Source: UNCTAD, 2013; RBI, 2014

fluctuations in Indian OFDI over the years until the end of 2013. The investments were made across 461 deals, with Reliance Communications, Apollo Tyres, Zee Entertainment Enterprises, Kirloskar Brothers Ltd, Aditya Birla Group, Tata Communications and VLCC, an Indian wellness and slimming firm, being the major players behind the increase. Overall, India's M&A activity value touched US$1.5 billion in July 2013, increasing the year-to-date M&A value by 36% from 2012 (Grant Thornton, 2013).

The main motives for Indian OFDI have been the need to achieve economies of scale and the acquisition of skills, technologies and distribution networks in order to increase the global competitiveness of Indian firms (Nayyar, 2008; Pradhan, 2008). Moreover, the search for strategic and complementary locational assets in metals, oil, gas and other raw materials, and the desire to diversify globally are also relevant (Hattari & Rajan, 2010). Finally, the geographic distribution of Indian OFDI has changed in the course of economic liberalization. Pre-liberalization Indian OFDI was concentrated largely in developing economies in Asia and Africa and went mainly into specific manufacturing sectors where Indian firms faced little competition. Post-liberalization, and particularly since the 2000s, Indian OFDI flows mainly to developed countries in the form of M&As and covers a broad spectrum of manufacturing and services sectors (Pradhan, 2007; Singal & Jain, 2012).

Indian OFDI in Germany

Industry experts observed that Indian companies have been shying away from the EU due to the turbulent economic environment in Europe (Charlie, 2012). However, the evidence points to the contrary. Even as Europe underwent a turbulent economic phase, with slow growth, high unemployment and a spiralling debt crisis, Indian firms were not deterred from moving into Europe.

For example, despite the economic crisis, TCS has doubled its revenue from Europe to nearly US$3 billion over the last four years. Its revenue from continental Europe alone has jumped more than 60% to US$1.1 billion (Thoppil, 2013). Evidence also shows a renewed interest in Europe, despite tough labour laws, language barriers and high costs of operation. For example, at the beginning of 2013, Cognizent acquired six companies from Germany's C1 group. Geometric Ltd. acquired three cap technologies with 110 employees in Germany for €11 million. Infosys bought Swiss-based Lodestone Holding Company along with its German subsidiary for US$350 million. Elsewhere, TCS acquired French company Alti SA for €75 million, and first week of October 2013, saw Cognizant acquiring France-based Equinox Consulting an undisclosed sum.

To strengthen this argument further, a survey conducted by Federation of Indian Chambers of Commerce and Industry reports that over the years, Indian companies have shed their pessimism and seen an upsurge in their business prospects in the region (FICCI, 2013). According to a report by Europe India Chamber of Commerce (EICC, 2012), Indian companies have invested US$56 billion across the continent during the 2003–2012 period, shown in Figure 10.2, of which US$38.47 billion was invested through M&A transactions. Furthermore, Indian firms employ 134,000 professionals in Europe, including in 40,000 new jobs created by 511 greenfield investments, three times more than the jobs created by firms from other emerging markets, like China (EICC, 2012). And, most of this investment was directed toward Germany, India's largest trading partner in Europe and India's sixth largest trading partner globally. Germany is also India's second largest technology partner. India's significance as a trading partner for Germany is also on the increase. Currently, India ranks at 28th among trading partners for Germany worldwide, and ranks 5th among Asian exporters to Germany (FICCI, 2012).

India and Germany have been in a strategic partnership since the year 2000. Economic and commercial relations between India and Germany date back to the early 16th century when German trading companies from Augsburg and Nuremberg developed a new sea route around Africa, as they sailed in search of precious stones and spices.

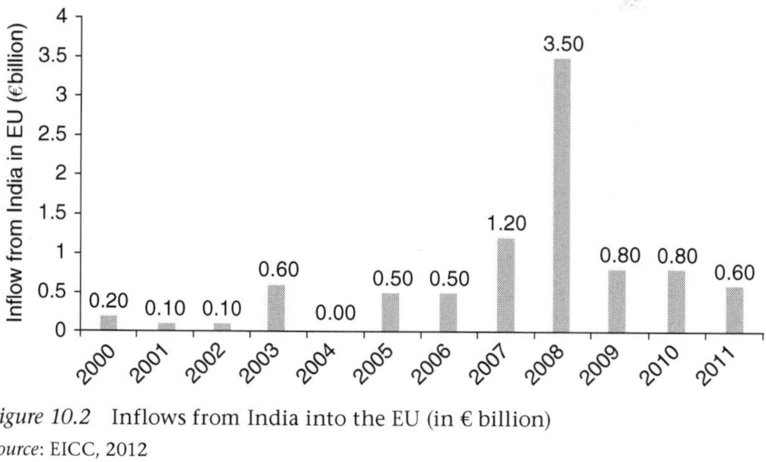

Figure 10.2 Inflows from India into the EU (in € billion)

Source: EICC, 2012

In the 16th and 18th centuries, a number of German companies were established with the express purpose of trading with India and other Asian countries (EICC, 2012; FICCI, 2012). And, over the years Germany has emerged as India's largest trading partner in Europe. Indian investments in Germany have also shown a remarkable increase in the last few years. Bilateral trade reached €15.18 billion in October 2011 (FICCI, 2012). However, the "€20 billion mark", the ambitious goal that German Chancellor Angela Merkel and Indian Prime Minister Manmohan Singh hoped their countries would reach in 2012, remained elusive owing to the dynamic economic environment in the year 2012–2013; but even then, it was apparent from the industry evidence that Indian investments continued to scale-up in the period.

Indian investments in Germany are not a new trend. From the period of 2000 onwards, Indian investors frequently acquired major German companies. While Germany is not among the top destinations of Indian OFDI, it still plays a significant role in terms of cross-border activities by Indian firms. One of the largest cross-border activities in Germany by an Indian firm was the acquisition of Germany's REpower Systems SE (now Senvion SE), the world's fifth largest wind turbine manufacturer, by the Suzlon Group for US$1.7 billion. Transactions such as this and others by Indian firms established India as a significant investor in Germany. By 2010, India's OFDI stock in Germany was €4 billion, and 134 firms operated in Germany, as did 190 subsidiaries (Tiwari and Herstatt, 2010).

Despite the economic slowdown elsewhere in the EU region in 2011–2012, Indian firms continued to invest heavily in Germany. Apart from the acquisitions by the Indian IT industry in Germany, as detailed above, the Indian manufacturing sector also actively scaled up its investments in the country. Table 10.5 shows some of the major acquisitions in Germany by Indian firms. Some other prominent examples are the acquisition of Germany's Rutgers Group, a leading manufacturer of chemical raw materials by Rain Commodities, for €702 million; PCM Group's acquisition of Railway equipment manufacturer Rail. One GmbH for €36 million; Amtek Auto's acquisition of German engineering and design firm Neumayer Tekfor Holding for an undisclosed amount; and Peguform, a German auto component company with a turnover of US$1.37 billion, acquired by Motherson Sumi Systems Ltd. In first half of 2012, 11% of India's overseas investments involved Germany, an increase of an average 6% from 2011 (Hoffmann-Theinert & Wright, 2013).

Owing to increased investments in Germany during recent years, the number of Indian firms operating in Germany has increased

Table 10.5 Major Indian acquisitions in Germany

No.	Indian firm	Acquired German entity	Sector	Deal amount (billion)
1	Suzlon Group	RePower Systems SE (now Senvion SE)	Renewable energy	US$1.7
2	Rain Commodities	Rutgers Group	Chemical	US$0.96
3	Dr Reddy's Laboratories Ltd	Betapharm Arzneimittel GmbH	Healthcare	US$0.65
4	Mahindra & Mahindra Ltd	Jeco Holding AG	Automotive	US$0.13
5	Shakti Auto Component	Intermet Europe GmbH	Automotive	US$0.12

Source: Author's own research

substantially and every fourth acquisition is reported to be by an Indian firm (EICC, 2012). Currently, there are approximately 280 Indian firms, employing about 26,000 people, active in Germany (Tiwari, 2013). Although Indian firms are spread throughout Germany, they are mainly focused in the states of North Rhine-Westphalia, Hessen, Bavaria and Baden-Württemberg (FICCI, 2012). Table 10.6 shows the 20 largest Indian employers in Germany, along with the sector and region they are active in.

It is quite apparent from the information provided in the above sections that sectors such as software and automotive components are clear favourites among the Indian firms. To date, almost all of the Indian investments in Germany have been in sync with the traditional avenues of Indian overseas ventures: technology, manufacturing, services and renewable energy. Germany provides an ideal platform for Indian firms to move up the value chain, and the great number of Indian firms already operating in Germany highlights the fact that Indian firms can be successful and run a sustainable business in the most economically progressive country in EU.

Investments in Germany have also helped Indian firms to focus more on using existing German facilities as a launch pad for a broader European presence, instead of just seeking know-how and brands. OFDI has also helped Indian companies to enhance their R&D, sales and after sales capabilities. In addition, bigger firms have benefitted from a deeper EU presence, which has reduced their dependency on the US. For big Indian IT firms, such as TCS, Wipro and Infosys, for whom success in

Table 10.6 Indian firms in Germany

No.	Indian–German entity	Number of employees	Place	Sector
1	Corus Deutschland GmbH	4,230	Koblenz	Steel
2	REpower Systems SE	2,508	Hamburg	Renewable energy
3	Novelis Deutschland GmbH	2,221	Gottingen	Aluminium
4	ALUMINIUM NORF Gesellschaft mit beschränkter Haftung	2,199	Neuss	Aluminium
5	Tata Steel Germany GmbH	1,336	Düsseldorf	Steel
6	SONA BLW Präzisionsschmiede GmbH	1,336	Munich	Automotive
7	Mahindra Forgings Europe Aktiengesellschaft	1,131	Aalen	automotive
8	RÜTGERS Holding Germany GmbH	934	Duisburg	Chemical
9	RÜTGERS Germany GmbH	650	Castrop-Rauxel	Chemical
10	Bilcare Research GmbH	626	Staufen	Chemical
11	Service Center Gelsenkirchen GmbH	576	Düsseldorf	Steel
12	Tata Consultancy Services Deutschland GmbH	537	Frankfurt	software
13	SCHÖNEWEISS & CO GmbH	528	Hagen	Automotive
14	CDP Bharat Forge GmbH	473	Ennepetal	Automotive
15	Reddy Holding GmbH	428	Augsburg	Healthcare
16	Gesenkschmiede Schneider Gesellschaft mit beschränkter Haftung	411	Aalen	Automotive
17	MeridianSpa Deutschland GmbH	402	Hamburg	Wellness
18	Infotech Enterprises GmbH	292	Leonberg	Software
19	Havells Sylvania Germany GmbH	274	Erlangen	Electrical
20	Peiner Umformtechnik Gesellschaft mit beschränkter Haftung	265	Peine	Engineering

Source: Dafne 2014, author's own research

continental Europe is so far limited so far to the UK and Nordic countries, Germany also provides a strategic opportunity to diversify business risks. Acquisition of German firms also provides Indian firms with a crucial advantage in terms of local trust, sales and as distribution base with intimate knowledge of local markets (Hoffmann-Theinert &Wright, 2013).

Indian firms have also been bold and proactive in buying out distressed or insolvent German firms. Most notable among them were: Megha Mittal's of Mittal Family Trust acquisition of Escada, a German fashion luxury brand for €30 million; Hindustan National Glass's acquisition of Agenda Glass AG for €50 million; ChinaKiri Dyes and Chemicals (KDCL) through its special-purpose vehicle Kiri Holding, Singapore's acquisition of Dystar, a dyes and related solutions manufacturer for €55 million including its brand, patents, technical know-how and most importantly around 21% global market share; and Ashok Minda Group's acquisition of Schenk Plastic Solutions for an undisclosed amount. What is more remarkable is that Indian firms acquired these companies not during the crisis years but during the growth period of 2004–2005. However, not all the Indian firms could manage to turn around the fortunes of their acquired entities as is shown by Ruia Group's investment in Bauer & Schaurte, and Reliance Group's investment in Trevira – both ventures declared insolvency in 2012 (Hoffmann-Theinert &Wright, 2013). Even though scholars believe that targeting insolvent or ailing companies is a major mistake (Williamson & Raman, 2011), an investment in a distressed business might win the support and goodwill of the local community (Hoffmann-Theinert &Wright, 2013), thus, providing a much needed impetus to the local population to recognize the brand and name of a foreign firm, and help to negate the costs associated with a greenfield project.

Analysis of Indian OFDI in Germany also revealed that Indian investors sought access to advanced markets and strategic assets to speed through the resource accumulation process. For example, Suzlon's acquisition of REpower instantly provided it with the status of a global player. Additionally, Germany has graduated from solely a gateway for overseas investment in Europe to also being a springboard for India's investment in the rest of the world, including the untapped and non-English-speaking Eastern European markets.

Even though India's overseas investments have a relative shorter history as compared to, for example, China, Indian firms have emerged as bold, proactive and competitive investors in Germany.

Summary and conclusion

Although, Indian investments continue to grow considerably in Germany, they have faced overwhelming odds to operate in the country.

Apart from the differences in the market environment, language barriers, high operating costs and regulatory barriers, Indian firms compete with not only the firms from developed markets, but also firms from other emerging markets. This complex dynamic of competition has opened three fronts for Indian firms – competition with firms from developed markets in the domestic market, as well as both from the firms from the developed markets and other emerging markets, such as China, in the overseas market – thus forcing the Indian firms to stretch their resources to the maximum, putting an overall strain on their budgets and performance. Furthermore, according to Holtbrügge et al. (2013), differences can also be observed concerning the role of the home government. While the internationalization of Indian firms is mainly market-driven, Chinese and Russian firms also receive strong support from their governments to invest abroad and to become world leaders in their particular industries.

Another major challenge that has emerged for Indian firms is that of building a strong and positive brand image. So far, their success has mostly been based on manufacturing excellence, low-cost production and economies of scale, while they have not yet successfully built a strong brand image. Nargundkar & Bajaj (2002, p. 71) state that, "at best, low-cost services can be an entry point into developed-world markets. But companies must leverage the entry to graduate to high-value service offerings". As a consequence, firms from emerging markets like India have to place more emphasis on marketing and increasing their brand image to succeed in international markets (Kreppel & Holtbrügge, 2012).

Firms from emerging markets require managerial resources in order to be successful in highly competitive business environments (Child & Rodrigues, 2005). In this context, one of their greatest challenges is to attract qualified local employees in order to exploit and extend their own capabilities (Milelli et al., 2010). To grow in Germany, Indian firms may have to endure higher costs, as it is imperative to have local presence. Unlike in the US, where IT companies have access to a number of skilled-worker visa programmes to bring in inexpensive employees, in Germany, and also in the rest of Europe, there are very limited options. Furthermore, it takes a long time for companies to hire someone in Europe, which leads to the severe shortage of technology professionals in some European countries (Thoppil, 2013). A key prerequisite for this ability is to stand out against their competitors and to be regarded as attractive employers. While this is important for companies in general, it is even more relevant for firms from India because they have been operating in developed markets for only a short time and are therefore not well known by potential employees. Moreover, firms from India are often faced with a negative country-of-origin image (Fetscherin & Toncar, 2010; Pappu et al., 2007).

Germany is really attractive from a market standpoint as it provides access to rest of the Europe. Indian firms are also trying to hedge their risks by developing markets other than the US. Europe, and Germany in particular, is considered as a next good region for sales as the markets are opening to outsourcing. Indian firms have become more streamlined and competitive since the liberalization of the economy. However, they have to continue to be proactive, focused and better positioned to explore and exploit the opportunities that Germany has to offer in order for them to become more competitive global players.

References

Athukorala, P. C. (2009). Outward foreign direct investment from India. *Asian Development Review*, 26(2): 125–153.

Berning, S. & Holtbrügge, D. (2012). Chinese outward foreign direct investment – A challenge for traditional internationalization theories? *Journal für Betriebswirt-schaft*, 62(3/4): 169–224.

Bhutani, J. (2007). *Study on FDI Outflow and Role of Manufacturing in the Mergers and Acquisitions Front.*New Delhi, India: Associated Chambers of Commerce and Industry, Research Bureau.

Charlie, A. (2012). *Indian Companies in the European Union: Reigniting Economic growth*. Brussels: EICC.

Child, J. & Rodrigues, S. B. (2005). The internationalization of Chinese firms: A case for theoretical extension? *Management and Organization Review*, 1(3): 381–410.

Chowdhury, M. B. (2011). India's outward foreign direct investment: closed doors to open souk. Available at: http://mpra.ub.uni-muenchen.de/32828/1/MPRA_paper_32828.pdf.

Dafne (2014). Dafne: Bureau Van Dijk, Jahresabschlüsse deutscher Unternehmen. Available at: https://dafneneo.bvdep.com/version-2014729/home.serv?product=dafneneo..

De Beule, F. & Van Den Bulcke, D. (2012). Locational determinants of outward foreign direct investment: An analysis of Chinese and Indian greenfield investments. *Transnational Corporations*, 21(1): 1–34.

Fetscherin, M. & Toncar, M. (2010). The effects of the country of brand and the country of manufacturing of automobiles. An experimental study of consumers' brand personality perception. *International Marketing Review*, 27(2): 164–178.

FICCI (Federation of Indian Chambers of Commerce and Industry) (2012). India-Germany bilateral relations. Available at: http://www.ficci.com/international/54525/Add_docs/India-Germany-Bilateral-Relations-21–12–12.pdf.

FICCI (Federation of Indian Chambers of Commerce and Industry) (2013). Is the worst phase over for Indian companies doing business in Europe? Available at: http://www.ficci.com/Sedocument/20255/europe-Survey-Report-2013.pdf.

Grant Thornton (2013). *Dealtracker: Providing M&A and private equity deal insights.* New Delhi, India: Grant Thornton India LLP.

Hansen, M. W. (2007). Outward foreign direct investment from India: Theory and evidence. Available at: www.cbs.dk/cbds.

Hattari, R. & Rajan, R. S. (2010). India as a source of outward foreign direct investment. *Oxford Development Studies*, 38(4): 497–518.

Hoffmann-Theinert, R. & Wright, C. J. (2013). *Indian Appetite for German Targets Likely to Stay Strong Throughout 2013*. Berlin: Görg.

Holtbrügge, D., Berning, S. C., & Garg, R. (2013). Outward foreign direct investment of emerging market firms. In Dyker, D. A. (ed.), *Foreign Investment in Eurasia and the Pacific Rim*, London: Imperial College Press (in press).

Jormanainen, I. & Koveshnikov, A. (2012). International activities of emerging market firms: A critical assessment of research in top international management journals. *Management International Review*, 52(5): 691–725.

Kreppel, H. & Holtbrügge, D. (2012). Determinants of the perceived attractiveness of Chinese products by German consumers. *Journal of Global Marketing*, 25(2): 79–99.

Krishnan, M. (2013). Indian investments in Africa soars. Available at: http://www.dw.de/indian-investment-in-africa-soars/a-16951164.

Kumar, N. (2007). Emerging TNCs: trends, patterns and determinants of outward FDI by Indian enterprises. *Transnational Corporations*, 16(1): 1–26.

Lall, S. (1983). *The New Multinationals: The Spread of Third World Enterprises*. New York: Wiley.

Mckinsey Global Institute (MGI) (2013). *Urban World: The Shifting Global Business Landscape*, : Mckinsey & Company. Available at: http://www.mckinsey.com/insights/urbanization/urban_world_the_shifting_global_business_landscape.

Milelli, C., Hay, F., & Shi, Y. (2010). Chinese and Indian firms in Europe: Characteristics, impacts and policy implications. *International Journal of Emerging Markets*, 5(3/4): 377–197.

Morris, S. (1987). Trends in foreign direct investment from India (1950–1982). *Economic and Political Weekly*, 22(45): 1909–1918.

Nargundhar, R. & Bajaj, C. (2002). International marketing Strategy for Indian companies: Value, image and other issues. *ICFAI Journal of Marketing*, 1(1): 67–73.

Nayyar, D. (2008). The internationalization of firms from India: Investment, mergers and acquisitions. *Oxford Development Studies*, 36(1): 111–131.

Pappu, R., Quester, P. G., & Cooksey, R. W. (2007). Country image and consumer-based brand equity: Relationships and implications for international marketing. *Journal of International Business Studies*, 38(5): 726–745.

Pradhan, J. P. (2007). Growth of Indian multinationals in the world economy: Implications for development. Working paper No. 04, Institute for Studies in Industrial Development, New Delhi.

Pradhan, J. P. (2008). The evolution of Indian outward foreign direct investment: Changing trends and patterns. *International Journal of Technology and Globalization*, 4(1):70–86.

Ramamurti, R. (2012). What is really different about emerging market multinationals? *Global Strategy Journal*, 2(1): 41–47.

Reserve Bank of India (RBI) (2013). Overseas Direct Investment for December 2012. Available at: http://rbidocs.rbi.org.in/rdocs/PressRelease/PDFs/IEPR1193OD0113.pdf.

Reserve Bank of India (RBI) (2014). Reserve Bank of India bulletin, January 2014. *RBI Bulletin*, 68(1): 1–118.

Sauvant, K. P. & Pradhan, J. P. (2010). *The Rise of Indian Multinationals. Perspectives on Indian Outward Foreign Direct Investment.* New York: Palgrave Macmillan.

Singal, A. & Jain, A. K. (2012). Outward FDI trends from India: Emerging MNCs and strategic issues. *International Journal of Emerging Markets*, 7(4): 443–456.

Thoppil, D. A. (2013). Indian IT firms step-up shopping in Europe. Available at: http://blogs.wsj.com/indiarealtime/2013/04/09/indian-it-firms-step-up-acquisitions-in-europe/.

Tiwari, R. (2013). Indian firms in Germany: Recent developments and the road ahead. *Indo-German Chamber of Commerce, Annual Review 2013*, India: 119–123,

Tiwari, R. & Herstatt, C. (2010). Indian firms in Germany: Recent FDI trends and critical success factors. *Indo-German Chamber of Commerce, Annual Review 2010*, India: 119–123

United Nations Conference on Trade and Development (UNCTAD) (2012). *Towards a New Generation of Investment Policies. World Investment Report – 2012.* Geneva: United Nations Publications.

United Nations Conference on Trade and Development (UNCTAD) (2013). *Global Value Chains: Investments and Trade for Development. World Investment Report – 2013.* Geneva: United Nations Publications.

Verma, R. & Brennan, L. (2011). The investment development path theory: Evidence from India. *International Journal of Emerging Markets*, 6(1): 74–89.

Williamson, P. & Raman, A. P. (2011). How China resets its global acquisition agenda. *Harvard Business Review*, 89(4): 109–114.

Index

Printed and bound by CPI Group (UK) Ltd, Croydon, CR0 4YY